Forex Analysis and Trading

Also available from
Bloomberg Press

Making Sense of the Dollar:
Exposing Dangerous Myths about Trade and
Foreign Exchange
by Marc Chandler

Sentiment Indicators—Renko, Price Break, Kagi,
Point and Figure:
What They Are and How to Use Them to Trade
by Abe Cofnas

Far From Random:
Using Investor Behavior and Trend Analysis to
Forecast Market Movement
by Richard Lehman

Market Indicators:
The Best-Kept Secret to More Effective Trading and Investing
by Richard Sipley

The Trader's Guide to Key Economic Indicators
Updated and Expanded Edition
by Richard Yamarone

A complete list of our titles is available at
www.bloomberg.com/books

Forex Analysis and Trading

Effective Top-Down Strategies
Combining Fundamental, Position,
and Technical Analyses

T. J. MARTA
and
JOSEPH BRUSUELAS

BLOOMBERG PRESS
NEW YORK

This publication contains the authors' opinions and is designed to provide accurate and authoritative information. It is sold with the understanding that the authors, publisher, and Bloomberg L.P. are not engaged in rendering legal, accounting, investment-planning, or other professional advice. The reader should seek the services of a qualified professional for such advice; the authors, publisher, and Bloomberg L.P. cannot be held responsible for any loss incurred as a result of specific investments or planning decisions made by the reader.

First edition published 2009

1 3 5 7 9 10 8 6 4 2

Library of Congress Cataloging-in-Publication Data

Marta, T. J.
    Forex analysis and trading : effective top-down strategies combining fundamental, position, and technical analyses/T. J. Marta and Joseph Brusuelas. -- 1st ed.
        p. cm.
    Includes bibliographical references and index.
    Summary: "Two foreign exchange trading professionals share their unique top-down approach to currency analysis. Their approach combines the best of fundamental, sentiment, and technical analysis to reveal the most profitable trading opportunities in one of the world's largest markets"--Provided by publisher.
    ISBN 978-1-57660-339-0 (alk. paper)
    1. Foreign exchange market. 2. Foreign exchange futures. 3. Currency convertibility. 4. Investment analysis. I. Brusuelas, Joseph. II. Title.
    HG3851.M315 2009
    332.4'5--dc22

                                                                    2009039852

Mixed Sources
Product group from well-managed forests, controlled sources and recycled wood or fiber
www.fsc.org Cert no. SW-COC-003264
© 1996 Forest Stewardship Council
FSC

This book is dedicated first to my wife, Melissa, and my children, Alexis and Joseph, who have supported me during this effort; second, to Don Alexander and Robert Sinche, who provided solid and steady mentorship; and third, to all who embark on the quest for the Holy Grail of currency valuation.

—T. J. M.

This book is dedicated to my wife, Amanda Jefferis: a woman of extraordinary intelligence, sweetness, and grace without whom life would be far less meaningful.

—J. B.

ACKNOWLEDGMENTS

I'd like to acknowledge the support of my wife, Melissa, and children, Alexis and Joseph, who put up with numerous lost weekends and cancelled and delayed plans. From a professional perspective, this book would not have been possible without Don Alexander, who gave me my first shot on Wall Street and provided me with the framework by which to analyze long-term currency trends. Bob Sinche, my manager at Citigroup's institutional foreign-exchange research group, provided a tireless example of leadership and multifaceted analysis of foreign-exchange valuation and trading opportunities. I'd also like to thank the numerous professionals I've had the pleasure of meeting and discussing Forex with over the years. Finally, special thanks to Stephen Isaacs of Bloomberg for his editorial skills in guiding me through the process of putting years of thoughts and experience into some semblance of organized layout.

—T. J. M.

I would like to acknowledge the support of my father, Herman, and my mother, Donna, and thank my brothers Jason and James and my sister Rebecca, and her husband, A. J., for their love and encouragement. On a professional level, Robert Since, Ryan Sweet, Aaron Smith, Chris Cornell, Nathan Topper, and Michael

Bratus have all provided valuable insight during the writing of this text. Finally, I would like to thank our editor, Stephen Isaacs, whose editorial skills made a complex and time-consuming effort so much easier than it should have been.

—J. B.

CONTENTS

Introduction   *1*

PART I   Fundamental Analysis

Chapter 1   Purchasing Power Parity   11

Chapter 2   Real Exchange Rates and the External Balance   27

Chapter 3   Exchange-Rate Determination over the Medium Term: Parity Conditions, Capital Flows, and Current Account   43

Chapter 4   Fair-Value Regressions   59

PART II   Market Sentiment and Positioning

Chapter 5   Futures Non-Commercial Positioning   97

Chapter 6   Risk Reversals   117

PART III   Technical Analysis

Chapter 7   Trend-Following Indicators   137

Chapter 8   Oscillators   167

Chapter 9   Technical Pattern Recognition   195

Case Studies   211

Conclusion   *245*

Index   *249*

INTRODUCTION

How far will the dollar adjust? Within the context of a $3-trillion-a-day foreign-exchange market, the very question of the basic value of the greenback is perhaps the single biggest day-to-day issue in the global economy. Given the recent turbulence experienced by the global economy, the size of the U.S. current account deficit, the rate of consumption in China, and the structural impediments to growth in the European Union, the fundamental question of the adjustment of the dollar has become more—not less—important in the basic functioning of the global economy.

An economist can primarily focus on how larger macroeconomic changes will affect the value of the euro/dollar in the long run. Yet the larger macroeconomic questions that may affect the valuation of a currency pair over the long run may not be so useful in determining the fair value of a pair over the course of weeks or days, and almost never in the course of a single trading session. Portfolio managers and investors with position horizons of days and weeks cannot wait for long-term theory to "kick in," and traders must instantaneously digest news, economic data releases, and trade flows. A currency strategist interacts with all three types of market participants both as a consumer of those groups' information and as a provider of information to those groups. The range of both inputs and demands requires the application of a variety of methods by which to determine the value of the dollar.

Unlike many texts on foreign-exchange analytics, this text will not present one overarching methodology as "the way" to determine fair currency values. Rather, our approach, which relies on a multidisciplinary examination, provides an analytical framework for institutional analysts to utilize in making successful investment decisions regarding the currencies of major countries. Rather than presenting the disparate disciplines that are employed to make currency decisions in separate vacuums, this book recognizes that different perspectives take on key relevance in markets under varying conditions, and therefore, that the best investment decisions are based on inputs from the full spectrum of considerations.

Our analytical paradigm consists of three main groupings: fundamental, positioning, and technical. By employing this analytical framework, we believe that this text provides an accurate and realistic look into how foreign-exchange analysts, economists, investors, and traders actually seek to put together profitable investment and trading strategies and mitigate risk in the open global economy.

The foundation and starting point of our framework consists of fundamental analyses to provide macroeconomic and cross-asset perspectives. The second grouping consists of positioning

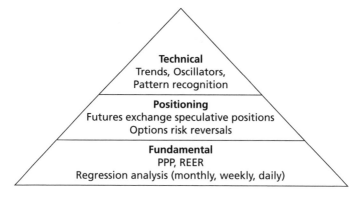

Figure I.1   Comprehensive Currency Analysis Framework

analysis, which attempts to identify extremes in positioning—and so potential turns in market sentiment/direction. Finally, technical analysis provides even more precise price action "triggers" for investment and trading decisions.

Fundamental Analysis

We begin the analysis of any currency using fundamental variables. The very broadest considerations involve purchasing power parity (PPP) and real effective exchange rate (REER) analysis. These frameworks permit an analyst to establish a contextual perspective regarding the "value" of a particular currency. These analytical tools are well suited to long-run exchange-rate determination and are useful to buy-side firms that practice buy-and-hold strategies or global firms that are engaged in long-term planning in a dynamic foreign-exchange environment.

However, the limits of the long-run approach favored by academics and some buy-side institutions are quite observable. Long-run valuations are so broad in scope, they often provide only modest value to traders or risk managers who require more detailed analysis to determine value and potential price action over a more actionable time horizon.

A more precise valuation of a currency's fundamental fair value for the medium term can be obtained using regression analysis based on monthly economic and financial data. Regressing the currency against financial data using fifty-two weeks of weekly data further refines this estimate. Finally, recognizing that different fundamental considerations can dominate price action over shorter time horizons, one can employ regression analysis of daily price action using sixty-day time horizons to obtain short-term valuations.

Positioning Analysis

Whereas the above methods provide a robust analysis using macro-economic and cross-asset underpinnings to explain valuations and price action, they do not always lead to profitable decisions. Too often, a purely fundamental approach ignores the psychological aspect of market behavior. According to an old, wise adage, "the markets can stay irrational longer than an investor can stay solvent." Thus, we incorporate a second level of analysis based on measures of market positioning that allows market actors and risk managers to identify extremes and potential changes in the direction of the market.

Two publicly available measures of market sentiment are the positions reported to the U.S. Commodity Futures Trading Commission (CFTC) by non-commercial traders (sometimes referred to as speculators) and options risk reversals. The CFTC positions are collected by the CFTC once per week on Tuesdays and released on Fridays. Extremes in the positions of non-commercial traders relative to the CFTC positions in recent months allow an analyst to identify when at least one segment of the trading/investing community has not only likely exhausted its ability to contribute further to a price trend, but also could be more likely to begin trading the other way in a market, precipitating a reversal in price action. The drawback of the data is that it is published late on Friday afternoons in the United States when liquidity is low, and that it is three days old when released.

A timelier positioning indicator, although one measuring a different segment of the market, is the risk-reversal skew in the options market (risk reversals). Risk reversals measure the difference in premium for puts versus calls on a particular currency. Extreme readings suggest that options traders are "off balance" in their view regarding future price action, which suggests an increased potential for a reversal in price action. Whereas shifts in both the CFTC and risk reversals tend to correspond to shifts in price action relative to trend, they are frustratingly ambiguous in providing concrete entry or exit levels, and this leads us to the third section of our currency analysis: technical analysis.

Technical Analysis

Detractors liken technical analysis to reading tea leaves. Technical analysts retort that price action "says it all" regarding what is going on in the market and scoff at how often "fundamentalists" obstinately hold a position when price action is screaming that one's view of how the world works "just isn't so." We remain firmly neutral in this bitter debate, noting only from a pragmatic perspective that if enough market participants decide that price action in regards to a channel support, a head-and-shoulder neckline, or a 76.4 percent Fibonacci retracement is important, then it probably *is* important.

Consequently, we are not looking to establish "black box" technical trading models, but to offer a framework that incorporates changing market sentiment and an appreciation of which specific levels or patterns could be decisive in influencing behavior and price action. In viewing the foreign-exchange markets through a multidimensional prism, a decision maker can make more informed—and profitable—decisions.

PART

I

Fundamental Analysis

As we write this in the spring of 2009, the near collapse of the global financial system in 2008 has ushered in the most severe economic downturn since the Great Depression. Dislocation in financial markets caused by the breakdown of monetary discipline, lack of financial regulation, and imprudent lending standards by financials has unleashed a sea of volatility in the global market for foreign exchange.

This market, with a volume of close to three trillion dollars per day, has perhaps experienced its greatest volatility of any time during the era of floating exchange rates. Between January 2007 and February 2009, the exchange rate of the euro/dollar (EUR/USD) has moved from a position of overvaluation to undervaluation and back. The yen has seen highs not experienced since 1995, and the stabilization of emerging market currencies such as Mexico's has been lost amid 10 percent declines in valuation in a single day against the dollar.

From December 2008 to February 2009, market sentiment swung from expecting the long-term secular decline of the dollar to the greenback threatening to drive towards parity with the euro. A few short months later, the new quantitative easing policy of the U.S. Federal Reserve, which provides an outsized risk to the long-term inflation prospects of the United States, has swung the market back in the other direction. The euro once again, as of June 2009, appears to be ascendant and the dollar in decline. Unless, of course, the European Central Bank adopts its own version of quantitative easing that will engender another period of volatility in currency markets. Of course, the Chinese call for the adoption of a new global reserve currency, due to the problems in the advanced economies, carries with it the possibility to reorder the global economic landscape.

Under such conditions, the attempt by economists and currency strategists to construct short-term trading strategies or corporate actors to manage foreign-exchange risk is fraught with extreme difficulty. But the advent of a global economy that demands the exchange of currency on a continuous basis does not provide such a luxury.

Yet what on one hand may seem to be a curse, on the other offers tremendous opportunity. For the seasoned foreign-exchange trader this is a difficult but potentially lucrative environment in which to put into practice the ideas, tactics, and strategies at the heart of this text.

So, under such conditions, how does one derive the fair value of the dollar versus the other major currencies? Where should one start, given the significant disturbances in the foreign-exchange markets observed over the past forty years and the probability of further volatility ahead? What value does fundamental analysis have for the currency analyst in such an environment? The first section of this text intends to provide an answer to those potent questions by presenting the theoretical backbone of fundamental analysis, which still plays a significant role in assessing fair exchange-rate values.

1 | Purchasing Power Parity

Purchasing power parity (PPP): three words that are sure to warm the heart of any currency economist. But that same concept is certain to cast a glaze over the eyes of most observers of foreign-exchange markets and send a surge of skepticism up the spines of experienced foreign-exchange traders. Yet, the value of such a tried-and-true method of deriving foreign-exchange rates has not diminished.

The Organization for Economic Cooperation and Development (OECD) defines PPP as the rate of currency conversion that equalizes the purchasing power of different currencies by eliminating the differences in price levels between countries. Put a bit more simply, PPP is a method through which one can evaluate how changes in the absolute or relative price level drive changes in the underlying exchange rate between two currencies. This chapter discusses the relative usefulness and shortcomings of employing PPP in foreign-exchange analysis.

Law of One Price

To obtain a solid grasp of the concept of PPP, it is necessary to first understand the law of one price. The law of price reflects the idea that if two firms in different countries produce identical goods, assuming that transportation costs are stable and trade barriers low, then the cost of that good should be the same throughout the global system. Thus, if American-made desktop computers cost $90.00 per unit in the United States, and an identical Japanese computer costs 8,100 yen in Japan, the exchange rate must be 90 yen per dollar ($0.011 per yen). If this condition holds, then one U.S. computer must sell for 8,100 yen in Japan, and one Japanese desktop must sell for $90 in America.

If the exchange rate were to increase to 180 yen to the dollar, then the cost of a Japanese desktop computer would be $45.00 per unit, and the price of the same American product in Japan would be 16,200 yen. Thus, the cost of a Japanese computer would be reduced by roughly half, due to the change in the relative exchange rate, increasing the purchasing power of all those holding dollars. (See **Figure 1.1**.)

In theory, due to Japanese computers being relatively cheap, demand for these computers in both America and Japan should increase and demand for U.S. computers should fall to close to zero. Since U.S. computers are more expensive than the identical machine in Japan, the net impact is that the resulting increase in supply of U.S. computers will be reduced as the exchange rate falls back to $90.00, which would bring the price of identical computers in Japan and the U.S. back into alignment.

Purchasing Power Parity

Economists often use PPP to ascertain the fundamental value in foreign-exchange markets between two currencies. It asserts that the exchange rate between any two currencies will adjust in light of changes in the price levels of the two home countries of the units of exchange. At its core, PPP is an attempt to explain the relationship between the prices of tradable goods and the exchange rate. Thus, the theory of PPP states that the long-run equilibrium value (E) of a currency is primarily determined by the ratio of domestic prices (P) in the home country relative to those abroad (P^*).

$$E = P/P^* \tag{1.1}$$

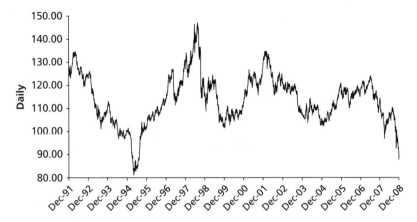

Figure 1.1   Dollar/Yen Exchange Rates

Source: Federal Reserve Board.

Using this framework, the theory of PPP would suggest that the long-term equilibrium value of the dollar/yen rate ($/¥) would be determined by the ratio of the price level in the United States (P_{US}) relative to the price level in Japan (P_J).

$$\$/¥ = P_J/P_{US}$$

According to PPP theory, one can fairly derive the fundamental value of a currency by estimating what an identical product can be purchased for at home and abroad. In our example, the relative cost of an identical computer in the United States should be exactly the same as it is in Japan.

However, theory does not always approximate reality. Should exchange rates overshoot or undershoot equilibrium PPP levels, opportunities for individuals to engage in arbitrage would ensue. For example, if computers in the United States due to a change in the exchange rate were to become cheaper than those in Japan, opportunistic individuals and firms could then buy low in the United States, sell high in Japan, and capitalize on the relative change in the exchange rate. Thus, capital and goods would flow between the two countries until such a time (no doubt a very short period of time) when the cost of purchasing identical computers in both the United States and Japan falls back into equilibrium.

Variation on a Theme

Inside the investment community most economists and foreign-exchange analysts use some variation of purchasing power parity to derive what they consider to be a reliable and robust estimate of the fair value of exchange rates. Should exchange rates of a currency pair deviate too far from PPP, many if not most analysts would expect over the long term that the pair would move back towards equilibrium.

Yet, as Keynes stated, "in the long run, we shall all be dead." Thus, it is of little surprise to observe that there is more than one version of PPP and several factors that affect exchange rates in the long run.

Absolute Purchasing Power

The theoretical underpinning of PPP rests on a set of assumptions. Thus, by conveniently assuming away differences in transportation costs, transactions costs, restrictions in trade, and taxes, it is possible that tradable goods that are identical should be available at the same price anywhere in the global economy after accounting for exchange rates. This is often referred to as the absolute version of PPP simply because it deals with an absolute price level. This is easily understood by the following: Let S indicate the U.S. dollar/yen exchange rate, $\$/\yen$. Then let P signify the price level in the United States and P^* denote the price level in Japan. Thus, we can express the absolute version of PPP as

$$P = S \times P^* \tag{1.2}$$

Put a bit more simply, the price level of the domestic currency should be absolutely equal to the foreign price level multiplied by the spot exchange rate. This version of PPP can be applied to all identical tradable goods and services. Thus, P is a representation of a wide range of goods, but not a single good. This strongly suggests that the activity of arbitrage plays a critical role as a catalyst for the convergence of prices implied by the law of one price that lies at the heart of the idea of absolute purchasing power parity.

Shortcomings in Absolute Purchasing Power Parity

However conceptually attractive the absolute variant of PPP is, there are several shortcomings to this potent explanation of long-term exchange rates. Paramount among these shortcomings is the fact that as a short-term predictor of exchange-rate movements, PPP does not have the best record. How could a basic theoretic explanation that is used in just about every introductory and intermediate economic textbook be so deficient? The answer is located in the basic assumptions behind absolute PPP.

First, the basic assumptions of no differences in transportation costs in an era of volatile energy costs and the variation in energy subsidies from country to country cast considerable doubt upon this idea.

Second, the variations in tariffs and taxes from country to country are quite dramatic, and these factors play a significant role in shaping the incentives to produce and the relative costs of goods.

Simplification of reality through the use of such assumptions is quite useful for the development of theory and the models to support it. Yet, for the spot trader or forward-desk analyst, theoretical elegance or long-term efficacy is of little use in formulating day-to-day or near-term strategies.

Relative Purchasing Power

Due to the limitations of the absolute version of PPP, some analysts rely on a bounded version that focuses on price changes as opposed to a singular emphasis on absolute price levels. This is best understood by the following. Let %Δ denote the percentage change of a variable, S the spot rate, P the price level, and P^* the foreign price level. Thus, the concept of relative purchasing power can best be expressed by the following:

$$\%\Delta S = \%\Delta P - \%\Delta P* \qquad (1.3)$$

This implies that a change in the exchange rate equals the difference in percentage change in prices between the two economies. Foreign exchange-rate analysts would then focus on the public rate of inflation. Keeping within the framework of our earlier example, then let Π be the rate of inflation in the United States and $\Pi*$ be the rate of inflation in Japan. Then if a foreign-exchange analyst were interested in seeking to estimate the possible appreciation or depreciation of the dollar/yen spot rate, he would investigate the differences between the two countries' inflation rates. Thus, we can rewrite the expression for relative PPP as

$$\%\Delta S = \Pi - \Pi* \qquad (1.4)$$

For example, assume that the nominal exchange rate for the USD/UK pound ($/£) in a given base year was $1.50. Then assume that the price of goods and services in the United States had risen by 8 percent, and the cost of those same goods and services in the United Kingdom had risen by 4 percent. Then the PPP spot rate would be $1.50/£1 × 1.08/1.04 = $1.557/£1. The nominal exchange rate of $1.557/£1 can be used to establish a PPP comparison to the base period. Thus, a nominal exchange rate greater than $1.557/£1 implies that the British pound is overvalued, and a nominal exchange rate less than $1.557/£1 suggests that the U.S. dollar is overvalued.

PPP and Exchange-Rate Analysis

Without a doubt, PPP is a useful method in the toolbox of any economist. Over the long run, PPP can provide a fairly effective tool for predicting exchange rates. Yet, like many theoretical propositions in the dismal science, the reliability of either version of PPP is a function of the conditions under which it is used. For example, if one were to observe a monetary-induced shock to an equilibrium position, PPP will tend to hold up very well. Why?

Because, under the quantity theory of money, the supply of money relative to the demand for money affects the price level of a currency. Using PPP theory, one would find that currency values would adjust as prices on an international basis adjust. If one assumes that the supply of money determines the price level, changes in relative prices would then act as the primary catalyst for a change in the exchange rate. Under such conditions, it is fair to conclude that a change in monetary policy can facilitate a change in exchange rates and does provide a fairly convincing validation of the theory of PPP. (See **Figure 1.2**.)

However, not all shocks to a general equilibrium position are monetarily induced. Real factors such as changes to the terms of trade, the discovery of scarce resources, productivity shocks, and changes in the rate of growth will often alter the current account balance of a country and have an impact on exchange rates. A change in the underlying long-term trend in the current account will often occur outside of any change in the relative price levels. Such a change in the long-term trend inside a country's current

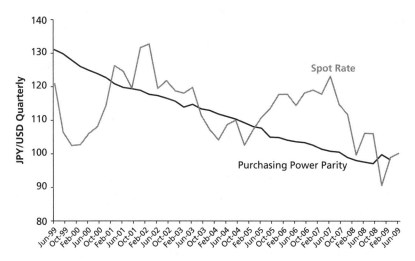

Figure 1.2   Japanese Yen Purchasing Power Parity vs. Spot Rate

Source: Bloomberg.

account will often stimulate a change in exchange rates to reflect a positive or negative change in the current account balance.

Thus, a change in real factors such as a productivity shock can cause a fundamental reorientation of how the market perceives the fair value of an exchange rate that is not accompanied by a change in the underlying price level. This strongly implies that an equilibrium exchange rate can deviate from that which would be predicted by the theoretical propositions put forward by PPP and does suggest that there are a range of factors and methods that can be used to explain changes in exchange rates. More pertinently, the absolutely unbounded version of PPP may not provide a satisfactory explanation of exchange rates under a wide range of conditions.

Calculating PPP

One of the major issues surrounding the use of PPP to determine the fair value of exchange rate is that there are an extraordinarily large number of ways to calculate it. The method that one chooses may alter the outcome that one derives. For the foreign-exchange analyst, this is a particularly problematic issue since choosing a method to calculate PPP will determine the extent to which a currency is overvalued or undervalued. Thus, whether one uses a particular price level, price deflator, or price index will provide the framework in which an analyst may take a position in the market on a short- or long-term basis. Thus, whether one chooses to employ the consumer price index (CPI), producer price index, or personal consumption expenditure deflator in an attempt to derive the correct value of a currency pair is crucial and will cause variation in outcomes.

For example, if one were to choose the consumer price index between the United States and the European Union as a basis to derive the fair value of the EUR/USD, one would run into two problems. First, the composition of relative price indexes varies between countries and regions. The consumer price index inside the United States is quite different from that of the European Union. In the U.S. CPI, the cost of shelter is given an extraordinarily large weight of over 40 percent in the index, whereas in the European Union, it is given far less. The weightings inside the relative indexes reflect the different tastes and preferences of the respective consumers inside each economy. As such, there is no optimal benchmark to compare relative prices across international boundaries for a foreign-exchange strategist.

Second, both the absolute and relative version of PPP depend on the assumption of tradable and identical goods. It is without a doubt that within the design of price indexes, non-tradable goods make their way into the constructs and affect the relative price level. Thus, one can lean toward using wholesale price indexes and producer price indexes that are composed of tradable goods, but that too is fraught with risks. An overdependence on the use of such indexes presents problems in that a prediction of an exchange rate would be of dubious value, since a fair value estimate based on purely tradable goods could conceivably constitute a tautology and provide a misleading and costly set of erroneous information for a trading operation.

Finally, there are always issues surrounding the choice of a base year for the construction of an index or providing a profitable PPP calculation. One of the primary assumptions behind PPP is that a change in an exchange rate can be traced to a change in the price level that is based on the selection of a carefully crafted and appropriate base year. Therein lies the problem. The choice of a base year can decisively influence the assessment of whether a currency is fairly valued.

It is typical for analysts to choose a base year that corresponds with major structural changes in the international economic system when an index could plausibly be constructed to reflect a zero current account balance between two countries. Such years as 1973, when the United States abrogated the gold standard, or perhaps the last year the U.S. current account was in balance, 1980, are often chosen by savvy analysts as base years to construct a meaningful index.

In truth, just about any choice of a base year can be criticized as arbitrary. There is some truthfulness to this criticism due to the difficulties of accurately estimating the long-run value of an exchange rate in any given year over the long term.

So, how does one solve this problem? One useful approach to solving the base-year problem is to construct the long-run moving average of an exchange rate. Given the volatility of exchange rates during the era of floating rates, any analyst worth his salt can attest to the fact that there are sustained and persistent deviations away from the long-run equilibrium path as would be predicted by PPP. Thus, the construction of a moving average around the long-term equilibrium value that would be predicted by PPP is a useful way to predict exchange-rate movements.

Should there be a structural change driven by a productivity shock or a change in real factors, this construct may not provide a satisfactory valuation of an exchange rate. Under such conditions, the construction of the long-run moving average may tend to undershoot the true value of the exchange rate, and it may be more useful to construct a weighted moving average of past trends in the underlying exchange rate. Whatever the case, it is paramount that a currency economist or a foreign-exchange analyst be cognizant of the change in the monetary environment and real factors in order to construct profitable trading strategies or manage risk in the foreign-exchange market.

A second way of dealing with problems associated with choosing a base year is to use the constructs of the International Monetary Fund (IMF) and the Organization for Economic Cooperation and Development (OECD). The recent updating of PPP by the International Comparison Program is benchmarked to the year 2005. This update, which is used to derive estimates of PPP, sought to take into account price differences between countries, and permit comparisons of market size, structural differences between and among economies, and the purchasing power of national currencies. The update brings together the efforts of the ICP and the OECD PPP program, provides estimates of GDP per capita for 146 countries, and constructs a price level index that intends to demonstrate which economies are the most inexpensive and expensive using foreign-exchange rates. Although this effort has proven somewhat controversial, the survey conducted during 2005 collected prices for more than one thousand goods and services,

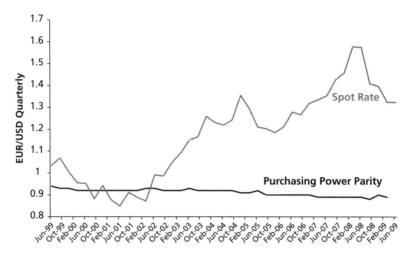

Figure 1.3   Euro and USD Purchasing Power Parity vs. Spot Rate

Source: Bloomberg.

according to the ICP, using innovative data validation tools to improve the quality of the data.

PPP—An Empirical Assessment

There is a heavy volume of academic literature that empirically tests the basic theoretical propositions behind PPP. There is a preponderance of evidence that implies that over the long term exchange rates do tend to converge toward their PPP values, albeit with sustained and persistent deviations in the short and medium term. (See **Figure 1.3**.)

The major question that most analysts ask is how long these deviations from the long-term trend take. The empirical literature strongly suggests that the rate of convergence is somewhat slow and it can take up to five years before a deviation from the longer-term underlying trend can evaporate.

Is the Dollar Overvalued?

There has been much ink spent on the question of whether the greenback is overvalued. Indeed during the period from July

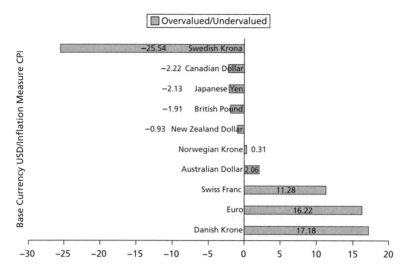

Figure 1.4 G10 Purchasing Power Parities

Source: Bloomberg.

2002 to August 2008, one did see a fairly strong secular downward trend in the value of the dollar. Many analysts attributed this to the combination of the persistent imbalances in the global economy due to overspending on the part of American consumers and oversaving on the part of Chinese consumers. (See **Figure 1.4**.) Others attribute the weak dollar to the accommodative monetary stance of the Alan Greenspan and Ben Bernanke Fed regimes during that time.

However, during the most intense portion of the global financial and banking crisis of 2007 to 2009—between October and December of 2008—the dollar became a safe haven. Thus, the market observed a sharp correction upward in the value of the dollar vis-à-vis the euro. (See **Figure 1.5**.)

The synchronized global recession that became quite apparent in late 2008 was the primary catalyst behind a severe bout of risk aversion among global investors. Under the extreme conditions wrought by a global banking crisis, the relative safety of U.S. Treasury instruments caused euros, pesos, and Swiss francs to be exchanged for U.S. dollars.

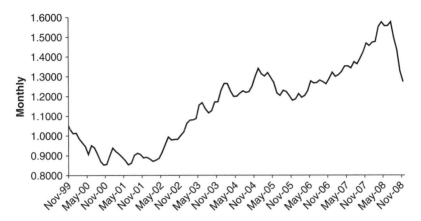

Figure 1.5   Euro/USD Exchange Rate

Source: Federal Reserve Board.

This behavior was primarily a function of the long-standing role the dollar has played as the reserve currency of the global economy. Another part represented the inertia of traders, who in a crisis fall back on the relative safety of the dollar.

Quantitative Easing

As the global economic crisis deepened, global central banks engaged in quantitative easing. Quantitative easing involves a central bank forgoing its independence and effectively driving its target rate to zero. Once the central bank takes the policy rate to zero, it removes any need to keep pressure on bank reserve positions to ensure that its target rate remains positive. Thus, without any need to keep control of its balance sheet, the central bank can begin to inject liquidity into the economy, or in the case of the United States, recapitalize the banks and repair the credit system.

Whereas it is technically possible for a central bank to engage in quantitative easing and still maintain a positive policy rate, the point here is that as the central banks engaged in quantitative easing policies, the foreign-exchange market became unmoored.

The strong rally in the value of the dollar that began in late 2008 accompanied the reduction in policy rates across the major trading states. However, once the U.S. Federal Reserve announced that it would engage in a robust policy of quantitative easing the greenback experienced a sharp reversal against the euro and the yen.

Yet, due to the pervasive problems in the European banking sector and the severe contraction in the euro zone economies, the duration and intensity of that correction was limited. Market participants doubted the resolve of European Central Bank authorities to maintain their policy stance of avoiding the quantitative easing regimes adopted by the Federal Reserve, Bank of England, Bank of Canada, Bank of Japan, and Swiss National Bank. At the first sign of weakness, the greenback saw gains against most major currencies as the financial crisis continued to roil global markets.

New Reserve Arrangements?

The near collapse of the global system of finance left the United States unable to provide the economic leadership necessary to coordinate global action to mitigate the synchronized slowdown in the international economy. Dissatisfaction with the role that the world's reserve currency, the dollar, had played in the transmission of the crisis built among the countries in possession of capital account surpluses. At the April 2009 G-20 meeting one of the largest surplus countries, the People's Republic of China (PRC), called for the creation of a new global reserve currency.

The PRC suggested that the special drawing rights (SDR), a reserve asset created by the International Monetary Fund in 1969 to supplement the reserves of member countries, be considered as a potential replacement.

The SDR, which serves as a unit of account based on a basket of currencies, would provide the IMF with the capacity to increase the global money supply in a crisis. Under the initial proposal, this would bestow upon the IMF a powerful tool to address problems in the emerging world and would provide a greater voice in the body to emerging economies.

Of course, it goes without saying that the advanced economies will be loath to surrender their power in the body or bequeath to an international body the ability to create money to pursue a political agenda that may have little to do with sound macro-economic policy.

Beyond the considerable technical considerations and political hurdles, it is highly unlikely that the dollar will lose its position as the global reserve currency anytime soon. To create a market for a synthetic currency, such as a supersovereign SDR, would require a large and wealthy nation, not an international organization, to subsidize the cost of attracting buyers and sellers to participate in the creation of a new market over a period of time before it can become institutionalized.

The type of deep and liquid markets that would hold the attention of market participants are typically not the artificial creations of supranational authorities. Rather, they spontaneously develop based on the needs of buyers and sellers or savers and borrowers to fill unmet needs in the wider universe of markets.

Moreover, China holds nearly $2 trillion worth of U.S. Treasury securities, and central banks hold trillions more in dollars and dollar-denominated securities. The dollar is still the preeminent unit of account in much of the world. The question is, should the quantitative easing policy pursued by the U.S. central bank not succeed, will the dollar continue to be the primary reserve asset?

Many analysts would still contend that the large current account deficit run by the United States should continue to facilitate a secular decline in the value of the dollar. Yet, with the global financial system still quite shaky after a tumultuous 2008 volatility in the foreign-exchange market, the deficit seems poised to remain the rule rather than the exception. It is our assessment that because of the damage wrought by the financial crisis and the ensuing process of the deleveraging of U.S. consumers, global financials will compress the normal secular cycle of deviations from PPP from five years into a much shorter time frame.

It may be premature to state that the six-year upswing in the euro may have come to a conclusion. Firms in an era of heightened risk have opted for the relative safety of U.S. Treasuries, which has caused many holders of euros and other foreign currencies to exchange those holdings for greenbacks to purchase

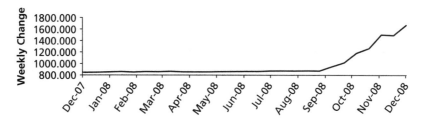

Figure 1.6   Adjusted Monetary Base

Source: St. Louis Fed.

U.S. government bonds. It is too soon to know the full impact on the long-term value of the dollar, due to the shift in monetary policy by the Fed towards quantitative easing. The flood of the market with newly minted dollars (see **Figure 1.6**) to recapitalize the U.S. banking system and flood the domestic economy with liquidity to stabilize credit markets may ward off any deflationary impulse wrought by the process of deleveraging.

But over the long term, it could unleash the demon of inflation. One danger is that the Fed could prove lax on hiking rates once the U.S. economy recovers. Another danger is that the Fed's independence becomes compromised due to political pressure on the part of the federal government and political appointees who intend to use inflation as a method to monetize the debt of both the U.S. federal government and individual consumers. In either case, markets will respond dramatically. Long-term interest rates will increase and the value of the dollar will plummet. Should that occur, there is no country or confederation such as the European Union ready to assume the mantle of international economic leadership and put forward its own currency as the primary reserve asset in the global economy.

Over the long term, the use of PPP as a method to fairly value exchange rates will remain a useful and attractive option for those interested in the longer-run value of a given currency. Yet in the near term it is certain that analysts and traders will continue to rely upon a range of methods and models to fairly value currency and estimate future currency movements. The remaining chapters of this book will concentrate on those methods and models that drive currency analytics and trading in financial markets.

2 | Real Exchange Rates and the External Balance

Deriving the probable path that a currency will take over the medium to long run is a required task for any foreign-exchange analyst. The use of PPP models is often the foundation for completing such a task. Yet, as the previous chapter demonstrates, the shortcomings in the PPP approach are many. More important, exchange rates will often see large deviations from their true long-run values for extended periods of time.

The inability of PPP theory to account for such persistent and sizable deviations away from what PPP would predict demands that traders and analysts rely upon other methods. One fundamental approach that is widely used to ascertain long-run values is the internal-external balance approach. The method focuses on the long-run equilibrium real exchange rate, which we define as that currency value that reflects the resting of the external and internal balance in a stable equilibrium.

The internal balance is best defined as the obtainment of some full level of employment. The external balance can be defined as some sustainable target associated with the current account. Whereas it can be argued that for the long-run equilibrium real exchange rate to be obtained, the current-account balance will have to reach zero, we think that this may be slightly overstating the case. The current account does not necessarily need to fall to zero but needs to reach a steady, stable, and sustainable level.[1]

Perhaps the more pertinent question that needs to be addressed is whether current-account deficits are sustainable over the long term. Should they prove to be durable, then the short- to medium-run path of a given exchange rate should be roughly accurate. If not, as is often the case, the long run exchange rate will have to adjust to ensure that the current account moves towards a much more sustainable level over the long term.

For example, consider a country which is experiencing full employment and a growing current-account deficit fueled by expansionary fiscal policy. Such a hypothetical country would face quite a quandary. Excessive domestic demand, which has acted as a catalyst for growth, trade, and current-account deficit, shows no signs of abating. To correct such an imbalance, the foreign-exchange rate of the country would have to experience depreciation to restore some semblance of macroeconomic balance. This is a fair description of what occurred in the Mexican currency crisis in 1994, when government officials in Mexico City were forced to accept a sharp devaluation of the peso to reflect the unsustainable level in the country's current account.

Changes in the internal-external balance can provide a powerful dose of gravity on real long-run exchange rates. Clearly, there is no single factor model of exchange-rate determination. In general equilibrium, the exchange rate responds to many shocks including productivity, changes in the terms of trade, and fiscal policy. The bulk of this chapter will address these ideas.

---

1. John Williamson, "*The Exchange Rate System*," Policy Analyses in International Economics 5, Peterson Institute for International Economics, Washington, DC, 1983.

Productivity Shocks and the Long-Run Equilibrium Exchange Rate

The long boom in the 1990s that the United States experienced is often associated with an increase in productivity driven by advances in information technology. Indeed, the period was characterized by a strong dollar vis-à-vis the mark and its successor, the euro, as well as the yen. According to conventional wisdom among market participants and in the opinion of former U.S. Fed Chairman Alan Greenspan, this development was partially a function of the unexpected increase in the rate of productivity in the United States.

Between 1995 and 1999, the strong acceleration in the rate of productivity growth in the United States accompanied a 5.8 percent appreciation of the dollar against the euro and a 4.8 percent climb against the yen, on an annual basis. (See **Figure 2.1**.)

According to Greenspan, the increase in demand for the dollar was a function of expectations forming among market participants that rates of productivity in the United States would see greater

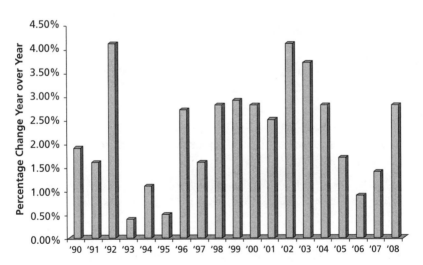

Figure 2.1   U.S. Productivity

Source: Bureau of Labor Statistics.

increases than those thought to be in Europe's future. This was part of the reason why the euro, the world's other major reserve currency, got off to such a tough start.

Differentials in total factor productivity across the G-20 during the 1990s do seem to have played a role in the appreciation of the dollar. However, that appreciation was accompanied by exploding trade deficits and an expansion of its current-account deficit. Thus, many bearish market participants and academic scholars of that era made a vigorous case that the dollar was fundamentally overvalued and that the United States would have to undergo a significant macroeconomic reorientation in response to the unsustainable internal and external imbalances that were forming.

Perhaps, it is of little surprise that following the bursting of the dot-com bubble, the recession of 2000 to 2001, the intense period of geopolitical uncertainty following 9/11, and the 2003 invasion of Iraq that market participants substantially changed their expectations regarding the value of the dollar. So to what extent has the dollar's depreciation since 2002 been a reflection of changing expectations about U.S. productivity and growth relative to the rest of Europe?

The probability of the United States sustaining differentials in the rate of productivity in contrast with that of the euro zone in coming years is often cited as a major factor in the relative decline in the value of the greenback since 2002. Moreover, given the significant development of macroeconomic imbalances in savings and consumption in the global economy, primarily due to China and the United States, market participants have shifted their focus and expectations toward a painful period of macroeconomic adjustment ahead.

With the global economy appearing to have entered a period of macroeconomic adjustment that looks to be organized around the near meltdown of the domestic system of finance in the United States, it is quite uncertain how exchange rates will respond. The U.S. rate of productivity has slipped below its average seen in 1995 to 2005, yet U.S. Treasury instruments and the currency itself still appear to be considered a safe haven for many in the international economy. How the market will absorb and interpret the rise of "quantitative easing" in the United States, Canada, England, Japan, and Switzerland and the substantial fiscal stimulus, which in part will be dedicated to some productivity-enhancing infrastructure, is perhaps one of the crucial questions hanging over the foreign-exchange markets over the next several years.

Terms of Trade and Exchange Rates

The very impressive gains in the value of the dollar seen in the mid-1990s may have been driven by the increase in productivity in the United States, but according to a study by the Federal Reserve, most of those gains were concentrated in the tradables sector of the U.S. economy. Indeed, changes in the terms of trade can often play a decisive role in the determination of real exchange rates.

The terms of trade, which we define as the relationship over time between the price of a country's exports to the price of its imports, has long played an important role in exchange-rate determination. If export prices are higher than import prices, the terms of trade are said to be favorable. Thus, the notion that the terms of trade should be an important factor in deriving the real long-run equilibrium value of a currency should be intuitive. As such, if a country observes deterioration (improvement) in its terms of trade, then a fall (rise) in the price of its exports (imports) relative to that of its imports (exports) should cause a fall in that country's real long-run equilibrium value.

Should such a development persist, a fall in the price of imports relative to exports should be facilitated by a decline in demand on an international basis for that country's exports. The ensuing decline in the current account should facilitate depreciation in the real long-run equilibrium value of the country's currency.

During the previous two decades, what in the foreign-exchange community are referred to as the *commodity currencies*—a loose

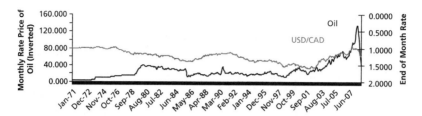

Figure 2.2   Oil and the U.S. Dollar/Canadian Dollar Rates

Source: St. Louis Fed.

term used to describe the Australian, Canadian, Norwegian, Swedish, and New Zealand currencies—have seen their relative valuations improve along with their terms of trade.

For example, the Canadian dollar (CAD), which just over a decade ago in December 1998 saw a low of 1.55 against the dollar, in mid-2008 dipped below parity in a show of strength associated with the surge in commodity prices, including that of oil, as shown in **Figure 2.2**.

Figure 2.2 demonstrates the structural change that occurred in the foreign-exchange market in the aftermath of the geopolitical and macroeconomic environment at the turn of the century. During the 1990s, traders had formed expectations that higher energy prices implied a bearish position should be taken on the CAD due to its deep integration with the U.S. economy.

Yet with hostilities breaking out in the Middle East after 9/11, increased globalization, and excessive liquidity provided by the Fed and the securitization process, the demand for oil (and commodities generally) from emerging markets exploded. As a result, the relationship between the value of the CAD and the price of oil changed. Beginning in 2002 as the price of oil began its steady ascent to $1.47 per barrel in the summer of 2008, the value of the CAD climbed along with it until it reached parity with the U.S. dollar. One can observe that the trading community, once the CAD reached parity, stepped on the brakes and did not fall into the bear trap associated with the overshooting of the price per barrel of oil.

Fiscal Changes and the Long-Run Real Equilibrium Exchange Rate

Attributing changes in the long-run real equilibrium exchange rate to fiscal changes until recently has been a secondary concern among many foreign-exchange analysts. The improvement in the fiscal condition in the United States during the 1990s, followed by relatively mild deficits in real terms through the middle part of the following decade, caused many market participants to discount this factor.

However, the onset of the global financial crisis beginning in 2007 and the robust fiscal response by the United States beginning in 2008 have again placed renewed attention on the sheer volume of fiscal spending on the part of the federal government. With the fiscal year 2009 deficit expected to exceed $2.5 trillion and the stimulus plan in 2009 to 2010 anticipated to exceed another $1 trillion, market participants have begun to assess just how all this will affect the long-run equilibrium value of the greenback. (See **Figure 2.3**.)

This renewed focus is not without precedent. According to a study by Froot and Rogoff, there is a strong correlation between government spending and the real exchange rate during the Bretton Woods era of 1950 to 1973.[2]

The financing of the expansion of the Vietnam War and the Great Society programs by the Johnson administration in the late 1960s is often thought to have contributed to a decline in the real exchange rate during that period, even though the nominal value of the dollar was fixed at the time. Indeed, the overvaluation of the dollar, fixed at a price of $35.00 per ounce of gold, resulted in a run on the U.S. gold stock and the ultimate abrogation of the postwar currency arrangements in 1973 by the Nixon administration.

---

2. Kenneth Froot and Kenneth Rogoff, "Perspectives on PPP and Long-Run Real Exchange Rates," NBER Working Paper No. W4952, 1994.

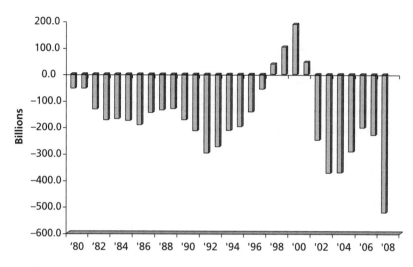

Figure 2.3 U.S. Fiscal Path 1980 to 2009

Source: St. Louis Fed.

This precedent is not without value. The combination of the extraordinary fiscal stimulus on the part of the U.S. federal government and the onset of the quantitative easing program by the Federal Reserve, under the guidance of Ben Bernanke, has stimulated much discussion regarding the status of the U.S. dollar as the world's reserve currency and if the current flexible international currency regime can survive in its current form.

At the 2009 G-20 meeting, member states allocated $250 billion in special drawing rights, the International Monetary Fund's synthetic global currency. This was done in part as a response to the growing dissatisfaction among the member states over the role played by the dollar in transmitting toxic mortgage-backed securities throughout the global system of finance.

International Investment and Exchange Rates

There is a positive long-run relationship between the net international investment position as a percentage of GDP and the real effective exchange rate of a country. This relationship tends to hold up over the long run for the following reasons.

A country may be able to attract a sufficient quantity of capital to finance its deficit in the near term, but it is very difficult to accomplish over the long run. In fact, on a monthly or quarterly basis, there may not be a positive relationship between a country's external deficit and the real exchange rate.

However, should its domestic economy suffer from an economic shock or the international rate environment change, such a country is likely to reach a point where its ability to attract capital at the rate it is willing to pay will be severely curtailed.

For example, until recently the United States has run a current-account deficit in excess of 5 percent of GDP for many years. In 2004 alone, the U.S. current account absorbed 75 percent of the combined current-account surpluses of Germany, Japan, China, and all the world's surplus countries.[3] This condition persists to this day, but the decline in the relative value of the dollar since 2002 will need to continue for the United States to be able to effectively meet its financial obligations to its foreign financiers.

So how has the United States been able to sustain such a large external account imbalance without triggering a run on the dollar? The dollar remains the world's reserve currency and still represents a store of value in a time of crisis. More important, the United States has earned a greater rate of return on its international investments than it has paid out on its external liabilities. Thus, the dollar has not only been resilient but it has also benefited from the dynamic corporate sector based in the United States that participates in the global economy.

But over time, even the United States will not be able to escape the reality of the very difficult position it finds itself in. Given the breadth and depth of the financial crisis of 2007 to 2009, it would be of little surprise to observe a depreciation in the real exchange rate of the dollar going forward until such a point that

---

3. Maurice Obstfeld and Kenneth Rogoff, "Global Current Account Imbalances and Exchange Rate Adjustments," accessed at http://www.econ.berkeley.edu/ ~obstfeld/global_current.pdf, p. 2.

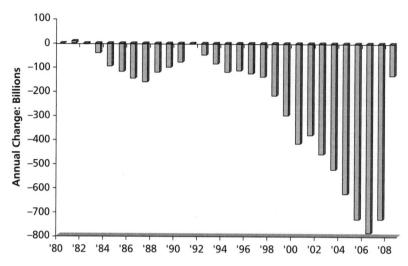

Figure 2.4   U.S. Current-Account Deficit

Source: Bloomberg.

the current-account deficit shrinks to a more sustainable level (somewhere below 2 percent of gross domestic product).

Not all countries are as fortunate as the United States. Until another global reserve currency comes into existence, all other currencies are required to play by a different set of rules. Should a country run a large external deficit over time there will be a real price to pay. For those currencies, there tends to be a positive relationship between the external deficit and the real exchange rate that leads to a loss of purchasing power.

Second, transfers of wealth from deficit to surplus countries tend to be associated with currency depreciation in states that run current-account deficits. Should the recent improvement in the U.S. current account not be sustained, Americans would slowly experience a transfer in their wealth to the foreigners that finance the current account. (See **Figure 2.4**.)

Conversely, a country that runs a current-account surplus will over time have to see the value of its exchange rate rise. (See **Figure 2.5**.) China, a major financer of the U.S. current-account deficit, employs a fixed-exchange-rate regime for the yuan. Given

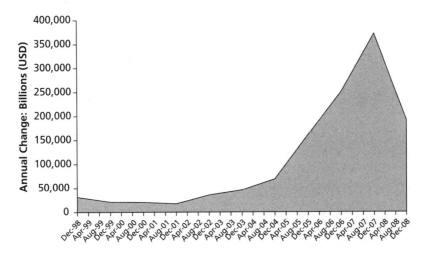

Figure 2.5 China Current Account

Source: Bloomberg.

the very large external surplus run by the Chinese, the fixed-exchange-rate regime over time may not be sustainable. The excessive savings on the part of China and the profligate consumption on the part of the United States that is responsible for the global macroeconomic imbalance cannot be sustained indefinitely. At one point, this very serious problem will have to be addressed. The primary mechanism through which that will occur will be the adjustment of the real exchange rate for both the dollar and the yuan.

Finally, most members of the global financial community prefer that their wealth be denominated in the currency of the country in which they live. This is what economists refer to as "home bias." Thus, investors who reside in surplus countries will tend to accumulate larger quantities of foreign currencies than may be optimal, relative to their holdings of their home currencies.

Each year just before the end of the Japanese fiscal year on March 31, the market observes home bias in action. The yen will typically observe an appreciation in its value during the final two weeks of March. Similarly, over time, if a country runs a large enough surplus, its investor class will rebalance their portfolios in favor of the home currency.

Case Study—A New Reserve Currency?

In advance of the 2009 G-20 meeting, the Chinese central bank's governor, Zhou Xiaochuan, called on the major trading states to consider the creation of a new reserve currency system. China's call for the creation of a novel global reserve currency was not simply a function of its newfound power, but a reflection of problems that can be linked to the long-term prospects for the dollar caused by its current-account deficit.

A global reserve currency is not a new idea. During the Bretton Woods Conference that designed the modern system of international finance, John Maynard Keynes proposed that such a currency unit be created. Keynes' idea of a new currency, which he called the bancor, was to be based on a basket of thirty commodities. Instead, the participants adopted the Bretton Woods standard, which valued the dollar linked to gold at $35 per troy ounce. This system lasted until 1973 when the Nixon administration abrogated the Bretton Woods Agreements.

Keynes' proposal was rejected by conference participants but the idea of a global currency has not withered. Most notably, Nobel laureate Robert Mundell has proposed the creation of a single global currency as a method of addressing instability in foreign-exchange markets and financial markets. Mundell considers a fixed system of exchange-rate regimes to be superior to that of floating rates.

The primary claim of those who support the imposition of a single global currency or a synthetic global reserve currency is that under the dollar standard post-1973, there have been five major banking crises, which have been accompanied by major fluctuations in exchange rates, often followed by changes in official exchange-rate regimes.

China's Request and IMF Action

According to the International Monetary Fund, roughly 64 percent of all currency reserves are held in dollars. Another 26 percent are held in euros, with the remainder spread out among sterling, yen, and Swiss francs. The use of the dollar confers upon the United States great advantage. Because it is able to borrow in its own currency, the ability of the United States to fund its own current-account deficit is much easier than it would be otherwise.

China's request for a new reserve currency is a function of its concern that the $1 trillion in dollar-denominated U.S. Treasury notes thought to be in its possession, and another $1 trillion in foreign reserves that it holds, are in danger of being devalued.

China and most other countries that hold vast reserves of dollars and dollar-denominated assets are concerned that the advent of quantitative-easing monetary policy by the United States will end up triggering a massive devaluation of the dollar. The U.S. Federal Reserve has engineered an expansion of its balance sheet from roughly $900 billion before the financial crisis to just over $2 trillion in early 2009, with the likelihood of moving to $4 trillion by the end of the year.

Zhou called for the member states of the G-20 to support using the unit of account issued by the International Monetary Fund known as special drawing rights (SDR), which is based on a basket of four currencies: the U.S. dollar, the euro, the pound sterling, and the yen.

Indeed, the first tentative steps at the global meeting were taken. The advanced economies allocated $250 billion to support a new SDR allocation. Emerging markets were given a greater voice in the operation of the fund, and it does appear that this issue will be on the agenda at future meetings. Should the evolution of the current financial crisis see continued volatility in the foreign-exchange and equity markets, demand for a new global reserve currency will only increase.

To institutionalize the use of the SDR, a settlement system between it and other currencies would have to be established, to ensure the acceptance of the new reserve currency as payment for international transactions. Next, SDR-denominated financial assets and markets would have to be established. This would require enthusiastic participation by the advanced economies. A fundamental decision would have to be made to make the SDR a paper currency or to put real assets behind it, to provide a benchmark for the financial community.

So does the IMF now have the power to engage in a global version of quantitative easing? Not quite. The move to make a synthetic SDR the currency reserve of choice will not be an easy or efficient affair. It would require significant changes in the global macro and micro environments.

Such a move would change the structure of currency markets but not alter their fundamental nature. The absolute hegemony of the dollar would come to an end, but like the sterling before it, the greenback would continue to play a vital role in international finance. The SDR would not be a Mundell-inspired global currency that would be used as a substitute for the dollar, the euro, or the yen. Rather it would take its place alongside them as a competitor subject to the same financial discipline as all other currencies.

While the establishment of the SDR as a potential reserve currency will be on the table for some time, it will not replace the dollar as the currency of choice among central banks or the investment community in a crisis. That would require that the global financial community put a non-trivial amount of monetary trust in an international institution that is widely reviled throughout the international community.

Second, the supply necessary to establish the SDR as a reserve currency would be enormous. During the era of Japan's ascendance in the early 1980s, it was thought that one day the yen would supplant the dollar as the currency of choice. However, due to the export-led economic framework of the Japanese economy at that time, domestic currency was used to pay exporting companies, which prevented the yen from circulating on a global level.

China, which is today's economy of choice to eventually supplant the United States as the dominant economic power, faces a slightly different problem. The yuan is not convertible. Although use of the yuan will certainly increase in the international system, especially in Asia, it is not widely used in the rest of the world.

A greater problem for China is the fact that it does not enjoy current-account surpluses with all its trading partners. China does run a healthy current-account surplus with the United States, but it runs deficits with several of the countries that supply it with commodities, such as Indonesia and Korea.

To support its growing trade operations, China has taken two important steps. First, to facilitate the import of critical commodities, Beijing arranged for yuan swaps equivalent to $95 billion that would permit importing companies to pay with yuans.

Second, China has recently permitted yuan settlement for international trade in Shanghai, Shenzhen, Zhuhai, and Dongguan. The action was taken to directly promote the use of the yuan as a global currency and help domestic companies hedge exchange-rate risk associated with volatility in the dollar.

Moreover, the evolution of a synthetic SDR that is sponsored by the IMF would not suppress volatility or relative mispricing of currencies. Foreign-exchange trading will still play an important role in the global economy, and arbitrage opportunities would not disappear. In the near term, the U.S. dollar will remain the reserve currency of choice. Important commodities such as oil will continue to be priced in dollars. Although countries may diversify their holdings going forward should the financial haircut taken by the United States over the next few years as it makes its painful structural adjustment become too onerous, it is likely that the U.S. current-account deficit will decline. Should that occur or should the United States begin to run a current-account surplus, then the move towards diversification away from the dollar will ease. This role of the current account is an important topic that will be addressed in the following chapter.

3 Exchange-Rate Determination over the Medium Term

Parity Conditions, Capital Flows, and Current Account

Thus far we have focused on exchange-rate determination in the long run. Given the rather unsatisfactory record of PPP to explain real exchange rates except over the long run, we now turn our focus to the medium term that is the bedrock of every year-ahead look at the foreign-exchange market.

Given that exchange rates are determined simultaneously by news flow, the short-term speculative community, changes in the business cycle, and longer-term structural transformations, it is not surprising that persistent deviations from a currency's long-term path are more often the rule rather than the exception, creating both a peril for the corporate risk manager and possibilities for the trader.

The construction of a medium-term outlook can be decisively influenced by a set of cyclical factors that can intensify the deviation of a currency from its long-term path. Over the longer term, these deviations tend to be smoothed out as cyclical factors run their course, but investment and risk managers must account for those short- to medium-term moves in their portfolio strategies.

In the medium term, macroeconomic data tend to provide a strong directional bias for the movement of currencies. Such factors as monetary and fiscal policy, differentials in economic growth and real interest rates, and trends in the current account all play crucial roles in influencing medium-term valuations of exchange rates.

Often, an analyst will find that a correlation between the movement in a currency and one of the aforementioned factors will break down and require change in outlook and strategy. More often than not, monetary policy and differences in real interest rates will provide the decisive factors behind medium-term movements in exchange rates. This chapter will focus on how parity conditions, capital flow, and the current account all influence exchange-rate valuation in the medium term and provide arbitrage opportunities for profit taking.

Parity Conditions

To obtain a solid foundation regarding how exchange rates are determined in the medium term, it is essential to consider parity conditions. Thus far we have considered PPP. Now we move to considering interest-rate parities, Fisher parities, and the unbiased forward rate.

Parity conditions demonstrate how exchange rates move based on differences in inflation rates, interest rates, and the forward exchange rate. These conditions provide crucial information on how the market is likely to value a currency of a low-inflation country and use the forward rate as an unbiased indicator of the future spot rate. Under such conditions, the currency of such a country can be expected to appreciate going forward, and the market can be expected to price in currency valuations in the short to medium term that reflect the low inflation rate of the hypothetical country.

The question that is often asked is whether parity conditions hold up any better than PPP. Just as with PPP, there are persistent deviations away from the medium-term path. Differences in inflation and interest rates often do not provide accurate forward-looking predictors of exchange-rate market movements. So why should traders and analysts pay attention to parity conditions? Because, if parity conditions held up at all times, under all circumstances, there would be zero chance to pursue arbitrage opportunities through the movement of capital from dollar positions to euros or yen. Indeed, the identification of the potential breakdown of those conditions will provide the greatest profit-taking opportunities and permit risk managers to avoid outsized losses to corporate balance sheets. The parity conditions discussed here often provide the foundation for many macro models of determining exchange rates and foreign-exchange analytics.

Interest-Rate Parities

The relationship between forward rates and spot rates is often a result of interest-rate differentials. If interest rates are higher in the United States than in a foreign country, the forward dollar value of the foreign currency will exceed the spot dollar value of the foreign currency. Analysts observe two types of interest-rate parities: covered and uncovered.

Covered Interest-Rate Parity

Covered interest-rate parity can best be understood as the equilibrium relationship between the spot and forward exchange rates. Based on this definition, an investment in Japan that is properly hedged against exchange-rate risk should provide the same return as a similar investment in the dollar. This can be expressed as the following:

$$(1 + i_\$) = (F/S)\,(1 + i_c), \qquad (3.1)$$

where

- $i_\$$ is the domestic interest rate;
- i_c is the interest rate in the foreign country;
- S is the spot exchange rate expressed as the price in domestic currency (\$) of one unit of the foreign currency c, i.e. \$/c; and
- F is the forward exchange rate implied by a forward contract.

For example, assume the following:

- One-year rate in the United States is 5 percent.
- One-year rate in the United Kingdom is 8 percent.

- Spot rate is 1.5$/£.
- Implied forward rate one year ahead is 1.5$/£.

Thus, the implied logic of covered interest-rate parity is that one should be able to borrow in the United States and invest in the United Kingdom without any risk. If this is true, one dollar invested in the United States will be

$$\$1 \cdot (1 + 5\%) = \$1.05. \qquad (3.2)$$

If the logic of the interest rate parity equation above holds, one dollar invested in the United Kingdom at the end of the twelve-month period after repatriation to the United States will be

$$\$1 \cdot (1.5/1.5)\,(1 + 8\%) = \$1.08. \qquad (3.3)$$

Using this information, a trader could carry out the following:

- Borrow $1.00 in the United States, where it is cheap
- Purchase sterling at the current spot rate of 1.5$/£ which translates to 0.67£
- Invest the funds in the United Kingdom for one year
- Purchase forward contract at current spot rate to hedge against exchange rate risk

Based on our working example using the current differential in interest rates, the spot rate and forward rate expectations one year out are as follows:

- The current 0.67£ should translate into 0.67£(1 + 8%) = 0.72£.
- Repatriate the 0.72£ back into the United States at 1.5$/£, providing $1.08.
- Repay the initial $1 to the U.S. bank with 5 percent interest, i.e., $1.05.
- The resulting arbitrage profit is $1.08 − $1.05 = $0.03 or three cents per dollar.

While acknowledging that arbitrage opportunities of this type would dissipate quite quickly, one should anticipate that interest rates in the United States will decline, the forward rate will appreciate, the spot rate depreciate, and the price of money in the United Kingdom will increase, thus restoring the original interest-rate parity condition and eliminating opportunities for arbitrage.

Uncovered Interest-Rate Parity

Whereas under covered interest parity the interest-rate differentials equal the forward exchange rate, under uncovered interest parity interest differentials equal the expected future exchange rate. The uncovered interest rate parity condition is best expressed as

$$(1 + i_\$) = E[S_{+1}]/S\,(1 + i_c). \tag{3.4}$$

The expression makes an a priori assumption of a zero-risk premium, risk-neutral investors, no transactions costs, and equal default risks for both domestic and foreign currency denominated assets. Should any one of those conditions not hold, or should investors prove not to be risk neutral, then the forward rate (F_{+1}) can differ from the expected future spot rate ($E[S_{+1}]$), and uncovered interest rate parity may not hold.

For example, consider an environment where interest rates in the United States and the United Kingdom are the same. Thus, investing in the United Kingdom and the United States, despite the always lurking exchange-rate risk, would yield the same return. Should the sterling experience a decline against the greenback, it would be intuitive to seek a more profitable return in the United States.

Due to the favorable exchange rate, investment in the United States and repatriation of capital back into the United Kingdom results in a higher return on the investment in the United States, in sterling terms, than in the United Kingdom. To attract more investment into the United Kingdom, the rate of interest paid would have rise equal to the amount of the depreciation of the sterling.

Fisher Effect

Consistent with the aforementioned example, according to the Fisher effect, all things being equal, the nominal interest rate

(i) in the United States will equal the real interest rate (r) plus the expected inflation rate (e_i). If the real rate of interest in the United Kingdom is equal to the inflation rate in the United States, $r_{UK} = r_{US}$, the yield spread between the United States and the United Kingdom will equal the expected difference in the inflation rate between the two countries, $i_{UK} - i_{US}$. However, as with parity conditions that this text has presented, practical experience strongly suggests that real interest rates often diverge quite significantly. As such, the difference in inflation rates are not always reflected by nominal yield spreads.

Covered Versus Uncovered Interest Parity

Assume a corporate manager for a multinational firm will need to buy a valuable input for production from Germany in thirty days. Because she must pay for the transaction in euros, the manager must consider various forms of risk. There are several ways to do this:

- Lock in the exchange rate by purchasing euros forward thirty days. Simultaneously, invest in dollars over the next thirty days and then convert them to euros at the end of that interval. By covering an action that one must take thirty days hence, one has covered that action with no exchange-rate risk. Using this approach a higher (lower) interest rate in the United States would be offset by the forward discount (premium).
- Simultaneously purchase euros at today's spot rate and buy a Eurobond for thirty days. At the end of the time period, due to interest earned, the manager will have to convert a few dollars to euros. The exchange risk has been covered by converting at the spot rate at the outset. Using this approach the higher (lower) interest rate in Europe is offset by the loss (gain) from converting spot instead of using a forward.
- Simply invest the amount in dollars and exchange them for euros at the end of the time interval to complete the transaction. This approach is uncovered. Yet, it is important to

note that according to interest-rate parity, the spot rate in thirty days *should* become the same as the thirty-day forward rate. The exchange risk under these conditions should be obvious.

- Based on interest-rate parity, one should obtain the same number of euros in all approaches. The first two approaches are covered while the final is uncovered.
- As a general rule, if the forward rate is less than that indicated by the interest-rate parity differentials, the optimal strategy would be to borrow euros, exchange dollars at the spot rate, and lend dollars. If the obverse obtains, then borrow dollars, exchange euros at the spot rate, and lend euros.

Capital Flows

The integration of the global economy has been the most important development in international finance over the past two decades. Without a doubt, the flow of capital around the globe and the development of a $3-trillion-per-day foreign-exchange market represent a revolution in global finance.

Yet the relatively short time span has stimulated only a limited quantity of work examining the linkages between capital flows and the foreign-exchange market. What is more interesting is that what little scholarly work that has been done suggests that many specific sectors that foreign-exchange analysts pay close attention to, such as the equity market and mergers and acquisitions, provide little evidence of having a statistically significant impact on exchange-rate determination. Yet these factors merit continued discussion given the fact that they continue to act as a catalyst for short-term movement and mid-term strategies.

Equity Markets and Foreign Exchange

It is often taken as a given among many traders that the yen moves in tandem with equities. While that may be true for short periods of time, is it true in the medium to long term? A look at the relationship between the yen and equity market tends to suggest that it is not always so.

Figure 3.1   Relationship Between Yen and U.S. Equities

Source: Bloomberg.

As illustrated in **Figure 3.1**, between 1997 and 2005 a positive relationship between the value of the U.S. equity market and the USD/JPY roughly held. However, that relationship broke down in 2005 as the U.S. economy begin to exhibit signs of a bubble in asset prices. At that point, the positive relationship between the USD/JPY and U.S. equities decoupled.

The volatility in foreign-exchange markets over the past twenty-five years tends both to support and challenge the best scholarly work in the field. In 2000, the IMF published a study titled "Exchange Rates and Capital Flows," which made the case that net-equities flows were insignificant when examining the USD/JPY rate but statistically significant when looking at the EUR/USD rate (see **Figure 3.2**). Yet a Bank of International Settlements study released that year finds no statistically significant correlation between stock market indexes and the exchange rates of the primary trading states.

Due to the absolute explosion of stock markets on a global basis and the continuing focus within the foreign-exchange community on capital flows, it is not surprising that many prognosticators continue to extol the virtues of the movement in equity

Figure 3.2   Relationship Between Euro/USD and U.S. Equities

Source: Bloomberg.

prices as an explanatory variable for movements in exchange rates. In fact, the very strong correlation between the movement of the Dow and the greenback in the late 1990s seems to have provided a powerful framework among many capital market participants. It is only the recent meltdown in global financial markets that has caused a general rethinking within the greater foreign-exchange community of the relationship between equity markets and exchange-rate determination.

Current Account

The era of international finance has ushered in a period of prosperity around the globe not seen since the great liberalization of the late nineteenth century, but it has also been characterized by substantial volatility in foreign-exchange markets and systemic crises. For the world's largest economy, the United States, the flow of capital around the world has been an enormous positive, permitting it to sustain its standard of living even with a negative rate of savings. (See **Figure 3.3**.)

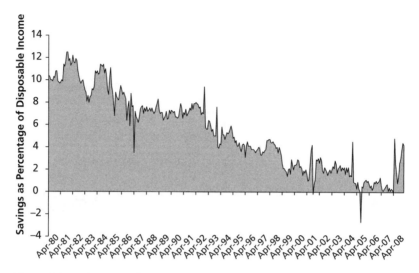

Figure 3.3 U.S. Personal Savings Rate

Source: Bloomberg.

The flow of capital into the United States since the early 1990s is not simply a function of the insatiable demand of the U.S. consumer; it is a result of capital flight out of the emerging world following the Asian currency crisis of 1994, the Russian debt default and Mexican currency crises of 1997 and 1998, foreign direct investment from Europe, and the huge purchase of U.S. Treasury instruments by China over the past two decades.

The combination of the aforementioned developments has provided enormous support for the significant global macroeconomic imbalance fueled by the unwillingness of the United States to save and the lack of domestic consumption on the part of China. Between 1995 and 2002, the development of the imbalance and the explosion of the current-account deficit did not have a deleterious impact on the value of the U.S. dollar, thus challenging the fundamental notion that the current account matters in the determination of exchange rates.

One would normally expect that nations with a current-account surplus would see appreciation of their currencies and those with a deficits would experience depreciation. In fact, this tends to occur

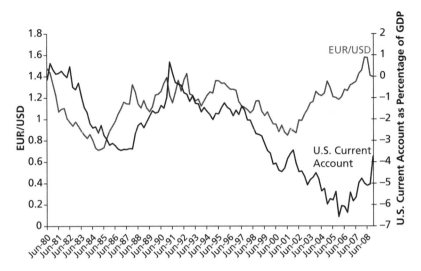

Figure 3.4   Current Account Suggests Dollar Weakness Ahead

Source: Bloomberg.

over time. A look at the comparison of the trade-weighted value of different national currencies versus their current-account positions tends to demonstrate an inverse relationship between the size of a current-account deficit and the value of a national currency.

Of course, over time one can expect to see persistent deviations from this logic, as was seen in the United States between 1995 and 2002. So how did the United States finance its current account during that time without a concomitant decline in the value of the dollar? The structural shift caused by the flow of capital away from emerging markets and towards the United States provided net support for the value of the dollar.

But that structural shift proved temporary. Beginning in mid-2002, macroeconomic factors began to reassert themselves, and flows of capital began again to move towards Asia and emerging markets. While China continued to purchase U.S. Treasuries, permitting the United States to sustain its standard of living and facilitating a further deterioration in its current account, the value of the dollar embarked on a cyclical decline through mid-2008. (See **Figure 3.4**.)

Competing Explanations

Market participants themselves differ substantially regarding the efficacy of the current account as a medium-term explanation of exchange rates. A straightforward balance of trade model would make a strong case that trade flows should determine the path that exchange rates take. Countries that run large current-account deficits, like the United States, should experience significant depreciation of their national currencies, whereas countries that run large surpluses should see increasing demand for their currencies and see markets drive up the value of those units of exchange.

An alternative explanation to current-account explanation would be the portfolio-balance model of exchange rates. Using this formulation, a change in the geographical location of capital wrought by a change in the current-account balance can facilitate a positive correlation between the current account and the determination of exchange rates.

Thus, as wealth is transferred from countries that run deficits to those that run surpluses, residents in the surplus countries prefer to possess assets denominated in their home currencies over those in a foreign country. Over time, a shift in wealth causes a change in the composition of demand for global assets that favor the currency of the surplus country over that of the deficit country, which should, in turn, cause an increase in demand for the currency of the former and a depreciation of the currency of the latter. A portfolio-balance model of exchange rate, then, strongly implies that it is not the flow of trade that determines exchange rates, but the transfer of wealth driven by a change in individuals' choice of asset denomination that provides the causal link between the current account and exchange rates.

Another competing explanation of medium-term exchange-rate trends is monetary or financial shocks. A sudden burst of fiscal activity or change in monetary policy can cause the current-account and exchange-rate trends to proceed in the same direction. For example, tight monetary policy pursued by a country would result in higher interest rates, an improved current-account position, and an increase in the value of the domestic currency. Thus, one would expect to see a highly positive correlation between the current account and the exchange rate. Should an accommodative policy path be pursued, one would expect to observe deterioration in the current-account position and the value of the national currency.

However, this may not always be the case. Under conditions of an accommodative monetary policy and a major expansion in fiscal policy, one might instead observe an appreciation of the currency due to higher real interest rates on the back of a increasing budget deficit: this describes the experience of the United States in the early 1980s.

Balance of Payments and Exchange Rates

Over the past two decades, there has been some discussion regarding the ability of the dollar to defy gravity given the massive expansion of the nation's current-account deficit. The underlying trend in the current account is important to foreign-exchange markets. The relative supply and demand of dollars in the foreign-exchange market is influenced by the current account.

To present the relationship between the current account and exchange rates, we turn to the classic balance of payments model, which explains how flows determine supply and demand for dollars.

Assume that Mexico maintains a floating currency regime. Thus, demand for pesos (D) is a function of external demand for Mexican goods and services. The supply of pesos (S) is caused by domestic demand for foreign goods and services. So, if current-account flows determine the supply and demand of pesos when the U.S. current account is in equilibrium, the supply and demand of pesos should also be in equilibrium.

Figure 3.5 shows that the equilibrium value of the x^1, as in Figure 3.5 is determined by the interaction between the supply and demand curves for pesos at point C. However, should Mexico run a current-account deficit due to an overvaluation of the peso relative to its medium-run equilibrium value, the supply of pesos in the global currency markets exceed demand for pesos.

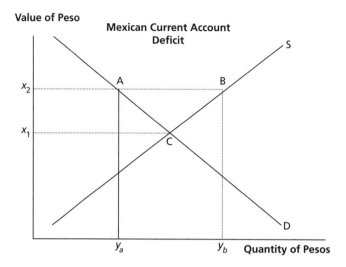

Figure 3.5   Balance of Trade Flow Model

The oversupply of pesos in the foreign-exchange market due to the current-account deficit run by Mexico is the gap between points A and B. The value of the peso at point x_2 is not sustainable due to the excess supply of pesos in the market. Under such conditions, participants in the foreign-exchange market would engage in speculative pressure on the peso, causing it to fall back towards its equilibrium value x_1. Thus a decline in the value of the peso would over time bring supply and demand for pesos back into equilibrium and the current-account deficit would shrink back towards point C.

Case Study: Mexican Currency Crisis

After a decade of stagflation, the Mexican government moved to liberalize the trade sector in 1985 and by 1988 had introduced a framework to support market-oriented financial institutions. For the first time in decades, Mexico experienced a sustained period of growth and a strengthening currency.

The subsequent years featured a substantial increase in securitized debt, simultaneous booms in real estate and stock markets, and elevated levels of private investment. Bank reserve requirements were eased and then eliminated. Financial liberalization accompanied privatization of the banks. A weak and overwhelmed system of government oversight presided over an unsustainable increase in the supply of credit. Hence, weak credit quality and unwise lending were the rule rather than the exception.

The expansion of credit was stunning. Between 1988 and 1994, credit issued by domestic commercial banks to the private sector increased in real terms by 277 percent.[1] Credit card liabilities rose at a rate of 31 percent, and mortgage loans increased at a rate of 47 percent, all in real terms.[2]

External credit flows to the private sector turned a $193 million deficit in 1988 into a $23 billion surplus five years later.[3] The ability to attract foreign investment, the underlying boom in the financial sector, and the rise in private sector demand fueled an unsustainable increase in the current-account deficit.

Rising interest rates and an appreciating equity market attracted hot money inflows. The Mexican peso trended towards elevated levels within the prescribed fixed-exchange-rate regime set by the government. However, as the trade deficit approached 6 percent of gross domestic product, the fixed-exchange-rate regime became an irresistible target.

The year 1994 proved a crucial one in Mexico's fortunes. Rising real interest rates in the United States put pressure on the value of the peso. Uprisings over the North American Free Trade Agreement began on New Year's Day in the impoverished state of Chiapas. On March 23, Luis Donald Colosio, the presidential candidate of the ruling political party, the Institutional Revolutionary Party (PRI), was assassinated in Tijuana, Baja California. The combination of domestic political turmoil and the change in the international rate environment triggered capital flight out of Mexico.

---

1. Banco de México.
2. Francisco Gil-Diaz, "The Origin of Mexico's 1994 Financial Crisis," *The Cato Journal* 17, no. 3 (Winter 1998): 303–314.
3. Ibid.

Speculative attacks on the peso began in late 1994, accompanied by a sharp increase in the interest rates, a flight to safety among the international investment community, and further devaluation of the peso. Between November 1994 and March 1995, the interest rates on short-term government paper increased from 14 to 70 percent. During that time, the peso depreciated in value from thirty cents to the dollar to fifteen cents. International reserves quickly evaporated, and the government abandoned its fixed-exchange-rate regime in December of 1994.

A misalignment of savings and investment fueled an untenable credit expansion. The expansion of credit was the primary catalyst behind the rise of an unsustainable trade deficit. The flight to safety by international investors and the attempt to defend the peso triggered a depletion of international reserves and ultimate collapse of the exchange rate regime. The 1994 to 1995 Mexican banking and financial collapse origins can be traced to an unsustainable current-account deficit and overvalued currency.

4 Fair-Value Regressions

Attempts to determine the appropriate value for a currency pair discussed in this chapter entail the use of regressions. We are not addressing attempts to forecast either the price level or the change in price, as to the extent forecasting can be done with any measure of success, it is performed by using time-series analysis such as autoregressive integrated moving average (ARIMA) modeling. Instead, we are attempting to establish the "fair value," or model estimation, of a currency pair based on the pair's historical relationships with macroeconomic, financial, and commodity data. Such models allow analysts to develop a feel for the drivers of currency valuation over various periods of time; to determine when the price of a currency pair has significantly overshot the valuation suggested by the values of other variables; and to engage in what-if analysis regarding the future path of exchange rates based on forecasts for the variables shown to be important in the valuation of a particular currency pair.

In this chapter, we will introduce three types of regression models. The first is a monthly model based on macroeconomic and financial prices, and in one case, commodity data back to the mid-1990s. The use of monthly data allows one to utilize economic data, which rarely is published more frequently than monthly.

Going back to the mid-1990s allows the model to pick up long-term relationships. However, we chose not to use data prior to the mid-1990s on the view that the world began to change significantly due to increased globalization—China and India integrating into the international economy, the end of the cold war, and the advent of the euro, which all facilitated a stunning increase in global trade and capital flows. We will use the models to burst some myths regarding the drivers of currency prices and also to show that the relationships are not necessarily stable over time, which highlights one of the limitations of this analysis.

The second type of model is based on weekly data over the prior twelve months. The high frequency makes the use of economic data impossible, and so explanatory variables are limited to financial and commodity prices. However, despite the limitations on the universe of potential explanatory variables, the shortened time horizon allows for narrower confidence bands in the fair valuations provided. This type of analysis involves reoptimizing the regression models each week, thus taking into account the changing nature of the relationships between the prices of currencies and other assets and indexes.

Having recognized that the coefficients and significance of variables can change dramatically over time, the third type of model attempts to home in even more closely on the most recent developments in currency markets. This model employs sixty days of daily price closes for financial and commodity variables. The daily updating of the regressions allows one to keep the tightest possible confidence interval and take into account the changing relationships of exchange rates with other variables.

Taken in tandem, fair-value regressions represent a relatively rigorous way to zoom in on potential investment and trading opportunities. The monthly model is able to look at the bigger picture relationships and incorporate macroeconomic theory in valuing currencies, while the shorter-term, weekly and daily models are able to indentify contemporaneous market drivers and pinpoint shorter-term misvaluations.

Long-Term Fair-Value Regression for EUR/USD

In attempting to describe the long-term valuation of the euro/U.S. dollar (EUR/USD), we note first that in going back to 1993, we predate the advent of the euro. However, by utilizing a proxy EUR/USD measure, created by combining the exchange rates of the various member countries, we are able to create a time series that encompasses the price action of European currencies against the U.S. dollar. In order to capture some of the purchasing price parity concept, we included the ratio of inflation in Europe to the inflation in the United States. To capture bond portfolio theory, we included the differential of the 10-year government bond yields. The euro is often characterized as a "bond" currency, and so we included the average of the U.S. and German 10-year government bond yields. Furthermore, rising equities are often thought of as bullish for the U.S. dollar against the euro, and so we included the S&P 500 Index.

The simple least-squares regression of the data series indicates that our intuitions regarding three of the four variables were correct. The ratio of European inflation to U.S. inflation is significant, and the coefficient is negative. The German bond yield minus the U.S. 10-year bond yield was significant and had a positive coefficient. The average of the German and U.S. 10-year bond yields was significant and negative. The only variable that turned out not to be statistically significant was the S&P 500. The F-statistic (a measure of the hypothesis that the proposed model fits the data set) of the overall regression was 16.7, suggesting a significant overall relationship, although the adjusted R-squared of 0.25 and standard error of 0.14 left quite a broad confidence interval.

Figure 4.1 illustrates that the explanatory variables of the model generally hold true. Additionally, the areas indicated by the ovals point out some very exceptional and interesting periods. The first highlighted period is from late 1999 to early 2001, when the model fair value bottomed and began to drift higher, while the EUR/USD continued to plumb new lows. The model fails to pick up two extraordinary events during this period. The first is the final surge in the Nasdaq from November 1999 before it finally peaked in March 2000. Subsequently, despite the bursting

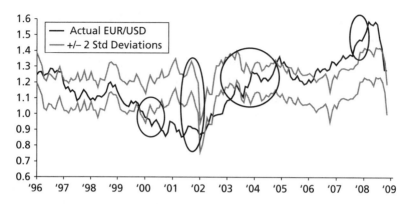

Figure 4.1 EUR/USD Relative to Model Fair Value Using Monthly Data

Source: Bloomberg and T. J. Marta calculations.

of the Internet bubble, the dollar remained buoyed by the surge in corporate debt issuance as companies attempted to keep the business expansion alive. Corporate debt issuance, on a 13-week moving average basis, reached over $16 billion by May 2001, a pace not attained again until March 2006. The second period in which the model's valuation and actual exchange rate deviated was during the months after 9/11, when the U.S. CPI fell sharply while Europe's stabilized.

The third period of interest is the late 2003–2004 period, when EUR/USD trended to a record high even as the model valuation slipped. Much of this deviation relates to global reaction to the U.S. invasion of Iraq. EUR/USD experienced an abrupt break from short-term regressions right around December 2002, which is when the United States signaled it was serious about initiating combat operations against Iraq. EUR/USD continued to rally over the next several years, experiencing a particularly sharp rally in the weeks after George Bush won reelection in November 2004. Indeed, a dummy variable inserted into the regression to reflect the pre- and post-Iraq invasion sentiment garnered a highly significant t-statistic of 11.6. Figure 4.1, in which the illustrated regression does not include the dummy variable, still reflects the structural shift in the pricing of EUR/USD, as the currency pair traded near the top of or above the 2 standard-deviation fair-value envelope in recent years. However, even within this deviant period, EUR/USD corrected lower beginning in 2005 after reaching not only a record high, but also trading more than 2 standard deviations above the estimated value.

The final period of interest is the February to May 2008 period, when EUR/USD spiked to above 1.60 even as the estimated value leveled off, causing EUR/USD to exceed the fair-value estimate by more than 6 standard deviations. This period was accompanied by a final spike in many commodities and subsequently proved to be the final blow-off top in many markets before liquidity began to collapse and markets generally began to deteriorate.

One note of caution regarding the use and interpretation of long-term regressions takes into account the unstable relationships between the dependent and independent variables. Rolling, 36-month correlations of the four explanatory variables with EUR/USD indicate that despite the significant long-term t-statistics for three of the four explanatory variables, the correlations for all four variables range widely from strongly negative to strongly positive. The 10-year bond spread (German less U.S.), which intuitively should—and does—have a positive coefficient in the regression, has experienced two periods of sustained negative correlation (2001 to 2003 and mid-2004 to 2007). The CPI ratio coefficient is significant and negative, but the rolling correlation suggests that the relation has been positive for extended periods, particularly in recent years. As to the notion that the euro is a bond currency, we can see that while for much of the time since 1993, the correlation between EUR/USD and the average of the German and the U.S. 10-year government bond yields has been negative, as would be expected, the correlation has also spend much time in positive territory—most particularly in 1998 and 2008. Finally, as to the notion that relative to the euro, the U.S. dollar is an equity currency, we can see support for that conclusion in the strong negative correlation between EUR/USD and the S&P 500 in the years just prior to and after the euro's advent. However, for almost the past five years, the correlation has been positive, which is likely why the S&P 500 is not a statistically significant explanatory variable in the regression.

In conclusion, the long-term, fair-value regression model for EUR/USD provides intuitively appealing explanatory variables: the 10-year yield spread, the 10-year average yield, and the CPI inflation ratio. However, the model is as important in what it fails to describe—the negative impact of U.S. foreign policy on the U.S. dollar, and the unsustainable bubble top in EUR/USD during 2008.

Long-Term Fair-Value Regression for USD/CAD

The long-term fair-value regression model for the U.S. dollar/ Canadian dollar (USD/CAD) that we present here employs data from 1994 and five statistically significant explanatory variables. The first two variables are the CPI ratio (Canadian/U.S. CPI inflation, attempting to incorporate purchasing power parity theory) and the 10-year government bond yield spread (U.S. minus Canadian, attempting to incorporate the notion of bond portfolio theory). Both variables are statistically significant, although the coefficient for the bond yield spread is counterintuitively signed.

Additionally, many analysts refer to the Canadian dollar, or loonie, as an oil currency. That characterization might actually overstate the relationship, as while a rise in the price of oil does increase Canadian oil exports, it also acts as a tax on the U.S. consumer, which dampens other Canadian exports. Nonetheless, the variable we have included that encompasses the price of oil—as well as natural gas—the Bank of Canada Commodity Price Index, has generally exhibited a strong, negative correlation with USD/ CAD, supporting the significant, negative coefficient in the regression. However, a stronger, more stable relationship exists between USD/CAD and *non*-energy commodities, particularly base metals, and the variable incorporating this relationship is the Bank of Canada's Ex-Energy Commodity Price Index.

A final variable, which was alluded to in the discussion of EUR/ USD, is the negative impact of U.S. foreign policy on the U.S. dollar when the United States went to war with Iraq. The incorporation of a dummy variable demarcating the pre- and post-December 2002 periods shows up as statistically significant.

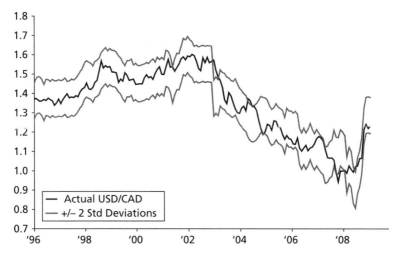

Figure 4.2   USD/CAD Relative to Model Fair Value Using Monthly Data

Source: Bloomberg and T. J. Marta calculations.

The resulting regression provides an adjusted R-squared of 0.92 with a standard error of 0.05 and is illustrated here as a chart of the actual exchange rate of USD/CAD and the ±2 standard-deviation band lines around the model's estimated value. **Figure 4.2** shows the overwhelming downward pressure on USD/CAD of the sharp commodity rally that began in 2003 and lasted until mid-2008. It also captures the sharp rally in both the model's estimated value and the actual exchange rate as commodity prices plummeted in the second half of 2008. During the 2003 to 2008 downtrend, extreme divergences of the actual exchange rate from the model valuation consistently provided signals that the downward price action either was about to stall, as in December 2004 and March 2006, or was about to resume, as in April 2004 and February 2007.

Long-Term Fair-Value Regression for AUD/USD

The long-term fair-value regression model for AUD/USD presented here employs monthly data from 1995 and four statistically significant explanatory variables. Note that while the Australian dollar is often characterized as a "gold" currency, and the long-term correlation of gold with AUD/USD is strong (0.70), the precious metal did not prove significant when employed in combination with other variables. Instead, the *Journal of Commerce* (*JoC*) base metals index, which registers a long-term correlation of 0.77, represents the only commodity in the model. It is also the most significant variable. Two of the variables regard interest rates: the U.S. 3-month Libor yield and the Australian less U.S. 10-year yield spread. The coefficients for these are both positive, consistent with yields rising during expansionary periods and with a yield advantage accruing to a currency's favor. The last variable is the ratio of Australian to U.S. year over year CPI. This variable is signed negatively, as one would expect given the negative effect of inflation on a currency.

The correlations of the Australian less U.S. 10-year yield spread and the Australian/U.S. CPI inflation ratio with AUD/USD are much less stable than that for the base metals index, which is why their *t*-statistics are lower. Nevertheless, the correlation for the yield spread is generally positive, which supports intuition and the positive regression coefficient for the yield spread. The CPI inflation ratio correlation has remained in negative territory for most of the period since 1998, also supporting both intuition and the negative regression coefficient. Finally, the rolling correlation of the U.S. 3-month Libor yield with AUD/USD has been generally unstable, although it does appear to spend a bit more time in positive than negative territory, which is consistent with the positive regression coefficient but low *t*-statistic.

The resulting regression provides an adjusted R-squared of 0.82 with a standard error of 0.05. **Figure 4.3** illustrates the actual exchange rate of AUD/USD and the ±2 standard-deviation band lines around the model's estimated value. The chart shows the downward pressure on AUD/USD during 1998 resulting from foreign-exchange carry-trade unwinds during the 1998 Russian default and LTCM collapse, which pushed the currency to the bottom of its fair-value range. The previously mentioned antipathy towards the U.S. dollar in light of the invasion of Iraq is evident

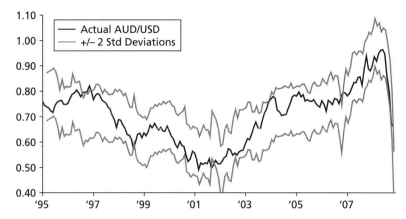

Figure 4.3   AUD/USD Relative to Model Fair Value Using Monthly Data

Source: Bloomberg and T. J. Marta calculations.

in the move in the actual exchange rate from the bottom to the top of the range during 2003. There are also two periods during which the model moves aberrantly, most recently in October of 2006, when the model estimate dropped precipitously and temporarily. This occurred due to an outsized jump in the CPI ratio because of a drop in U.S. CPI inflation stemming from the base effect of Hurricane Katrina the previous year. The other instance was around 9/11, when the model estimate spiked temporarily. This occurred because U.S. yields fell—both AUD/USD-positive—while the U.S. dollar rose on safe-haven bids.

Weekly Fair-Value Regressions

While the long-term fair-value models provide a decent picture of the price of a currency pair relative to longer-term relationships, they have at least two substantial shortcomings. First, the macroeconomic data used for explanatory variables are not published until at least weeks after the period they measure, making the models obsolete even as they are published. Second, the relationships of the explanatory variables with the currency pairs are generally unstable. Weekly fair-value regressions attempt to characterize the valuation of a currency pair relative to the values of other high-frequency data over periods short enough to describe the relationships in a more current form. In this section, we will consider regressions by looking back at the weekly closes of data for the prior fifty-two weeks. The regressions are based on a finite pool of intuitive data series such as interest rates, rate spreads, equities, and commodities, and they can and should be updated weekly to allow for fluctuating relationships/coefficients as market participants shift their focus.

Weekly Fair-Value Regressions for EUR/USD

As stated above, one reason for using rolling, fifty-two-week look-back periods for weekly fair-value regressions is to allow the model to reflect a current currency-price paradigm. For example, consider three different periods: July 2001, as EUR/USD limped along and appeared ready to retest its record low of 0.8230 set in October 2000; December 2002, when EUR/USD was consolidating around 1.00 during its multi-year uptrend; and finally, May 2008, when EUR/USD was testing 1.60.

Table 4.1 summarizes the weekly fair-value regression models for EUR/USD at the three stated times. We can see a fairly wide

Table 4.1   Weekly EUR/USD Models During Three Different Periods

Period	Significant Variables	Adjusted R-Squared, Standard Error
July 6, 2001: EUR/USD retesting record low	German–U.S. 10-year yield spread, U.S. 10-year yield, S&P 500, oil	0.7944, 0.0150
December 13, 2002: EUR/USD consolidating at 1.00 during multi-year uptrend	German–U.S. 2-year yield spread, 3-month yield, U.S. 10-year yield, S&P 500, oil	0.9404, 0.0127
May 2, 2008: EUR/USD testing 1.60 record high	German–U.S. 2-year yield spread, German 10-year yield, U.S. 2-year yield, oil	0.9672, 0.0136

Source: T. J. Marta calculations.

fluctuation in the models for the different periods. The adjusted R-squareds ranged from 0.7944 during the 2001 period to 0.9672 during the 2008 period. The most common significant variable is oil, which is also the only variable to show up as significant in all three models. The U.S. 10-year yield, 2-year yield spread, and S&P 500 showed up in two of the models. Finally, the 3-month Libor yield, German 10-year yield, and 10-year yield spread each showed up in only one model.

July 6, 2001   The worst-fit model was the one for July 2001. During this period, EUR/USD bounced along at very depressed levels even as the S&P 500 sold off, and the United States endured a recession that had led the Fed to cut its overnight target rate by 275 basis points to 3.75 percent in the preceding six months. Perhaps not surprisingly, the coefficients for three of the four variables were signed the opposite of what intuition would argue; the S&P 500 coefficient was positive, while those for oil and the 10-year spread were negative. The only "correctly" signed coefficient was that for the U.S. 10-year yield, which was signed negatively, as would be expected given the euro's reputation as a "bond currency."

At least part of the poor fit of the model in July 2001 resulted from two issues not captured in it. First, the head of the European Central Bank at that time, Wim Duisenberg, was perceived by many market participants as "out of touch" with the markets and the economy, which caused traders to sell the currency as a proxy vote regarding the competence of the ECB. Second, corporations were issuing a tremendous volume of U.S. dollar–denominated debt during early 2001. In the thirteen weeks leading up to May 25, 2001, corporations averaged $16.6 billion in U.S. dollar–denominated debt issuance per week, a pace not broken until 2006. These exceptional factors that caused the model to describe the price action for EUR/USD counterintuitively—and poorly—should serve as a reminder that a large deviation in the price of a currency does not necessarily indicate an automatic buying or selling opportunity. Rather, one must look to exogenous factors and assess how long those will have an impact on the currency.

December 13, 2002   In December 2002, EUR/USD closed—on a weekly basis—at 1.0241, breaking above the 0.9660–1.0130 range in place since June 2002. Undoubtedly, one of the reasons for the consolidation around 1.00 was the psychological importance of parity for traders. Another likely reason for the break higher stemmed from increased fear about U.S. intentions regarding Iraq. On December 7, 2002, Iraq delivered 12,000 pages of documents to the UN denying it had produced weapons of mass destruction, but fears of a U.S. attack continued to weigh and even gathered momentum when UN officials characterized Iraq's documents as failing to provide a thorough accounting of banned weapons and U.S. Secretary of State Colin Powell accused Iraq of having "totally failed" to meet UN demands.

The fair-value regression based on fifty-two weeks of weekly closing data run on December 13, 2002, provides a much better fit (adjusted R-squared of 0.9404) than did the model for July 2001. It is based on five variables: the German less U.S. 2-year yield spread, the 3-month Libor yield, the U.S. 10-year note yield, the S&P 500, and oil. The coefficients for all but one of the variables were signed as one would expect. The 2-year spread coefficient has a positive sign, consistent with yield advantage supporting a currency. The 3-month Libor yield coefficient is negative, consistent with a lower U.S. short-term yield being U.S. dollar–negative. The negative coefficient of the S&P 500 corroborates the notion of the euro being a "bond" currency relative to the U.S. dollar, while the positive coefficient of oil supports the notion of the price of oil—which is priced in U.S. dollars—rising as the U.S. dollar weakens. Only the positive coefficient for the U.S. 10-year yield is problematic, as one might expect that the rising inflation pressures suggested by a higher 10-year yield would show up in a weaker currency.

May 2, 2008   In late April 2008, EUR/USD first bumped up against a record-high 1.60. In the preceding fifty-two weeks, EUR/USD had moved higher in two stages as fears of a U.S. financial system collapse caused investors to retreat from the U.S.

dollar in favor of the euro. The period started with the currency pair drifting higher in a fairly wide channel from April 2007 to August 2007. However, the dislocation in the U.S. money markets that occurred in August prompted a surge in EUR/USD from 1.34 to 1.49 by late November. The pair then range traded until late February when EUR/USD spiked above 1.50 and to 1.59 by March 17 after Bear Stearns had been euthanized by the government's brokering of its sale to JPMorgan Chase. After consolidating for several weeks, EUR/USD finally breached 1.60—if only briefly—on April 22.

For the fifty-two weeks ending May 2, 2008, the value of EUR/USD is best explained by four significant variables: the German less U.S. 2-year government note yield spread, the U.S. 2-year government note yield, the German 10-year government note yield, and the price of oil. The signs of the coefficients generally were as would be expected. The 3-month Libor and 2-year note yield spreads were positive, suggesting that higher short-term rates for the euro area would support the euro versus the U.S. dollar. The coefficient for the German 10-year government note yield was negative, consistent with the common notion that the euro is a "bond currency." The positive correlation with oil can be tied to the weakness in the U.S. dollar, given that oil prices are generally quoted in U.S. dollars. The one variable that is counterintuitively signed, at least at first glance, is the U.S. 2-year note yield, which has a positive coefficient.

The adjusted R-squared for the overall regression was 0.97 with a standard error of 0.01, and **Figure 4.4** illustrates the actual path of EUR/USD along with the ±2 standard-deviation bands from the fitted value for EUR/USD. The graph also shows that the model was able to capture the overall trend and suggest when the currency pair was moving towards over- or undervalued levels. In late March and early April, as EUR/USD breached 1.55 and began testing 1.60, the model began showing the currency almost 2 standard deviations above the estimated value. This rich valuation suggested the ensuing retreat in EUR/USD. Interestingly, the decline in EUR/USD back below 1.55 left

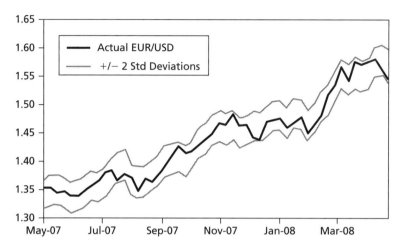

Figure 4.4 EUR/USD and Regression Based on Fifty-Two Weeks Ending May 2, 2008

Source: Bloomberg and T. J. Marta calculations.

it more than 2 standard deviations below the estimated value (1.5706), indicating that the currency would consolidate, as it did for four months, rather than begin a trend decline.

Weekly Fair-Value Regressions for USD/CAD

To highlight the changing drivers for the price action of USD/CAD, consider three different periods: January 2001 to 2002, as USD/CAD reached a record high of 1.6193; May 2005 to 2006, when USD/CAD was trending uniformly lower; and finally, November 2006 to 2007, when USD/CAD plummeted to a record low of 0.9058.

Table 4.2 summarizes the weekly fair-value regression models for USD/CAD at the three stated times, illustrating a fairly wide fluctuation in the models for the different periods. The adjusted R-squareds ranged from 0.8035 for the 2001 to 2002 period to 0.9428 during the 2006 to 2007 period. Natural gas proved to be the only variable significant in all three models. Base metals, the S&P Toronto Stock Exchange Index, the U.S. 3-month Libor yield, and the Canadian 3-month Libor yield each proved

Table 4.2 USD/CAD Weekly Models During Three Different Periods

Period	Significant Variables	Adjusted R-Squared, Standard Error
January 25, 2002: USD/CAD record high	S&P TSX, base metals index, natural gas, U.S.-Canadian 3-month Libor yield spread, U.S. 3-month Libor yield	0.8705, 0.0099
May 5, 2006: USD/CAD trending lower	Base metals index, natural gas, oil, U.S. 10-year yield, Canadian 3-month Libor yield	0.9492, 0.0099
November 9, 2007: USD/CAD record low	Natural gas, S&P TSX, Canadian 3-month Libor yield, U.S. 3-month Libor yield, U.S.-Canadian 2-year yield spread	0.9535, 0.0154

Source: T. J. Marta calculations.

significant in two models. The price of oil, the U.S. 10-year yield, and the spreads of the 3-month and 2-year yields were significant in only one model. The dominance of natural gas prices and the significance of base metals in two models attest to the loonie's general "commodity currency" reputation. Furthermore, the fact that oil was significant in only one model underscores that the loonie is not just an oil currency. The significance of the S&P TSX Index in 2001 and 2002 attests to the outsized effect of the Internet bubble's collapse on the Canadian dollar due to foreign investment in Canadian tech companies.

January 25, 2002   The fifty-two-week model run for January 25 encompasses a fairly extraordinary year. (See **Figure 4.5**.) The United States endured a mild recession, the popping Internet bubble finally reached a bottom, and 9/11 changed the world and threatened the global financial system. It is little wonder, then, that the model fit is the worst of the three periods chosen, with an adjusted R-squared of 0.8705. Nonetheless, the signage of the significant coefficients was mostly correct. The TSX coefficient was negative, consistent with the foreign-exchange impact of foreign investment outflows from Canadian tech companies. The negative coefficient of natural gas is consistent with the loonie being a commodity currency. The coefficient of the U.S. 3-month Libor spread being positive is intuitive in that a greater U.S. yield advantage should be U.S. dollar positive. The negative coefficient for the U.S. 3-month Libor yield reflects the slowing growth that was precipitating Fed easing. The only absolutely counterintuitive coefficient sign is the positive coefficient for base metals. Generally, rising commodity prices should be positive for the Canadian dollar, or negative for USD/CAD. However, in the midst of the other factors pushing USD/CAD, the world was also sagging towards

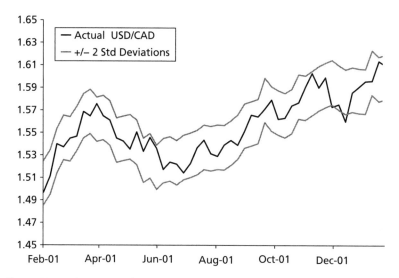

Figure 4.5 USD/CAD and Regression Based on Fifty-Two Weeks Ending January 25, 2002

Source: Bloomberg and T. J. Marta calculations.

deflation. In this situation, base metal prices and USD/CAD spuriously moved in the same direction.

The model accurately described the price action for the period, especially at extreme "misvaluations." For instance, during one pullback in late November to mid-December 2001, USD/CAD registered more than 2 standard deviations undervalued. The correction to 1.5665 proved a bottom from which the currency resumed its rally towards its record high.

May 5, 2006   On May 5, 2006, USD/CAD traded as low as 1.1014, having fallen sharply from 1.6193 in January 2002. In the prior twelve months, the currency pair had traded down in a relatively uniform, "channel" formation. The fifty-two-week fair-value regression model as of May 5, 2006, provides a strong fit (adjusted R-squared of 0.9492), and all the variables are correctly signed. (See **Figure 4.6**.) The presence of three commodities in the significant independent variables (oil, natural gas, and base metals) reflects not only that commodities were moving inexorably higher during the period on continued strong global growth, but also the bullish impact of Hurricane Katrina on oil and natural gas prices in the third and fourth quarters of 2005. The positive coefficient

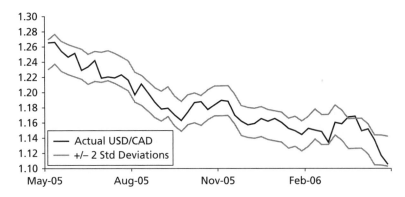

Figure 4.6   USD/CAD and Regression Based on Fifty-Two Weeks Ending May 5, 2006

Source: Bloomberg and T. J. Marta calculations.

for the U.S. 10-year note yield is intuitive in that a higher yield should support the U.S. dollar. The negative coefficient for the Canadian 3-month Libor yield reflects the idea that rising short-term yields in Canada make the Canadian dollar more attractive.

The model fits the actual price action relatively well, even through the post–Hurricane Katrina turbulence. Towards the end of the period, the price action became volatile, but the model was able to signal a trough and peak. Specifically, in late February and early March 2006, USD/CAD registered nearly 2 standard deviations undervalued, and the currency pair subsequently jumped from 1.1334 to 1.1686 in four weeks, at which point it registered overvalued and resumed its descent towards 1.10. By May 5, with USD/CAD closing at 1.1053, the model indicated that the currency was nearly 2 standard deviations undervalued. The currency subsequently bottomed and even began rising during the remainder of 2006.

November 9, 2007   The week of November 9, 2007, marked the last, desperate, unsustainable plunge in USD/CAD to a record low 0.9058. The beginning of the fifty-two-week period leading up to the record low was marked by a moderate rally in USD/CAD towards 1.20, but by March 2007, that run had stalled, and USD/CAD began to fall rather sharply. The price stalled around 1.05 from June through August, but then rolled over sharply as the U.S. commercial paper market became disrupted and collapsed to the low as the crisis reached a peak—at least up until that point.

The model for the fifty-two weeks leading up to November 9, 2007 (see **Figure 4.7**), captures most of the actual price action, achieving an adjusted R-squared of 0.9535. The significance and negative coefficient of natural gas is as expected for USD/CAD, in that Canada exports natural gas. The negative coefficient for the TSX is consistent with foreign buying/selling of Canadian equities in up and down markets. The negative coefficient for the Canadian Libor could be construed as part of the yield advantage accruing to the Canadian dollar or the repatriation flows as the banking situation worsened. The positive coefficient for the 2-year

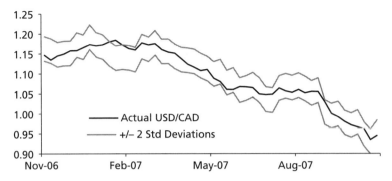

Figure 4.7 USD/CAD and Regression Based on Fifty-Two Weeks Ending November 9, 2007

Source: Bloomberg and T. J. Marta calculations.

yield spread and the U.S. 3-month Libor yield are consistent with the theory of yield advantage helping a currency.

Weekly Fair-Value Regressions for AUD/USD

To highlight the changing drivers for the price action of AUD/ USD, consider three different points in time: March 8, 2002, as AUD/USD was finishing a long bottoming process in which it traded a record low; March 24, 2006, when AUD/USD was reaching the end of a moderate, one-year decline; and finally, July 18, 2008, when AUD/USD reached a record—and unsustainable—close.

Table 4.3 summarizes the weekly fair-value regression models for AUD/USD at the three stated times and shows a wide fluctuation in the models for the different periods. The adjusted R-squareds range from 0.4434 for the 2001 to 2002 period to 0.9318 during the 2007 to 2008 period. Crude oil proves to be the only variable significant in all three models, although gold is significant in two, along with the U.S. 3-month Libor yield and the Australian 10-year yield. The 3-month yield spread, Australian 3-month Libor yield, and the S&P 500 and S&P/ASX 200 equity indexes are all significant in only one model.

March 8, 2002 The fifty-two-week model run for March 8, 2002, encompassed a year in which AUD/USD traded a flat,

Table 4.3 AUD/USD Weekly Models at Three Different Times

Period	Significant Variables	Adjusted R-Squared, Standard Error
March 8, 2002: end of flat-bottoming period that encompassed record low	Crude oil, U.S. 3-month Libor yield, S&P 500	0.4434, 0.0080
March 24, 2006: end of modest, one-year downtrend	Crude oil, gold, U.S. 3-month Libor yield, Australian 10-year yield, Australian-U.S. 3-month yield spread	0.7924, 0.0071
July 18, 2008: AUD/USD reaches record high	Crude oil, gold, base metals, Australian 3-month Libor yield, Australian 10-year yield, S&P/ASX 200 Index	0.9319, 0.0111

Source: T. J. Marta calculations.

0.4775–0.5392 range that included a record low. (See **Figure 4.8**.) Additionally, the events of 9/11 created extraordinary volatility within the range. Not surprisingly, the model fit is the worst of the three periods chosen. Nonetheless, the signage of the significant coefficients appears intuitive. The negative coefficient for the U.S. 3-month Libor is consistent with the Fed easing during the 2001 recession, as the slower growth environment would have weighed on the Australian dollar. Additionally, the Fed cut rates right after 9/11, at the same time the U.S. dollar was benefiting from a flight to quality bid. The positive coefficient for the S&P 500 reflects that except for the downtrend in equities at the beginning of the period, the two series traded almost in lockstep. Finally, the positive coefficient for crude oil is consistent with slowing economic activity, which generally weighs on both the Australian dollar and the demand for and price of oil.

About the best that can be said for the model is that its wide standard error allowed it to generally outline the trendless price

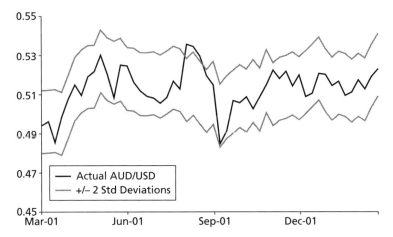

Figure 4.8 AUD/USD and Regression Based on Fifty-Two Weeks Ending March 8, 2002

Source: Bloomberg and T. J. Marta calculations.

action. The model did miss a volatile gyration—first higher in July 2001, and then lower through the aftermath of 9/11. However, in both these cases, the extreme "misvaluations" did point to an impending reversal of price back into the trend.

March 24, 2006 During the week ending March 24, 2006, AUD/USD traded down to 0.7086, a low since September 2004. (See **Figure 4.9**.) However, that close marked the end of the gentle slide in the currency that had started at 0.7950 in March 2005. The fifty-two-week fair-value regression model as of March 24, 2006, provides a reasonable fit (adjusted R-squared of 0.7924), with most of the variables signed in accordance with intuition. Oil and gold are both positively signed, consistent with the Australian dollar's reputation as a gold and commodity currency. The 10-year Australian yield and the U.S. 3-month Libor are positively and negatively signed, respectively, both consistent with the notion that a higher yield benefits a currency. Finally, the Australian less U.S. 3-month Libor spread is negatively signed, which is inconsistent with the yield advantage notion.

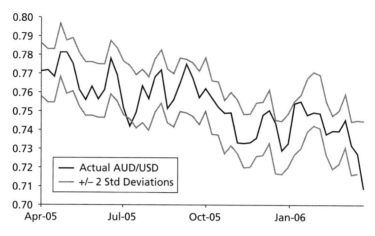

Figure 4.9   AUD/USD and Regression Based on Fifty-Two Weeks Ending March 24, 2006

Source: Bloomberg and T. J. Marta calculations.

The model fits the actual price action relatively well, even capturing many of the short-term price corrections in the downtrend. At one point during the fifty-two-week period, AUD/USD fell below the 2 standard-deviation envelope, and that point marked a low that held for the next four months despite the overall downtrend. At the end of the period, AUD/USD was falling sharply and moved more than 3 standard deviations below the estimated value. That proved to be the beginning of the AUD/USD's final rally to its eventual record high in July 2008.

July 18, 2008   The week ending July 18, 2008, represented the zenith of various risk assets, one of which included the Australian dollar as part of the foreign-exchange carry trade. (See **Figure 4.10**.) That week also encompassed one of the many "crises within the Crisis," the beginning of the downfall of the U.S. government–sponsored enterprises (GSEs) Fannie Mae and Freddie Mac. The prior fifty-two weeks encompassed the first shudders of the financial crisis, with the dislocation of the U.S. money markets in August 2007 precipitating a mini-meltdown of the foreign-exchange carry trade and a sharp, but temporary, sell-off in AUD/USD. The currency

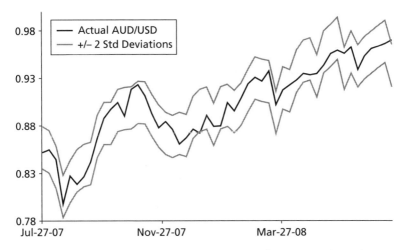

Figure 4.10   AUD/USD and Regression Based on Fifty-Two Weeks Ending July 18, 2008

Source: Bloomberg and T. J. Marta calculations.

pair resumed its grind higher, with modest sell-offs deriving from ongoing rumblings from the crisis in November 2007 (fears of year-end liquidity crunch and increased bank write-downs), January 2008 (a rogue trader and an intra-meeting 50 basis-point Fed rate cut), and March 2008 (Bear Stearns's demise). On July 15, AUD/USD spiked one last time to reach a record high 0.9850.

For all the extraordinary stresses on the global financial system, the model for the fifty-two weeks leading up to July 18, 2008, captures most of the actual price action, achieving an adjusted R-squared of 0.9319. The regression contains five significant variables. The presence of three commodity variables—gold, crude oil, and the *JoC* base metals index—along with the S&P/ASX 200 index, all with positive coefficients, testifies to the generalized nature of risk asset appreciation during that time frame. The Australian 10-year note yield coefficient is negatively signed, consistent with the move out of bonds and into risk assets like the Australian dollar during the period. AUD/USD traded outside the 2 standard-deviation band only twice during the period covered by the model. In the first instance, January 4, 2008, the model had jumped due to surges in the commodities and the S&P/ASX, but AUD/USD drifted lower. However, the misvaluation presaged a resumed rally in AUD/USD. The second misvaluation occurred at the very end of the period when AUD/USD continued higher even as crude oil, base metals, and the S&P/ASX began to buckle. The decline in the explanatory variables portended the subsequent meltdown for AUD/USD.

Daily Fair-Value Regressions

The fifty-two-week fair-value models provide a better description of medium-term currency drivers relative to longer-term, macroeconomic relationships. However, the dynamic nature of the relationships indicates that in some instances, even only fifty-two weeks of data might be too long to measure dynamics in a rapidly changing environment. Consequently, throughout the remainder of this chapter, we will consider regressions looking back at only sixty days of daily close data. These short-term fair-value regressions attempt to characterize the valuation of a currency pair relative to the values of other high-frequency data over periods short enough to describe the relationships in the most current form. The regressions are based on a finite pool of intuitive data series such as interest rates, rate spreads, equities, and commodities. A key element of this analysis is that the explanatory variables can change each day, and so the regressions should be reoptimized in order to maintain the most updated description of currency valuations.

Daily Fair-Value Regression for EUR/USD as It Reached 1.60

Using a 60-day regression, the value of EUR/USD can be explained by some permutation of interest rates (3-month, 2-year, and 10-year), interest-rate spreads, the price of gold, the price of oil, and/or the level of the S&P 500. (See **Figure 4.11**.) The regression optimized on May 1, 2008, just after EUR/USD first traded up to 1.60, is based on explanatory variables including the price of gold, the 3-month Euribor yield, the U.S. 2-year government note yield, the average of the U.S. and German 10-year government

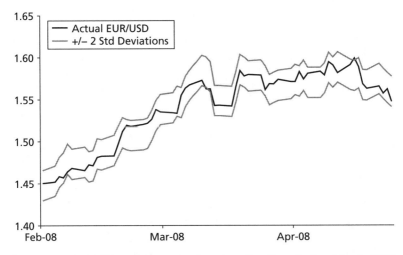

Figure 4.11   EUR/USD and Regression Based on Sixty Days Ending May 1, 2008

Source: Bloomberg and T. J. Marta calculations.

bond yields, and the level of the S&P 500. The adjusted R-squared for the regression is 0.95, and the graph illustrates the actual path of EUR/USD along with the ±2 standard-deviation bands from the fitted value for EUR/USD. The graph shows EUR/USD slipping towards the bottom of the 2 standard-deviation band in late April, suggesting that EUR/USD should trade higher during early May.

Indeed, as **Figure 4.12** shows, EUR/USD did bottom and traded higher in the first half of May. However, the graph also shows that the regression parameters established on May 1, 2008, began to break down and appeared visibly inaccurate by mid-June, with EUR/USD trading significantly above the estimated value on a persistent basis.

Figure 4.13 shows that the regression parameters became even more obsolete after EUR/USD failed to breach above 1.60 a second time and began to drop precipitously as the financial crisis worsened in July and August. At this point, the May 1 regression signaled that EUR/USD was extremely oversold and ready for a rebound, although the sharp deterioration in financial conditions, with the U.S. GSEs (Freddie Mac and Fannie Mae) skidding

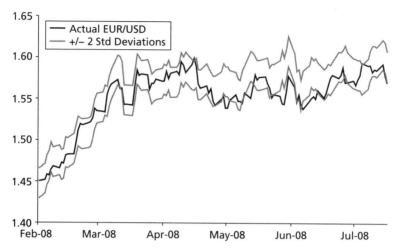

Figure 4.12 EUR/USD, February to July 2008, with Regression as of May 1

Source: Bloomberg and T. J. Marta calculations.

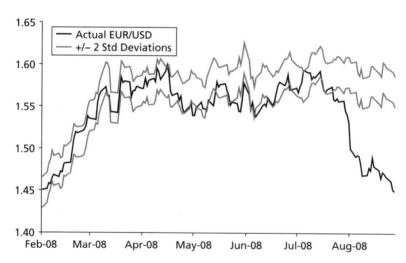

Figure 4.13 EUR/USD, February to September 2008, with Regression as of May 1

Source: Bloomberg and T. J. Marta calculations.

towards insolvency, strongly indicated the determinants of EUR/USD price action had shifted.

Figure 4.14 shows the path of EUR/USD from mid-August through November 1, 2008, with the regression reoptimized

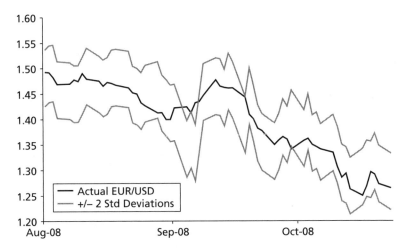

Figure 4.14 EUR/USD, August to November 2008, with Regression as of November 1

Source: Bloomberg and T. J. Marta calculations.

based on the sixty days up to November 1. The new regression has a lower adjusted R-squared (0.85), and the significant variables are reduced from five to two: the price of gold and the yield of the U.S. 2-year government note, suggesting that the EUR/USD was caught up in the same violent price action in which the market raced (1) to acquire gold in a safe-haven bid and (2) to shift pricing from expectations of inflation-fighting Fed rate hikes to financial crisis–fighting Fed rate cuts. The violence of the dislocation caused by the bankruptcy of Lehman Brothers on September 15, 2008, can be plainly seen as the estimated value lurched downward and then back up in the September 12 to 19 period due to the 2-year note trading a 94 basis-point range. The actual value of EUR/USD as of November 1 was well within the wide (2.8 big figure) standard error of the updated model.

Daily Fair-Value Regression for USD/CAD as It Reached Record Low at 0.9203 on November 6, 2007

Using a 60-day regression, the value of USD/CAD can generally be explained by various permutations of interest rates (3-month,

2-year, and 10-year), interest-rate spreads, levels of the TSX, and prices of the *JoC* base metals index, oil, and natural gas. For the sake of this discussion, we will focus on the November 6, 2007, record closing low of 0.9203. During the sixty days leading up to November 6, the financial crisis exploded. The Fed reversed an early-August inflation-fighting stance as the U.S. commercial paper market became severely dislocated and actually cut rates 50 basis points at its September 17 Federal Open Market Committee (FOMC) meeting.

The sixty-day model for this point in time is made up of three variables: the *JoC* base metals index, the price of crude oil, and the U.S. 3-month Libor yield. The variable coefficients are correctly signed. Those for base metals and oil are negative—or Canadian dollar supportive, while that for the U.S. 3-month Libor yield is positive, consistent with the Fed rate cuts during the period weighing on the U.S. dollar. The adjusted R-squared of the regression is 0.9499, and **Figure 4.15** below illustrates the actual price action along with the ±2 standard-deviation bands from the fitted value for USD/CAD. The model standard-deviation bands

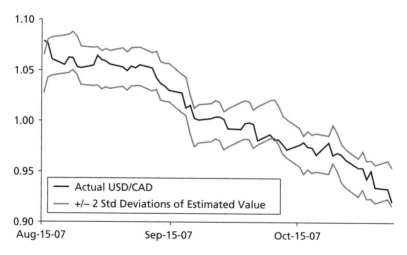

Figure 4.15   USD/CAD and Regression Based on Sixty Days Ending November 7, 2007

Source: Bloomberg and T. J. Marta calculations.

exhibit a sharp move downward around mid-September that derives from the Fed's 50 basis-point target rate cut on September 17, 2007. Near the end of the time period, USD/CAD slid towards the bottom of the model range even as the model estimate began to stabilize. This dynamic suggests that USD/CAD was oversold, and subsequently, USD/CAD rebounded sharply.

By January 31, 2008, sixty days after the November 6 bottom, the financial crisis had deteriorated even further. The Fed had cut rates another 150 basis points, including an intra-meeting 75 basis-point cut on January 22, likely due to the Fed getting spooked that the financial system was collapsing. In reality, the precipitating event was "only" a rogue trader whose losses caused a $7 billion write-down at a bank. However, the Fed was correct to be edgy, as less than two months later, Bear Stearns came to an inglorious end.

With the changes in the real world from November 2007 to January 2008, the model describing USD/CAD price action changes drastically. Instead of three independent variables and a strong, 0.9499 adjusted R-squared, the model for the sixty days to January 31, 2008, employs six variables to obtain a more modest adjusted R-squared of 0.7823. The *JoC* base metals index, crude oil, and the U.S. 3-month Libor are still part of the equation. However, the price of natural gas, the U.S. 2-year yield, and the U.S. less Canadian 10-year yield spread enter the model. The coefficient for natural gas is counterintuitively positive, as natural gas prices continued to rise during the period with little regard for the financial crisis. The U.S. 2-year yield coefficient is negative, likely as unwinding risk capital moved out of Canadian dollar–based positions and into the safe haven of short-dated U.S. Treasuries. Finally, the 10-year U.S.-Canadian yield spread coefficient is positive, consistent with the theory that a yield spread advantage supports a currency.

Figure 4.16 illustrates that the model captured the broad dynamics of the price action during the period. At two points, USD/CAD tested the upper band of the 2 standard-deviation envelope. On the first occasion, November 15, 2007, USD/CAD traded to 0.9854, 1.99 standard deviations above the estimated

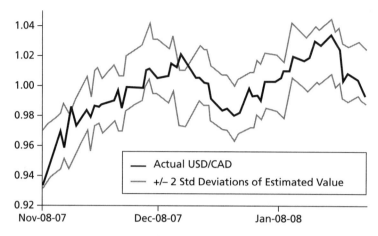

Figure 4.16 USD/CAD and Regression Based on Sixty Days Ending January 31, 2008

Source: Bloomberg and T. J. Marta calculations.

value of 0.9671, and subsequently the currency pair retreated slightly before resuming the uptrend at a more moderate pace. On the second occasion, December 13 and 14, 2007, USD/CAD tested 1.02, roughly 3 standard deviations above the estimated value. Furthermore, the estimated value of the currency had been trending lower since December 5. Subsequently, USD/CAD began trending lower in tandem with the model estimates through late December.

Daily Fair-Value Regression for AUD/USD as It Reached Record High at 0.9793 on July 15, 2008

Using a 60-day regression, the value of AUD/USD can generally be explained by various permutations of interest rates (3-month and 10-year), interest-rate spreads, levels of the S&P/ASX 200 and S&P 500, and prices of the *JoC* base metals index, gold, and crude oil. (See **Figure 4.17**.) For the sake of this discussion, we will focus on the July 15, 2008, record closing high of 0.9793. During the sixty days leading up to July 15, the key concern in the market regarded inflation as the price of crude oil approached $150 per barrel. The implosion of Bear Stearns was in the past,

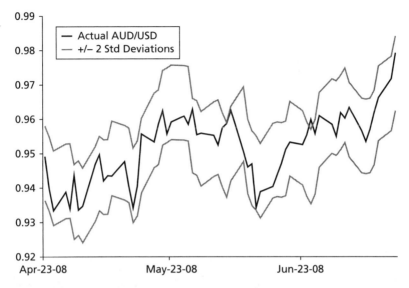

Figure 4.17 AUD/USD and Regression Based on Sixty Days Ending July 15, 2008

Source: Bloomberg and T. J. Marta calculations.

the problems that led to nationalization of the GSEs were just beginning to seem imminent, and the bankruptcy of Lehman Brothers and bailout of AIG had yet to occur.

The sixty-day model for this point in time is made up of three variables: the price of gold, the U.S. 3-month Libor yield, and the Australian 10-year yield. The coefficient for gold is positive, as would be expected of a "gold" currency. The negative coefficient for the U.S. 3-month Libor yield relates to the increased appetite for risk assets even as the Fed had begun to cut its target rate sharply in September 2007. Finally, the positive coefficient of the Australian 10-year yield is consistent with higher yields supporting a currency. The model captures most of the dynamics of the price action during the period. AUD/USD closed outside the 2 standard-deviation bands only once, on June 25, when it registered overvalued. The currency subsequently stalled for two weeks before making its last rally to the record.

By October 7, 2008, sixty days after the July 15 peak, the financial crisis had deteriorated to an entirely new level. The U.S.

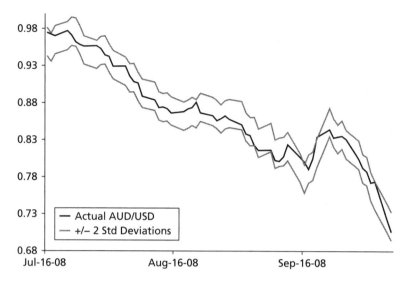

Figure 4.18   AUD/USD and Regression Based on Sixty Days of History as of October 7, 2008

Source: Bloomberg and T. J. Marta calculations.

government had placed Fannie Mae and Freddie Mac into receivership, Lehman Brothers had been allowed to fall into bankruptcy, AIG was in need of propping up, and policymakers were dealing with the very real prospects of financial Armageddon. AUD/USD had collapsed 27 percent to 0.7059, having retraced more than four years of gains in less than three months.

Given the unhinging of the financial markets during the period, the model describing AUD/USD price action changes dramatically. Gold drops out as a significant variable, as it originally sold off with the Australian dollar but then rebounded as a safe-haven play. The U.S. 3-month Libor yield also drops out despite the Fed continuing to cut rates, and the 3-month Libor yield spiked as interbank lending collapsed in the wake of the Lehman bankruptcy. The 10-year Australian yield remains significant and is joined by the U.S. 10-year yield, both of which collapsed along with AUD/USD as market participants fled risk assets like the Australian dollar in search of government bonds. The model also includes the *JoC* base metals index and crude oil, both signed positively, as they sold off sharply as part of the flight from risk assets. The model retained a strong adjusted R-squared of 0.9785. (See **Figure 4.18**.)

Conclusion

This chapter has explored fair-value regression estimates for currencies based on valuations assessed over varied time periods. At the highest level, fair-value regression analysis allows an analyst to quantify from a high-level, long-term view when a currency pair is over- or undervalued. As such, it attempts to implement the macroeconomic theory and analysis discussed in prior chapters in such a way as to suggest when a currency has entered an over- or undershoot period and so is ripe for a long-term trend reversal. However, currencies do not often wander into such excessive valuation territory (and once there, can remain for months—if not years), and so such a measure misses many investment opportunities that exist even when long-term valuations are not over-extended. Regression analysis based on fifty-two weeks of weekly closing data can be used to "zoom in" from the long-term analysis in order to select more frequent investment and trading opportunities. Additionally, analysis based on sixty days of daily closing data can be utilized to analyze the most current drivers of a currency pair's price in order to observe trends and deviations from fair value that might represent a sign of a consolidation in trend or a reversal of trend.

Market Sentiment and Positioning

At the most basic and benign level, the waning and waxing of human sentiment provides markets with their almost-life-like "breathing" behavior as an asset price oscillates around the trend it establishes in adjusting to macroeconomic determinants. Consequently, extremes in sentiment and positioning, whether measured by Commodity Futures Trading Commission (CFTC) non-commercial positioning data or by risk reversals in the options market, tend to correlate strongly with extreme deviations of price action from various trend measures such as moving averages.

At another level, shifts in sentiment can lead to structural breaks in the price action of a currency. In the previous chapter, we noted the statistically significant negative change in the sentiment towards the U.S. dollar that developed after the U.S. decision to invade Iraq.

At a third level, in the most extreme circumstances, human greed and aversion can lead to the violent booms and busts in asset prices. British economist John Maynard Keynes is usually credited with the famous saying that "the markets can stay irrational longer than [traders or investors] can stay solvent." This persistent irrationality lay behind the sharp rise in the Nasdaq more than three years after Federal Reserve Chairman Alan Greenspan warned of irrational exuberance in December 1996. It also caused many doomsayers, who eventually proved so terribly correct about the damage to the financial system that loomed, to sound like noisy gongs for years prior to the actual crisis unfolding in 2007. Examples in the G-10 currency universe include the sharp rise and collapse of USD/JPY in 1998, when carry trade activity spiked and then imploded, as well as the sell-off in the U.S. dollar during late 2007 and early 2008 as global investors recoiled from the greenback in fear of the collapse of the U.S. financial system.

Some analysts decry positioning analysis as useless in forecasting exchange movements, and therefore refuse to consider positioning at all. Given the poor record of currency price forecasters, we find such highbrow discounting of the information contained in positioning data to be naïve. Sentiment and positioning, like "fair-value" regressions, PPP measures, and technical analysis oscillators, can be used to assess the likelihood that price action has gone "too far." The important information content is not in forecasting but rather in highlighting the increased risk that a trend could reverse—or at least consolidate. For the investor and trader, such signals can be used to lighten up on exposure, buy insurance protection against downside risks, sharpen one's focus on positions in the opposite direction, or even take on contrarian positions.

5 | Futures Non-Commercial Positioning

The U.S. Congress created the Commodity Futures Trading Commission (CFTC) in 1974 as an independent agency to regulate the futures and options markets for commodities in the United States. As part of its regulation of the commodities markets, the CFTC issues Commitments of Traders (COT) reports each Friday at 3:30 p.m. (EST). These reports provide data about positioning as of the Tuesday of the reporting week. The reports detail the "commercial," "non-commercial," and "non-reportable" trader positions in futures for many of the major currencies, including the euro, British pound sterling, Swiss franc, Japanese yen, and Canadian, Australian, and New Zealand dollars.

The CFTC designates a trader as "commercial" if the trader uses futures for the hedging of primary business activities. An example might be a U.S. distribution company with accounts payable that include overseas counterparties. A trader is otherwise deemed a "non-commercial" trader, and is often referred to as a "speculator." "Non-reportable" positions merely represent the difference between the total open interest and the sum of the commercial and non-commercial traders' positions.

The net long (short) positions of traders often correlate strongly with some aspect of the price action of a currency. An analyst can use either the net positions of commercial traders or the net positions of non-commercial traders, as the positioning of these two groups tends to exhibit a very strong negative correlation. Furthermore, an analyst can transform the net positions and price action in order to filter out trends in price action or variances in total open interest.

There are two drawbacks to the CFTC data. The first is that they are three days old by the time they are published, and so the chance exists that a correction in price action will already be under way prior to the report's release. Second, the report is released late on Friday afternoon in the United States—hardly the best of times for liquidity and also potentially just ahead of weekend market risk. Nevertheless, the data do serve to provide warning of the rising potential for price action trend reversals.

Which Measures for Position and Price Action to Use?

The CFTC reports provide a great deal of data that can be used in different ways to characterize the positioning for a currency. The options raise the question of which permutation of the data is most useful. In particular, we will address whether to use commercial or non-commercial positions, how to measure a net long position, whether to use futures-only data or the data including both futures and options contracts, and finally, what the positioning data can tell us about the foreign-exchange price action.

One baseline question is whether to use the commercial or the non-commercial positioning. The historical data indicate an extremely tight, negative correlation (around -0.99) between the net long non-commercial and net long commercial positions for the major currencies (see **Figure 5.1** for illustration of EUR positions). Given that either positioning generates very similar signals, albeit in opposite directions, we will use the non-commercial positions.

The strong, negative correlation between commercial and non-commercial traders' positions highlights an issue that has been seized upon during the financial crisis regarding equity trading: namely, whether non-commercial traders, or speculators, provide

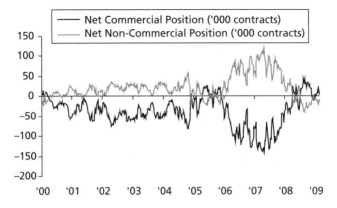

Figure 5.1 Net Long Commercial and Non-Commercial Positions in EUR

Source: CFTC, Bloomberg and T. J. Marta calculations.

a useful service in the marketplace, or whether they represent a disruptive—and destructive—force that regulators need to suppress. During 2008, as equities, particularly bank stocks, came under pressure, regulators and lawmakers issued harsh rhetoric and even limitations on the speculators and their capacity to "short" an equity. While some view short sellers with some type of judgment—as if selling a stock, or any asset, produced some moral judgment on the underlying asset—the reality, as evidenced by the strong negative correlation between the activities of commercial and non-commercial traders, is that the speculators provide the liquidity with which commercial actors can protect legitimate business interests. Were it not for the speculators and their role in the world of foreign exchange, a U.S. company looking out its forecasting budget at accounts payable in foreign currency would be hard-pressed to buy the hedge on that exposure. Without the hedge, the company's well-being would be put at risk from forces outside its business expertise to control. For our purposes, the strong negative correlation means that whether we use commercial or non-commercial positioning data makes no difference; that said, we will use non-commercial data.

With the question of whether to use commercial or non-commercial data answered, we can begin the analysis by charting

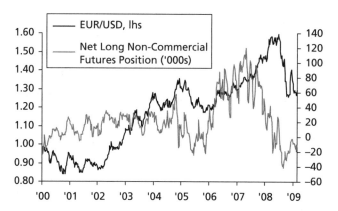

Figure 5.2   EUR/USD and CFTC Non-Commercial Futures Positioning

Source: CFTC, Bloomberg and T. J. Marta calculations.

the net long non-commercial EUR position against EUR/USD back to 2000 (see **Figure 5.2**). An initial visual inspection shows some potential signaling power: the peaks and troughs in positioning during 2000 and 2001 tend to align with peaks and troughs in EUR/USD. However, there are also disappointing disconnects. EUR/USD rallied from 2002 to 2004 while the net long position ranged roughly from zero to 40,000 contracts. From 2006 to 2008, EUR/USD rallied again, but during this period, the net long positioning first attained new highs and then began to drop precipitously. And it was not just the price of EUR/USD that "wandered"; while a 40,000 net long position would have been extreme in 2001, it would have been low during the 2006–2007 period. The correlation of the net long position to EUR/USD from 2000 to 2008 is a weak 0.27. Nonetheless, peaks in the net long position do tend to align with peaks during the rallies, which suggests that perhaps the positioning and currency price action need to be transformed, or measured against some base, to better determine a relationship.

That the peaks (troughs) in positioning appear to align with peaks (troughs) within a trend for EUR/USD suggests that we attempt to measure EUR/USD price action as a deviation from some trendline. We transformed the EUR/USD data to express it as the

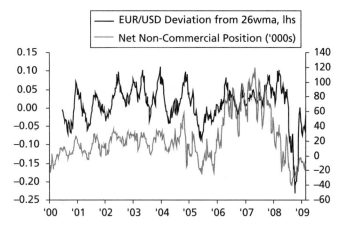

Figure 5.3   EUR/USD Deviation from 26-Week Moving Average and Net Long Non-Commercial Position

Source: CFTC, Bloomberg and T. J. Marta calculations.

difference between the closing price for EUR/USD in a given week and the 26-week moving average of the closing weekly values. **Figure 5.3** shows that the transformation of the EUR/USD time series has rendered it more stationary, and the peaks and troughs appear to align more closely with peaks and troughs in the positioning.

A second issue is how to measure a net position. The simplest measure is simply the difference between the number of long and short contracts outstanding, as illustrated in Figure 5.3. The problem with using simply the net contract figure is that the same position size could mean different things at different times. For instance, in 2000, the average open interest in the euro for commercial and non-commercial traders averaged 24,000 on any given Tuesday, whereas during 2008, the open interest averaged 109,000 contracts. Consequently, similar net long positions would have very different implications for how "overbought" or "oversold" the non-commercial community was. For example, the non-commercial net long euro position of 9,450 contracts on June 16, 2000, came at a time when 84 percent of the contracts held by non-commercial accounts were long contracts, an overwhelmingly lopsided position stance. In contrast, on May 23,

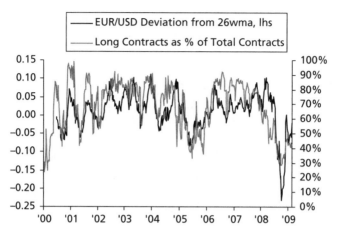

Figure 5.4   EUR/USD Deviation from 26-Week Moving Average and Long Non-Commercial Contracts as Percentage of Total

Source: CFTC, Bloomberg and T. J. Marta calculations.

2008, the non-commercial net long registered 10,788 contracts, but this similar net long position came with only 54 percent of the non-commercial positions being long, a relatively neutral stance. We have found that using the percentage of long contracts relative to the total contracts held by non-commercial traders ("percentage long measure") provides a more stationary time series from which to assess the potential impact of positioning on price action. **Figure 5.4** shows that the percentage long measure closely tracks the deviation of the EUR/USD from its 26-week moving average.

A final issue is whether to measure the percentage of long contracts to all open contracts using futures-only positions or futures and options positions. So far, we have used futures and options data. The correlation between the futures-only and the futures and options data from 2000 to 2008 was 0.998, suggesting neither would result in significantly different signaling results. Furthermore, we tested EUR/USD, GBP/USD, USD/CHF, USD/CAD, and USD/JPY from 2000 to 2008 for the correlation of the percentage positions to price action, defined as the deviation of the spot price from its 26-week moving average. The The correlation for CAD was –0.66 for both futures-only and futures and options data. Of the four remaining currencies, two, USD/CHF and GBP/USD, had stronger correlations using futures-only data, although the difference was small: −0.79 versus −0.78 for USD/CHF and 0.67 versus 0.65 for GBP/USD. In contrast, the correlations for EUR/USD and USD/JPY were significantly stronger using futures and options data: 0.67 versus 0.58 for EUR/USD and −0.63 versus −0.51 for USD/JPY. Consequently, we would choose to employ futures and options data over futures-only data.

In conclusion, the considerations and analysis above lead us to look at CFTC positioning as a relationship between the percentage of long non-commercial contracts relative to the total contracts held and the deviation of the currency price from its 26-week moving average.

EUR/USD and CFTC Non-Commercial Positions

For the discussion of EUR/USD and the CFTC non-commercial positions, we will refer to the figures already presented in this chapter. Plotting EUR/USD and the net long non-commercial positioning suggests little relationship between the two. Indeed, the correlation is only 0.27. In 2000 and 2001, as EUR/USD languished near its bottom, the bullish sentiment in the non-commercial community market built up. In 2002 through 2004, as EUR/USD trended higher, the bullish net long position held relatively steady. Both EUR/USD and the net long position fell in 2005. During 2006 and the first half of 2007, both rose. However, in late 2007 and the first half of 2008, even as EUR/USD established a new record high just above 1.60, the bullish sentiment in the non-commercial community began to fade. The two series began to trend together again, lower for most of the second half of 2008, but with a December 2008 rally.

Transforming the EUR/USD time series to the deviation from the 26-week moving average and the long position to the percentage of long contracts to total outstanding contracts allows the correlation to rise to 0.67, and the graph does suggest a tighter relationship from 2001 to 2007. It is only in late 2007 that the non-commercial community apparently began to lose its bullish fervor, as the percentage of longs dropped towards 60 percent even as EUR/USD spiked higher. This divergence could have derived from a combination of forced unwinds by hedge funds as liquidity began to seize up at the same time the global investment community remained convinced that the financial crisis would remain quarantined in the United States. In any event, the distortion in the relationship stands as testimony to the disruptions in the financial markets to the extent that traders could not rely on indicators and relationships that had worked for years. By the second half of 2008, when EUR/USD began to sell off sharply, the non-commercial community even began to establish a net short position (percent longs below 50 percent) that moderated only when EUR/USD showed signs of stabilizing.

GBP/USD and CFTC Non-Commercial Positions

The deviation of GBP/USD from its 26-week moving average and the percent long measure of the non-commercial CFTC positions exhibit a 0.65 correlation. (See **Figure 5.5**.) This is marginally better

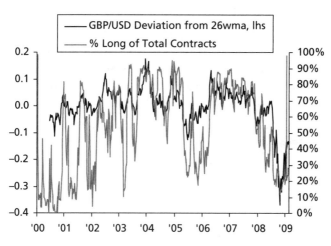

Figure 5.5   GBP/USD Deviation and Longs as Percentage of Total Contracts

Source: CFTC, Bloomberg and T. J. Marta calculations.

than the 0.61 correlation of the net long measure and the deviation of GBP/USD, and much better than the 0.55 correlation of GBP/USD with the net long measure. Extremes in the percent long measure generally coincide with extremes in the deviation of GBP/USD from its trend. Unfortunately, the percent long level associated with reversions back to trend in GBP/USD shifts over time.

As to troughs in percent long positioning, as GBP/USD fell and bottomed in the 2000 to 2002 period, the percent long level associated with a reversion to trend by GBP/USD was below 20 percent. As GBP/USD rallied in 2003 and 2004, the percent long associated with a reversion in price rose to 40 percent. As GBP/USD retraced in 2005 and early 2006, the percent long level dropped to below 30 percent. During the final spike in GBP/USD into 2008, the percent long level rose above 60 percent.

The percent long level peaks associated with moves lower in GBP/USD back towards trend are a bit less volatile. In the bear market of 2000, the percent long level dropped to 40 percent. During the troughing during 2001 and 2002, the percent long level rose to 80 percent. During the bull runs of 2002 to 2004 and 2006 to 2007, the percent long level associated with a correction lower back towards trend rose to 80 to 90 percent. The bad news here is that the person analyzing the data has a moving benchmark for determining a signal for a potential correction, depending on the market direction. The good news is that once one has established whether the market is flat, bullish, or bearish, the benchmarks are relatively clear.

As an example, consider the early February 2002 period. For the week of February 1, the percent long measure dropped to 6.3 percent, and it dropped even further to 4.0 percent the following week. During the preceding weeks of 2002, GBP/USD had collapsed from 1.45 to nearly 1.40. However, even as the percent long measure became more extreme, GBP/USD began to trade higher lows. By April 2002, GBP/USD had traded higher to 1.43 and closed the gap with its 26-week moving average.

For a second example, look at the December 2004 period. The week of December 3, GBP/USD closed at 1.9438. During the remainder of the month, it continued to test higher, even breaching 1.95 three consecutive weeks. For the weeks of December 17 and 24, the percent long measure jumped to 95 percent and 94 percent, respectively, clearly signaling imminent risk of a correction in GBP/USD. By the week of February 14, 2005, GBP/USD traded as low as 1.8510, below the 26-week moving average.

USD/CHF and CFTC Non-Commercial Positions

The deviation of USD/CHF from its 26-week moving average and the percent long measure of the non-commercial CFTC positions exhibit a −0.78 correlation. (See **Figure 5.6**.) This is better than the −0.61 correlation of the net long measure and the deviation of USD/CHF, and much better than the −0.07 correlation of USD/CHF with the net long measure. Extremes in the percent long measure generally coincide with extremes in the deviation of USD/CHF from its trend. Unfortunately, the percent long level associated with reversions back to trend in USD/CHF, particularly for reversions lower in USD/CHF, shifts over time.

As to corrections lower in CHF (higher in USD/CHF) back towards trend, the percent long level associated with a reversion

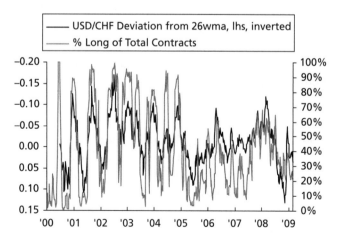

Figure 5.6   USD/CHF Deviation and Longs as Percentage of Total Contracts

Source: CFTC, Bloomberg and T. J. Marta calculations.

up through 2005 remained fairly steady at 80 to 90 percent. This stability likely resulted from the relatively steady decline in USD/CHF during the period. Beginning in 2005, USD/CHF rallied before beginning to trend down again. This increased two-way risk for the price caused the percent long level associated with moves lower in CHF (higher in USD/CHF) to fall towards the 40 to 60 percent range.

The percent long level troughs associated with moves higher in CHF (lower in USD/CHF) back towards trend are less volatile. For most of the 2000 to 2008 period, a percent long level below 20 percent would have been enough to signal warning of an imminent reversion to trend. Only during the highly aberrational period in late 2007, to early 2008, when CHF rallied sharply as markets feared a financial meltdown, did the percent long level associated with a move higher back to trend for CHF shift. During that highly exceptional period, the percent long level rose to 40 to 50 percent.

During the July 2002 period, for example, the percent long reading climbed through 96 percent and up to 99 percent. At the same time, USD/CHF collapsed to 1.44, causing it to fall well below the 26-week moving average, which remained above 1.60. In the ensuing weeks, as the percent long reading moderated, USD/CHF both corrected and consolidated, allowing USD/CHF to move back to its 26-week moving average by October.

By the week of October 25, 2002, as the deviation of USD/CHF closed in on the lowest deviation from the 26-week moving average since January 2002, the percent long reading had dropped to 17 percent, a low since March 2002, right before USD/CHF collapsed from 1.70 to 1.50 in four months. The warning provided by this short position proved accurate, as USD/CHF made another sharp leg down from 1.50 to 1.35 over the course of the next three months.

USD/JPY and CFTC Non-Commercial Positions

The deviation of USD/JPY from its 26-week moving average and the percent long measure of the non-commercial CFTC positions

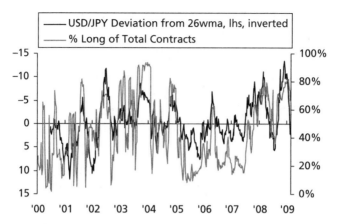

Figure 5.7   USD/JPY and Net Long Non-Commercial Positions

Source: CFTC, Bloomberg and T. J. Marta calculations.

exhibit a −0.63 correlation. (See **Figure 5.7**.) This is better than the
−0.50 correlation of the net long measure and the deviation of
USD/JPY, and much better than the −0.30 correlation of USD/
JPY with the net long measure. Extremes in the percent long measure generally coincide with extremes in the deviation of USD/
JPY from its trend. Unfortunately, the percent long level associated with reversions back to trend in USD/JPY shifts over time.

Troughs in percent long positioning proved relatively stable
from 2000 to 2007, with a percent long level of 20 percent generally associated with a correction higher in JPY (lower in USD/JPY).
However, as USD/JPY peaked and began a sharp, sustained descent
in 2007, the troughs in the percent long level associated with a
reversion to trend by USD/JPY moved higher towards 40 percent.

The percent long level peaks associated with moves lower in
JPY (higher in USD/JPY) back towards trend are a bit more
volatile. As USD/JPY peaked in 2002, the percent long level
associated with a correction lower in JPY (higher in USD/JPY)
slipped to 70 percent. As USD/JPY collapsed in late 2003, the
percent long level associated with a reversion to trend rose to 90
percent. In 2006 and 2007, as USD/JPY trended higher again,
the percent long reading associated with a reversion to trend fell

to 40 to 50 percent. Finally, during the 2007 to 2008 bear market, the percent long reading signal rose back to 80 percent.

As an example, consider the October to November 2004 period. During this time USD/JPY fell sharply from 110 to 102 and eventually tested four-year lows. The spot rate also fell to more than six big figures below the 26-week moving average, which was still registering 108. At the same time, the percent long level rose to 80 percent, a high since February 2004 when USD/JPY had bottomed at 105 before rebounding back to 112 in the course of three weeks. The warning provided by the percent long proved timely, as USD/JPY drifted slightly lower in December even as the non-commercial community pared back its JPY longs, bottomed through February 2005 and commenced a strong rally to above 120 by the end of 2005.

In June 2007, USD/JPY touched 124 just before entering a long swan dive to below 90 in late 2008. At the top, USD/JPY rose more than three big figures above its 26-week moving average, an extreme since January 2007 just before USD/JPY retraced from 121 to 115. The percent long level in June fell to 15 percent, a low since February, again, when USD/JPY corrected from 121 to 115. The warning provided in June proved timely. USD/JPY stalled around 123–124 before beginning its long descent by mid-July.

USD/CAD and CFTC Non-Commercial Positions

The deviation of USD/CAD from its 26-week moving average and the percent long measure of the non-commercial CFTC positions exhibit a −0.66 correlation. (See **Figure 5.8**.) This is roughly the same as the −0.65 correlation of the net long measure and the deviation of USD/CAD, but much better than the −0.29 correlation of USD/CAD with the net long measure. Extremes in the percentlong measure generally coincide with extremes in the deviation of USD/CAD from its trend. Unfortunately, the percent long level associated with reversions back to trend in USD/CAD shifts over time.

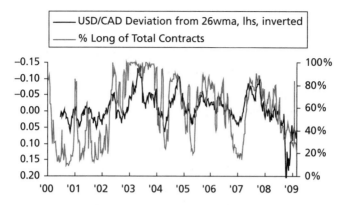

Figure 5.8 USD/CAD and Net Long Non-Commercial Positions

Source: CFTC, Bloomberg and T. J. Marta calculations.

Troughs in percent long positioning proved relatively stable from 2000 to 2003, with a percent long level below 20 percent generally associated with a correction higher in CAD (lower in USD/CAD). However, as USD/CAD topped in 2002 and began to decline sharply in 2003, the low in percent long positioning associated with a strengthening in CAD back toward trend moved sharply higher to above 50 percent. In 2004, as the rate of decline in USD/CAD moderated, the percent long troughs associated with CAD rallies back toward trend fell back towards 20 percent.

The percent long level peaks associated with moves lower in CAD (higher in USD/CAD) back towards trend are a bit less volatile, having ranged from 100 percent to 60 percent. With USD/CAD trading above 1.50 in July 2001, the percent long reading topped out at 61 percent. This presaged a stall in the rally until the wake of 9/11. As USD/CAD topped and began to fall sharply in 2003, the percent long readings associated with CAD retracing towards trend rose to near 100 percent. When the pace of decline moderated in 2004, so did the percent long level associated with reversions to trend—back towards 80 percent.

As an example, consider the June 2002 period. USD/CAD had peaked in January at 1.6193, stabilized through April, and then traded sharply lower through June. The percent long measure spiked to 100 percent, and two weeks later, USD/CAD had fallen to 1.5173, an extreme 5.5 big figures below the 26-week moving average. However, by the end of June, the decline in USD/CAD had stopped, and by the week of August 9, USD/CAD had rebounded to test back above 1.60.

During the first half of 2004, USD/CAD had rallied from 1.27 in January to test 1.40 during the weeks of May 14 and 21. During the week of May 14, USD/CAD was trading significantly higher than the 26-week moving average of 1.3260, while during the week of May 21, the percent long measure had dropped to 23.7 percent, a low since 2002. In the next six weeks, USD/CAD had fallen to close at 1.3239, back below the 26-week moving average.

AUD/USD and CFTC Non-Commercial Positions

Before 2003, CFTC reporting of AUD positions was inconsistent due to light trading volumes. During many weeks prior to 2003, traders did not hold enough positions to meet the threshold requirement for reporting. Even during 2003 and 2004, the liquidity remained low enough that the data proved exceedingly volatile and consequently provided little information regarding price action. As a result, the data are robust enough for analysis starting only in 2005.

The deviation of AUD/USD from its 26-week moving average and the percent long measure of the non-commercial CFTC positions exhibit a 0.74 correlation, better than both the 0.65 correlation of the net long measure and the deviation of AUD/USD and the 0.51 correlation of AUD/USD with the net long measure. (See **Figure 5.9**.) Extremes in the percent long measure generally coincide with extremes in the deviation of AUD/USD from its trend. Unfortunately, the percent long level associated with reversions back to trend in AUD/USD shifts over time.

Troughs in percent long positioning were generally quite high from 2005 to mid-2008, with a percent long level of 50 to 60 percent generally associated with a correction higher in AUD/USD.

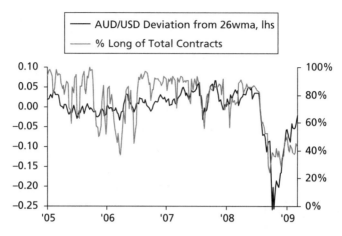

Figure 5.9   AUD/USD and Net Long Non-Commercial Positions

Source: CFTC, Bloomberg and T. J. Marta calculations.

The high level reflects that AUD/USD remained in a strong bull market for most of the period with few sharp, sustained pullbacks. However, as AUD/USD peaked and began a sharp, sustained descent in 2008, the troughs in the percent long level associated with a reversion to trend by AUD/USD fell to the 20 to 40 percent range.

The percent long level peaks associated with moves lower in AUD/USD back towards trend are consistently extremely high, also reflective of the persistent bull market that existed. The percent long level associated with a correction lower in AUD/USD remained above 80 percent up through 2008. Since the crash in AUD/USD during the second half of 2008, there have been few instances of overbought conditions leading to a further sell-off.

The second half of 2007 did provide two instances in which AUD/USD corrected fairly sharply and led to extremely (on a relative basis) "short" readings. In August 2007, when the U.S. commercial paper market froze and risk positions were eliminated, AUD/USD broke lower from 0.8872 the week of July 27 to 0.7675 the week ended August 17. This decline was prompted by a drop in the percent long reading to 56 percent for the week ended August 24, the lowest level since June 2006, just as AUD/USD was ending a three-year consolidation and beginning a two-year rally. The extremely low percent long reading presaged a sharp rally back to a new high of 0.94 by the week of November 9.

During November 2007, concerns grew regarding year-end liquidity, and risk positions, including long AUD/USD trades, were exited in a violent manner. From the 0.94 traded the week of November 9, AUD/USD fell to 0.8554 by the week of December 21. This move lower was coincided by a decline in the percent long reading to 56 percent (the same as in August). Subsequently, AUD/USD rallied the next seven months to trade a record high of 0.9850 on July 18, 2008.

NZD/USD and CFTC Non-Commercial Positions

If the lack of liquidity in AUD presented a problem, the issue for NZD is even more pronounced. Consistent weekly reports were not available until 2006, and there are no option data to supplement that for the futures positions. Nevertheless, in the period since 2006, the deviation of NZD/USD from its 26-week moving average and the percent long measure of the non-commercial CFTC positions exhibit a 0.84 correlation. (See **Figure 5.10**.)

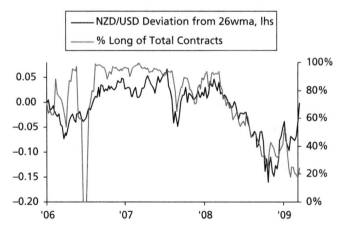

Figure 5.10   NZD/USD and Net Long Non-Commercial Positions

Source: CFTC, Bloomberg and T. J. Marta calculations.

This is the same as the correlation of the net long measure and the deviation of NZD/USD, and better than the 0.64 correlation of NZD/USD with the net long measure. Extremes in the percent long measure generally coincide with extremes in the deviation of NZD/USD from its trend. Unfortunately, the percent long level associated with reversions back to trend in NZD/USD shifts over time.

Troughs in percent long positioning proved unstable over the period. From mid-2006 to early 2008, NZD/USD rallied persistently, faltering only temporarily when the crisis first erupted in August 2007. However, the declines in NZD/USD during the first part of 2006 and August 2007 provided trough readings of 50 to 60 percent before NZD/USD began rallying back toward trend. Note that even in 2006, illiquidity bedeviled the analysis, as for three weeks in late June and early July no CFTC reports were required or made. The demise of Bear Stearns in March 2008 precipitated a sharp sell-off in NZD/USD from 0.82 to below 0.50 11 months later. The violence and persistence of the move affected the trough in the percent long reading associated with a trend reversal, driving it down towards 20 percent.

The percent long level peaks associated with moves lower in NZD/USD are similarly unstable. During the rally through March 2008, the price action was so unidirectional that percent long readings in excess of 90 percent became commonplace, thus providing little useful warning for the August 2007 correction. During the sharp sell-off of 2008 and 2009, the move was so forceful and unidirectional that there was only one incident in which a bear-market rally provided a surge in percent long positioning that presaged a renewed decline in NZD/USD. From December 2008 to January 2009, NZD/USD rallied from 0.52 to more than 0.60, and during that time, the percent long reading jumped from 31 percent to 52 percent, which coincided with the peak just before NZD/USD dropped sharply to below 0.50 within three weeks.

At the beginning of 2006, NZD/USD was experiencing an acceleration in the downtrend that had started in early 2005.

By the end of March, NZD/USD had fallen to 0.5993, testing lows that had held in May 2004. At the same time, the percent long reading had fallen to 58 percent, and a week later, the reading had dipped further to 53.5 percent. By the week of May 5, NZD/USD had rallied to 0.64 and the percent long position had jumped back to 95 percent. The next time that the percent long reading fell to a similar reading was in August 2007. From the week of July 27 to the week of August 17, NZD/USD collapsed from 0.8110 to 0.6643, and the percent long reading collapsed from 93.2 percent to 64.7 percent. This low reading proved a harbinger of the ensuing rally in NZD/USD back not only towards trend, but to a retest of the July high by February 2008.

Finding the Data:
Setting Up CIXs in Bloomberg

Analysts can obtain the data for net long, futures-only, non-commercial positioning either from the CFTC's Web site or from the Bloomberg Professional Service ("Bloomberg"). In Bloomberg, one must create custom indexes ("CIX") to calculate the net long positions. For example, to create the net long for EUR enter the following commands:

CIX < go > (to enter the CIX nest of commands)
1 < go > (to create a new CIX)
1 < go > (to create a custom index)
Enter a ticker name: i.e. "CFTCEUR"
Enter a short descriptive name
Enter the following formula: "IMFFENCL Index – IMMFFNCS Index <go>"
Enter "1 < go > " to save the CIX, and it can now be referenced as ".CFTCEUR < index > < go > " (remember the period at the beginning).

The pertinent codes for the net positions for other currencies are provided in **Table 5.1**.

Table 5.1   Codes for Net Positions

Currency	Ticker for Long Positions	Ticker for Short Positions
EUR	IMMFFNCL Index	IMMFFNCS Index
GBP	IMMOPNCL Index	IMMOPNCS Index
CHF	IMMTSNCL Index	IMMTSNCS Index
AUD	IMMOANCL Index	IMMOANCS Index
CAD	IMMOCNCL Index	IMMOCNCS Index
NZD	IMMTZNCL Index	IMMTZNCS Index
JPY	IMMOJNCL Index	IMMOJNCS Index

Source: Bloomberg.

Conclusion

The purpose of this chapter is to provide analysts with a tool to identify the warning signs of when the non-commercial community is overstretched to a point at which price action for a currency pair would be likely to revert back towards its trend. We found that percent long readings for the futures and options non-commercial positions provided the most consistent signals regarding when a currency might revert back towards its trend (26-week moving average). Unfortunately, the percent long readings associated with reversions to trend are not consistent but rather must be viewed in the context of the trend of the currency. However, the characterization of the price trend allows analysts, investors, and traders to at least gauge whether the positioning is providing a warning signal. The next caveat is a reminder that any warning is merely signaling a potential reversion to trend, and that such may involve a correction in price action, a consolidation of price action, or some combination of the two. Nevertheless, the warning signs provided—in conjunction with other forms of analysis—should allow traders and investors to snug up stop-losses, lighten up on exposure, buy insurance, or begin considering contrary positions.

6 | Risk Reversals

Risk reversals are a measure of options prices that can be used as a proxy for market positioning and sentiment. This chapter is not designed to provide any in-depth options discussions; rather, it will only provide enough detail to allow readers not familiar with options to have a basic understanding of how the concept works as it relates to market positioning/sentiment.

A risk reversal represents the difference in prices between a call and a put on a currency pair. The purchaser of a call (put) will generally profit if the currency goes up (down) during the term of the option. The "prices" in this case are actually quoted as the implied volatility ("vol" or "implied vol") of the option rather than the dollar price. Furthermore, as the price, or vol, of an option depends on multiple inputs, those inputs are controlled, or specified, in order to make the quoted vol differential meaningful. For the purposes of this chapter, we will be working with 3-month, 25-delta options. The timeframe of the option is important because the value of an option rises with the length of time in the option. The delta of an option is the change in dollar price of the option relative to the change in the value of the underlying currency, and it changes depending on a number of factors including the distance between the strike price of an option and the actual price of the underlying currency. Throughout this chapter, our reference to risk reversals

Table 6.1   Bloomberg Tickers for 3-Month, 25-Delta Risk Reversals for Major Currencies

Currency	Bloomberg Code for 3-Month, 25-Delta Risk Reversals
EUR	EURUSD25R3M Curncy
GBP	GBPUSD25R3M Curncy
CHF	USDCHF25R3M Curncy
NOK	USDNOK25R3M Curncy
SEK	USDSEK25R3M Curncy
JPY	USDJPY25R3M Curncy
AUD	AUDUSD25R3M Curncy
CAD	USDCAD25R3M Curncy
NZD	NZDUSD25R3M Curncy

will in all cases represent the implied vol of a 3-month, 25-delta call less the implied vol of a 3-month, 25-delta put. To the extent the volatility for the call is higher (lower) than that for the put, the market is interpreted to be willing to pay a higher premium for upside (downside) price action, and thus have a bullish (bearish) stance.

As with CFTC net speculative positioning, risk reversals are useful not in forecasting the future price action of a currency pair but rather in presenting a warning signal that the market is overly bullish (or bearish), so that a currency is at greater risk of a convergence between the spot price and the trend of the spot price (moving average). One advantage of risk reversals over the CFTC data is that the risk reversals reflect live market prices and so are updated in real time rather than with a three-day lag. **Table 6.1** presents the Bloomberg tickers for the 3-month, 25-delta risk reversals for the major currencies.

Analysis of Correlation with Price Action

For our analysis of risk reversals, we looked at the same major currencies as in Chapter 5 regarding futures speculative positioning: EUR, GBP, CHF, JPY, CAD, AUD, and NZD. We used daily data back

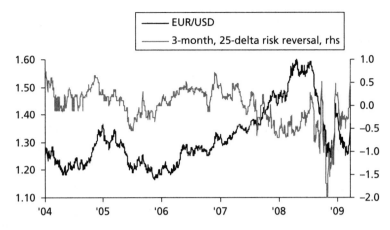

Figure 6.1   EUR/USD and 3-Month, 25-Delta Risk Reversal

Source: Bloomberg.

to October 2003, as that is when Bloomberg risk-reversal data begin. We will begin by determining what transformations, if any, of the data provide the most useful information regarding the potential for future price action.

Figure 6.1 illustrates the problems with using the untransformed data series to attempt to identify any type of signal regarding foreign-exchange price action. EUR/USD trended strongly during 2007 and the first half of 2008, while the risk reversal trended lower in 2007. Thus, not only did both series exhibit trends, which makes any type of consistent signal impossible, but they actually moved in opposite directions for significant periods. For example, in the second half of 2005, as EUR/USD continued to correct lower, the options market began paring back on its bearish stance. Eventually, EUR/USD did begin to rally, but as the rise continued during late 2006 and into 2007, the risk reversal stopped rising. Then, as EUR/USD surged above its late 2004 peak of 1.3666 to 1.60, players in the options market actually turned bearish on EUR/ USD. The result of these dichotomies is that the correlation of EUR/USD with its risk reversal for the 2003 to 2008 period was actually −0.36. That negative relationship makes EUR/USD an outlier among the currencies, as they generally exhibited a positive correlation. However, the correlation for USD/CAD proved to be a meaningless −0.03, while that for AUD/USD measured a weak 0.27, and so some type of transformation appears necessary in order to establish a robust signaling measure.

As **Figure 6.2** illustrates, the correlations for each of the currencies and their risk reversals from 2003 through early 2009 range widely—from −0.36 for EUR/USD to −0.03 for USD/CAD and +0.78 for USD/CHF. When we transformed the data, we obtained much more consistent results. Working from the success of the twenty-six-week period as a moving average from which to measure the deviation when analyzing weekly CFTC data, we chose to transform the daily currency price data to the deviation from its 130-day moving average. In order to de-trend the risk-reversal data, we chose to adopt the same measure—the deviation from the 130-day moving average. The correlation between the deviations of the currency and risk-reversal series proved much more consistent across the various currencies. The correlations ranged from + 0.40 for EUR/USD to 0.70 for AUD/USD. The remainder of the chapter analyzes currency prices and risk reversals via their deviations from trend to establish the positioning deviations that provide signals of increased risk that a currency will revert to trend.

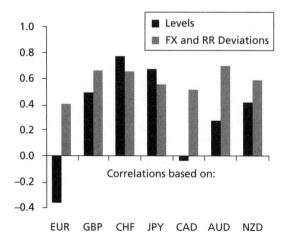

Figure 6.2   Correlations for Currencies and Risk Reversals

Source: Bloomberg and T. J. Marta calculations.

EUR/USD and Risk Reversals

Transforming the data for both EUR/USD and the risk reversal provides a correlation of +0.40. This still represents the lowest relationship of the currencies analyzed. (See **Figure 6.3**.) This low is consistent with the finding that the correlation of the deviations for the futures speculative positioning was also lower for EUR/USD. These lower correlations of EUR/USD with speculative and options positioning could reflect that the euro is less focused on by hedge funds as a carry trade currency than are other currencies such as the perennially low yielding JPY and CHF or generally high yielding (and less liquid) AUD.

In spite of the lower correlation, visually, the band for the risk-reversal deviations remained fairly consistent up until late 2008. The risk-reversal deviations associated with EUR/USD reversing higher relative to trend remained around −0.4 to −0.5 right up until the most violent part of the crisis in October 2008. The upper range for risk-reversal deviations remained around +0.25 to +0.30

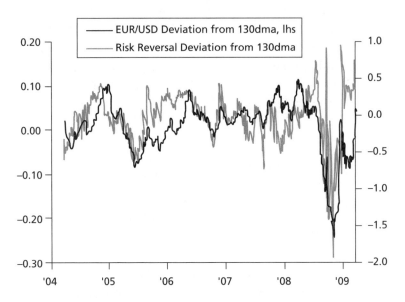

Figure 6.3 EUR/USD and Risk Reversal as Deviations from Trend

Source: Bloomberg and T. J. Marta calculations.

until mid-2008, when it shifted higher towards +0.50 as traders began to position for a potential collapse in the U.S. dollar.

Let us look in depth at the June 2005 period. From January to the beginning of June 2005, EUR/USD had traded down from 1.35 to 1.23. As June progressed, EUR/USD ground even lower. On June 14, EUR/USD closed at 1.2032 and a record low deviation from trend, which measured 1.2976. During this early June period, the risk reversal moved lower to −0.5, also at a record low deviation from its trend, which measured +0.12. The combination strongly warned of at least a consolidation, if not reversal in EUR/USD, and that is exactly what transpired. Over the next five weeks, EUR/USD consolidated, testing a bit lower for a few days. At the end of the five weeks, EUR/USD began to rally, eventually closing the gap with the 130-day moving average at 1.25 in early September.

For another example, consider the December 2006 period. On December 4, EUR/USD traded a multi-year high of 1.3368. The currency had rallied sharply from 1.2583 on October 13. The currency closed December 4 at 1.3343, 0.0601 above its trend, an extreme. That same day, the risk reversal closed at +0.7, with the deviation from its trend at 0.4, also an extreme. Subsequently, as indicated by the extreme readings, EUR/USD topped and then fell back to 1.2868 by January 12, 2007, almost fully closing the gap with the 130-day moving average.

GBP/USD and Risk Reversals

The deviations of GBP/USD and the risk reversal from their respective 130-day moving averages exhibit a 0.66 correlation, better than the 0.49 correlation of GBP/USD with the risk reversal. (See **Figure 6.4**.)

Until the financial crisis really heated up in August 2007, deviations of the risk reversal below −0.2 provided a warning of increased potential that GBP/USD would revert back towards its trend. After August 2007, the threshold moved lower to −0.5,

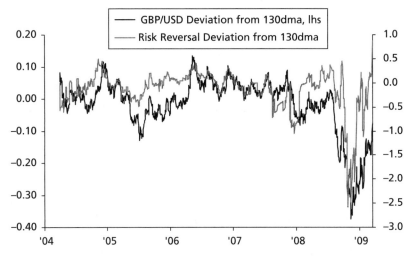

Figure 6.4   GBP/USD and Risk Reversal, Deviations from Trend

Source: Bloomberg and T. J. Marta calculations.

and in the wake of the Lehman failure, the deviation exploded to −2.5, evidence of the calamity unleashed by the government's failure to prevent Lehman's demise.

Regarding peaks in the risk-reversal deviation, readings in excess of +0.2 generally provided a warning signal. However, on occasion the reading reached towards +0.5, a warning in and of itself that a risk-reversal signal needs to be corroborated by price action. Another exception is during 2007 and 2008, when the deviation in trend for the risk reversals began to fade, as the options market established its maximum desired exposure to GBP/USD. During this period, the peak associated with a return lower to trend by GBP/USD was as low as −0.04.

Mid-2005 stands out on the accompanying chart as a period of extreme bearishness relative to trend for GBP/USD. GBP/USD had achieved a thirteen-year high in December 2004 and spent the first seven months of 2005 correcting from 1.95 to 1.70. By July 22, GBP/USD traded to a low of 1.7239, after which the currency rallied to 1.85 by early September. Now, the extreme in the risk-reversal deviation occurred several weeks earlier when, on June 30, the deviation fell to −0.49. However, the trough in the risk reversal had reached a similar low in April 2004 and also preceded a rally in GBP/USD by several weeks.

The week ending May 12, 2006, GBP/USD had just completed a sharp, four-week rally from 1.7510 to 1.8946. The violence of the move drove the GBP/USD deviation to a record-high 0.1352. Two days later, the risk-reversal deviation rose to 0.35, and the extreme measures presaged a move lower in GBP/USD. During the next six weeks GBP/USD fell to 1.8173, which closed the gap of GBP/USD with its 130-day moving average.

USD/CHF and Risk Reversals

Data for the USD/CHF 3-month, 25-delta risk reversals on Bloomberg begin only in March 2005, and so the deviation data do not begin until September 2005. (See **Figure 6.5**.) The deviations of USD/CHF and the risk reversal from their respective 130-day moving averages exhibit a 0.60 correlation. This is much better than the 0.27 correlation of the risk reversal and the deviation of GBP/USD, though not so strong as the 0.78 correlation of USD/CHF with the risk reversal.

Extremes in the risk-reversal deviation appeared fairly stable until early 2008. Peaks in the risk-reversal deviation of +0.15 or

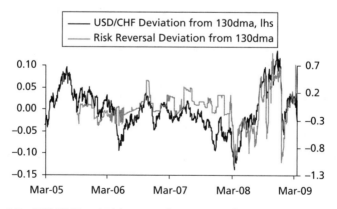

Figure 6.5 USD/CHF and Risk Reversal, Deviations from Trend

Source: Bloomberg and T. J. Marta calculations.

higher tended to suggest an increased potential for a reversion lower in USD/CHF towards its trend. In contrast, troughs below −0.15 tended to suggest an increased likelihood that USD/CHF would revert higher towards its trend. The historic events of 2008 caused the above ranges to give way. During the collapse of Bear Stearns, money flowed out of the United States and into Switzerland on a flight-to-quality trade, and the risk-reversal deviation collapsed to −1.13. Subsequently, beginning in July, when all risk trades were being unwound, the USD rallied against every currency, including the CHF, and the risk-reversal deviation shot up to +0.8. However, in anything like "normal" trading conditions, we should begin to look for reversions to mean when the risk-reversal deviation is below −0.15 or above +0.15.

The week of May 12, 2006, USD/CHF had just completed a sharp, four-week sell-off from 1.2983 to 1.1974. The risk-reversal deviation had fallen to −0.40, while the USD/CHF deviation had plummeted to −0.0945, a record. These extreme measures indicated an imminent reversion towards trend, which is what occurred. USD/CHF consolidated for four weeks before grinding higher to close the gap with the 130-day moving average on September 8 and eventually rallying to 1.2771 on October 13. By October, the deviation measures had flipped toward the opposite extremes. The USD/CHF deviation had risen to 0.03562 on October 13, a high since December 2005. Meanwhile, the risk-reversal deviation had spiked to a record high 0.44 on October 19. These extremes suggested that the October 13 high marked a high-water mark for USD/CHF, and the currency corrected lower to close the gap with its trend at 1.2505 on November 22, 2006.

USD/JPY and Risk Reversals

The correlation of the deviations in USD/JPY and risk reversals from their 26-week moving averages is 0.56, weaker than the 0.67 correlation of the currency price and the risk reversal but still strong and positive. **Figure 6.6** shows that the transformation has provided a relationship more amenable to trading and investing decisions.

More specifically, from 2004 through the beginning of the deleveraging crisis in August 2007, risk-reversal deviations in excess of either −0.5 or +0.5 could generally be associated with points at which the spot currency price and the trend currency price would converge, and the reversions generally entailed a roughly five big-figure shift in the deviation over a two- to three-month period.

As the crisis unfolded after August 2007, options players began to price in sharp USD/JPY price declines based on the view that the deleveraging in the financial markets would cause carry trade unwinds that would at least partially manifest themselves in USD/JPY selling. Consequently, negative deviations in the risk reversals associated with convergences between the currency and its trend shifted sharply lower—from −0.5 to below −1.0—and even as low as −5.65 during the most perilous time of the crisis in October 2008. The rally of USD/JPY from the sub-90 lows of late December 2008 and January 2009 on the back of veiled threats of intervention by the Bank of Japan caused the risk-reversal deviations to spike to above 3.0. Despite the increase in the risk-reversal deviations, the −0.5 to +0.5 levels should be considered as initial warning signs of an impending reversion to trend.

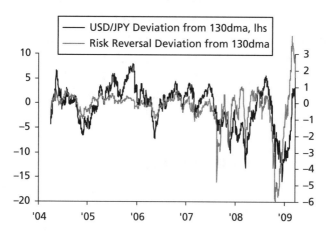

Figure 6.6 USD/JPY and Risk Reversal, Deviations from Trend

Source: Bloomberg and T. J. Marta calculations.

For example, in late November 2004, USD/JPY was testing lower towards lows near 100 last traded in 1999, having collapsed from 110 six weeks prior. The deviation of USD/JPY had reached an extreme—in excess of six big figures below the 130-day moving average. The risk-reversal deviation had also reached an extreme of −0.85. These readings portended the consolidation of USD/JPY through early February 2005 and the eventual rebound towards 120 by December 2005.

A less extreme example is provided by developments in mid-October 2006. Since May of 2006, USD/JPY had ground higher from 110 to 120. By October 10, the currency had closed at 119.78, an extreme 4.4 big figures above the 130-day moving average. From October 11 through 19, the risk-reversal deviation remained above +0.6. These readings warned of an imminent reversion to trend, and by November 23, USD/JPY eliminated the gap with the 130-day moving average, closing at 116.30.

USD/CAD and Risk Reversals

The deviations of USD/CAD and the risk reversal from their respective 130-day moving averages exhibit a 0.52 correlation, as illustrated in **Figure 6.7**. This is much better than the −0.03 correlation of USD/CAD with the risk reversal.

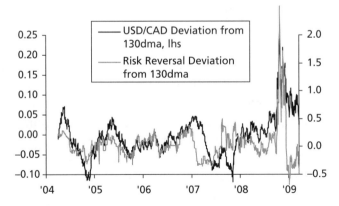

Figure 6.7 USD/CAD and Risk Reversal, Deviations from Trend

Source: Bloomberg and T. J. Marta calculations.

From 2004 through mid-2008, risk-reversal deviations in excess of +0.2 and below −0.2 generally signaled a reversion to trend for the currency. During the massive USD rally during the liquidation crisis of late 2008, the risk-reversal deviation spiked to 2.0. Additionally, after USD/CAD failed to breach 1.30 for the third time in as many months on December 5, 2008, and began to correct lower, the options market became very bearish on USD/CAD, sending the risk reversal from 2.03 to 0.26 by December 18 and creating a risk-reversal deviation of −0.43. Nonetheless, risk-reversal deviations of roughly above +0.2 or below −0.2 should trigger some warning of a potential reversal in the price action relative to trend.

For example, in mid-May 2004, USD/CAD ended a four-month, bear-market rally at 1.40 that had started at 1.2682 in January. From May 13 through 18, USD/CAD tested 1.40 unsuccessfully. Earlier in the month, on May 3, with USD/CAD closing at 1.3726, the risk-reversal deviation had risen to +0.29. That extreme reading in the risk reversal suggested that the USD/CAD rally was running out of momentum, which is what happened as USD/CAD topped and corrected, falling back to the 130-day moving average when it closed at 1.3328 on June 30.

On November 26, 2004, USD/CAD traded down to 1.1718, ending a sharp downturn that had begun on May 21 at 1.40. Indications that the end of the decline was near could have been picked up from the risk-reversal deviation, which had dropped to −0.17 on November, as well as the currency deviation, which dropped down to −0.1138 on November 25. Subsequently, USD/CAD mounted a short-term rally, closing the gap with the 130-day moving average at 1.2447 on February 4, 2005.

On August 16, 2007, USD/CAD traded to a three-month high of 1.0867. The next day, the risk-reversal deviation jumped to record high 0.49, portending at least a consolidation and possibly a correction lower. As it happened, USD/CAD consolidated just above 1.05 support through September 11 before beginning a strong downtrend through November.

AUD/USD and Risk Reversals

The deviations of AUD/USD and the risk reversal from their respective 130-day moving averages exhibited a 0.70 correlation, much stronger than the correlation of the untransformed levels (0.27).

The very tight risk-reversal deviation ranges during much of 2005 and into 2007 reflect the relatively trendless price action for AUD/USD during the period. During 2007, the trend picked up as AUD/USD began to rally, although the deviation in the price action from the trend remained low, and so the deviations from the trend remained subdued. Deviations in the risk reversal below −0.25 and above +0.15 generally suggested that the spot price for AUD/USD would converge with the trend. (See **Figure 6.8**.)

Periods of greater volatility led to wild fluctuations in the risk-reversal deviation. In the wake of the August 2007 commercial paper crisis, the risk-reversal deviation ranged from −3 to +0.6. After AUD/USD failed to breach 0.80 in February 2005, marking a second failure (the prior was February 2004), the market became very bearish, and the risk-reversal deviation plunged to −0.99. Finally, in October 2008, as AUD/USD was finishing its collapse from 0.9850 in July to 0.6005, the risk-reversal deviation plunged

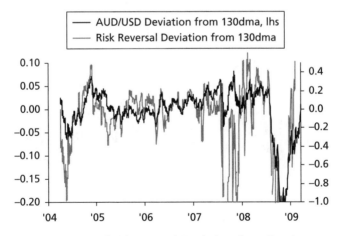

Figure 6.8 AUD/USD and Risk Reversal, Deviations from Trend

Source: Bloomberg and T. J. Marta calculations.

to below −6. As AUD/USD stabilized and began to rally in early 2009, the risk-reversal deviation spiked to above +3.

As an example of one of the more benign periods, consider late March 2006, when AUD/USD closed at 0.7016 to finish a gentle downtrend in place from 0.7990 in March 2005. By March 29, the risk-reversal deviation had dropped to −0.38, a low since March 2005. The deviation for AUD/USD had fallen to −0.0376 on March 28, and the combination of extreme readings indicated that a reversion to trend for AUD/USD was in the offing. By April 18, AUD/USD had rallied to close at 0.7420, above the 130-day moving average, and the currency would continue to rally to 0.7794 on May 11.

NZD/USD and Risk Reversals

The deviations of NZD/USD and the risk reversal from their 26-week moving averages exhibit a 0.58 correlation, better than the 0.40 correlation of the non-transformed data series. The range of risk-reversal deviations varies widely over time. (See **Figure 6.9**.)

As with AUD/USD, the risk-reversal deviations for NZD/USD can spike rather dramatically in the face of sharp corrections.

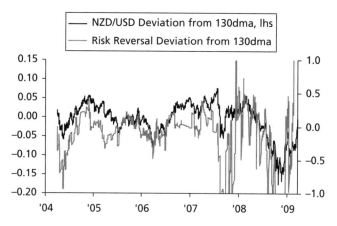

Figure 6.9   NZD/USD and Risk Reversal, Deviations from Trend

Source: Bloomberg and T. J. Marta calculations.

For instance, in February 2004, NZD/USD tested above 0.70 and was trading near the very top of the 0.40–0.70 range in place since 1982. When the rally failed, the sentiment turned very bearish, and NZD/USD collapsed to below 0.60 in three months. As a result of the violent downdraft in the currency, the risk-reversal deviation fell to −0.94. In the wake of the August 2007 commercial paper crisis, NZD/USD collapsed from above 0.80 to below 0.70 in the span of three weeks, and the risk-reversal deviation collapsed to below −5. And when NZD/USD rallied back to above 0.80 by early 2008, the risk-reversal deviation had spiked to +1.4. Unfortunately, the rollercoaster ride was not over. During the massive sell-off of risk assets in late 2008, the risk-reversal deviation again plunged below −5 and then lurched above +3 again when NZD stabilized in early 2009.

During the relatively calm period between late 2004 and early 2007, when NZD/USD ranged between 0.60 and 0.75, the risk-reversal deviations associated with a return to trend by the currency were generally above +0.15 and below −0.15. For example, by November 2004, NZD/USD had fully recovered from the early year sell-off and was testing toward 0.7250 and a new high since 1982. On November 26, the risk-reversal deviation had risen to 0.42, indicating an increased probability that the rally would stall. NZD/USD did manage to reach 0.7268 on December 6, but then fell to 0.6969 by December 10. From November 2006 to March 2007, NZD/USD traded within a 0.67–0.71 range. On March 5, the currency fell and closed at 0.6745, below the 130-day moving average. That same day, the risk-reversal deviation fell to −0.16, a low since June 2006 when NZD/USD bottomed just below 0.60. The extreme risk-reversal deviation marked the medium-term bottom for NZD/USD, which went on to test 0.75 by April 18.

Conclusion

Risk reversals provide important information regarding how bullish or bearish the options market is at any given point, which in turn can provide a warning sign that a trend is becoming exhausted and that price action will have to consolidate or perhaps even reverse.

One challenge in interpreting risk-reversal data is determining the level of bullishness or bearishness that makes the market vulnerable to a correction. On the discouraging side, data since 2004 show that the range varies widely over time, making any simple, consistent trading rule impossible. However, on the optimistic side, the time series for the risk-reversal deviations allow us to see how much the deviations have ranged under widely varying conditions. The data since 2004 provide examples of trendless markets, trending markets, and even severe financial dislocations. Consequently, once we have classified an environment as one of these three states, we can make reasonable assumptions about what constitutes an "extreme enough" reading to suggest an increased potential for a consolidation or correction in price action.

Remember that positioning analysis, whether for options risk reversals or CFTC non-commercial futures positions, is not an attempt to forecast price action. Rather, it is designed to provide a warning system that the deviation from trend in a currency is overdone and that an increased probability exists that the currency price will either consolidate, in which case the trend will converge with the price action; correct back towards the trend; or, as is most often the case, some combination of the two. In any event, the extremes in risk-reversal deviations often signal a consolidation and/or price correction that lasts from one week to six months.

Positioning analysis, especially when combined with other types of analysis, such as fundamental, inter-market, and technicals, can provide traders and investors with the signals to begin lightening up on an existing position, buying protection for an existing position, exiting a position, or even preparing to enter a contrary position.

Technical Analysis

Technical analysis encompasses attempts to utilize mathematical and visual descriptions of price action to divine future price action. Detractors liken technical analysis to tea leaf or entrails reading and complain bitterly that technicians are often chameleon-like in nature, rabidly declaring price action should hold a particular level or maintain some trend, but then switching their view 180 degrees in the course of a day when the price level or trend is broken. Technical analysts retort that price action "says it all" regarding what is going on in the market and that the market votes each and every moment regarding the outlook for an asset price. As for being taunted as taciturn, technicians will respond that they are reporting "just the facts"—that the "markets," not they, have turned. Technical analysts strike back against "fundamentalists," denigrating economic models as naïve and simplistic attempts to hang a paradigmatic frame on a market of immeasurable complexity and nuance. Going further, they argue that fundamental valuation analysis constitutes nothing more than one additional voice to the cacophony of the marketplace, and that if the fundamentalist is not trading, it's not even a voting voice!

We remain firmly neutral in this bitter debate, preferring to adopt a pragmatic approach (and keep our friends on both sides of the aisle!). For instance, to the extent a currency adjusts to changing fundamentals at a gradual pace, the "trend is one's friend" and so it cannot hurt to know where the trend is. Additionally, if enough market participants decide that price action in regards to a channel support, an inverse head and shoulders, or a 61.8 percent Fibonacci retracement is important, then it probably *is* important. Consequently, we are not looking to establish technical trading systems in this book, but rather to introduce some basic concepts, to offer a framework that incorporates a respect for the trend in price action and an appreciation of what specific levels or patterns could be decisive in influencing behavior and price action. In viewing the foreign exchange markets in a multi-dimensional, holistic manner, a decision maker can make more informed—and profitable—decisions.

In this book, we divide the discipline of technical analysis into three parts: trend following indicators, oscillators, and pattern recognition. Knowing the trend is important in that price action does tend to exhibit trend-like qualities, and so moving with—or least not moving against—the trend increases the chances one's positioning will be profitable. Currency prices also tend to fluctuate relative to their trend, and oscillators can help identify when price action is most at odds with the prevailing trend. At such points, traders and investors stand to gain the most from the resumption of the prevailing trend. Finally, many technicians rely on pattern recognition to categorize certain price actions as indicative of major developments in market psychology (i.e., key day reversals and head-and-shoulder patterns).

None of these analyses works all the time. Trends can change, and an oscillator might be reflecting a change in trend rather than an extreme prior to a return to trend. In general, trend-following systems are like a home run hitter in baseball. They have more losses (strikeouts) than wins (hits), but the wins (hits) are usually quiet large. In contrast, oscillator signals are more like singles hitters in baseball. They have a higher percentage of winning trades to losing ones (a better batting average), but the hits are less powerful. Patterns "work until they don't," which means that price action that begins to trace out a pattern only provides a hint of where traders might position—ultimately ending in either a confirmation or a break of the pattern. Finally, note that the chapters are not intended to provide an exhaustive account of technical analysis, but rather to provide enough of a description to address some major themes and allow the incorporation of technical analysis into a robust analysis of the currency markets.

7

Trend-Following Indicators

Trend-following indicators attempt to describe mathematically the direction of price action over some period of time, the thought—or hope—being that the old adage that "the trend is your friend" will hold true, or that price action will continue in the direction it has recently moved. In this chapter, we will examine some of the more common trend-following indicators. The purpose will be to expose you to the technical analysis concepts widely accepted by market technicians, particularly the subset of those that we have found most useful. These include moving averages, the Average Directional Movement Index (DMI), Parabolic SAR, and the Moving-Average Convergence Divergence Index (MACD). None of these works in all trading conditions, and not all mesh with how you might view the markets. This chapter introduces the key concepts and allows you to research further to determine which ones to incorporate in your analytical "toolbox."

Technical analysis can be employed for a variety of time frames. A short-term trader would employ tick-by-tick data, a swing trader looking for positions lasting from days to weeks would look at daily data, and a position trader looking for positions lasting weeks to months would be more likely to look at weekly data. We will utilize weekly data in this chapter, but note that the concepts can be applied to all time frames.

137

Simply looking at **Figure 7.1**, the weekly chart for USD/JPY going back to 1999, appears to suggest some very obvious trends: down from May to November 1999, then up through February 2002, down through December 2004, up through June 2007, and down through December 2008. The cumulative changes of these trends total 121.14 big figures, using weekly closing levels.

However, a cursory visual inspection may suggest an order to price action that would not stand up to the rigors of marking one's positions to market for any significant period of time. For instance, despite the uptrend from November 1999 through February 2002 noted in the paragraph above, would one have been so certain of that uptrend during the drop from 126 to 117 during the June through September 2001 period? And at what point in 2007 would we be able to say that the uptrend from either January 2005 or May 2006 was no longer valid and that a downtrend was in place? Various trend-following indicators, or statistics, have been

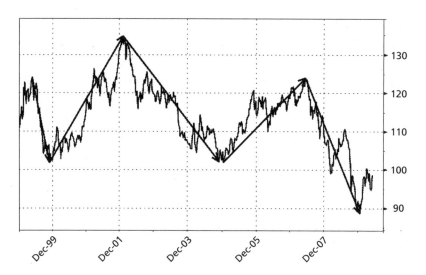

Figure 7.1   USD/JPY, Weekly, 1999 to 2008

Source: Bloomberg.

identified and are used by traders and investors to provide a more objective measure of the flow in price action.

Moving Averages

A moving average is simply a statistic based on the average closing price for a currency during a specified number of periods. The weekly graph of USD/JPY back to 1999 can be viewed by typing "JPY < curncy >< go >" on a Bloomberg terminal and then switching the period to weeks and typing "13" and "52" into the fields for moving averages. One can look at a variety of time frames, such as the 12-month moving average ("12mma"), the 13-week moving average ("13wma"), or the 15-day moving average ("15dma"). Alternatively, one can look at similar periods using different time units. Consider the 12-month moving average ("12mma"), the 52-week moving average ("52wma"), or the 250-day moving average ("250dma"). The 12mma would calculate the average of the closing values for the previous 12 months, while the 52wma would take the average of the closes for each of the previous 52 weeks, and the 250dma would take the average of the closes for each of the prior 250 days (the approximate number of trading days in a calendar year). Note that each of these measures would provide a similar value, but that the dma could be updated to the last day's close, whereas the weekly and monthly moving averages can only be updated to the close of the last week or month.

Moving-average signals generally entail the movement of either the spot price or a shorter-term moving average across a longer-term moving average. The rationale for employing moving averages is that at the beginning of a trend, price action will cross the moving average and then pull away, dragging the moving average with it.

Three main problems are generally encountered. The first is what happens if there is no trend, either because the price is locked in a range or because one trend is ending and a new one is just forming. A trendless situation is akin to trying to sail a boat on a windless day. The signal oscillates back and forth as the currency price trades to and fro aimlessly over the moving average. However, worse than sailing in a windless environment, in which case you go nowhere, is that trading in such an environment actually causes losses. The losses are generally small, but numerous, and the "death by a thousand cuts" nature of the situation can chew up a trading account and/or one's reputation with one's colleagues and clients.

The second problem comes during sharp but brief pullbacks from a trend. In such situations, the lagging nature of moving average signals is such that they tend to signal a reversal in the main trend just as the pullback is ending and the trend is resuming, and this generally results in a relatively large loss.

The final problem is that of optimizing the parameters of the moving-average signal. The hope here is that the number of periods the average looks back at will provide enough lag to keep the signal from getting whipsawed on a trend pullback but not so much that the signal misses significant trends. The issue here, of course, is that no currencies have the same optimization. Worse, no single currency remains optimized for any extended period. To continue with the sailing analogy, one must always be cognizant of and adjust to changing conditions, and this requirement of constant vigilance and adjustment makes blind allegiance to one rigid signaling system quite dangerous. Consequently, when one hears someone say to watch out because USD/CAD is approaching its 200-day moving average, one needs to understand the context of the statement and not just take the admonition on faith. For the remainder of the chapter we will work with 13- and 52-week moving averages. We have found from numerous tests that ratios of 3 to 4 for the longer-term to shorter-term moving averages tend to yield the most consistently positive result across time and different currency pairs.

USD/JPY and Moving Averages

Consider a rule that goes long (short) USD/JPY when the price closes above (below) the 52-week moving average. Visually, this

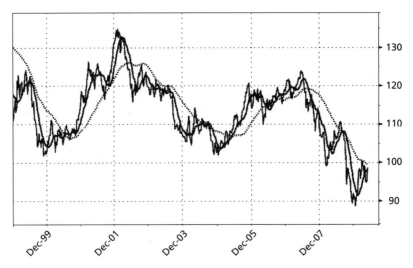

Figure 7.2 USD/JPY and 13- and 52-Week Moving Averages

Source: Bloomberg.

setting appears to roughly describe the big trends our visual inspection identified. However, the price/moving-average cross with the 52wma failed to catch substantial parts of both the beginnings and ends of the actual highs and lows. For instance, it did not signal an uptrend until July of 2000, eight months and six big figures after the low was established. And as USD/JPY peaked and began to trend down in 2002, the price/52wma cross rule provided a signal in May with the currency at 125, three months and ten big figures after the peak had been put in place. Consequently, employing the rule with the 52wma parameter provided an "up" signal for a move of only seventeen big figures (from 108 to 125), or 51 percent, of the thirty-three big-figure range from the low to the peak of the move. Additionally, the 52wma setting provided two false signals during the period when the price action dipped temporarily below the moving average. (See **Figure 7.2**.)

Overall, the rule provided thirty signals, only ten—or 33 percent—of which proved profitable. However, the average gain was 5.3 percent, while the average loss was only 1.3 percent. Combined, the win ratio and gain/loss ratio provided a net gain with the typical trend following characteristic of getting whipsawed numerous times for small losses and on occasion catching a large move.

Attempts to adjust the moving-average period fail to provide meaningful improvement in terms of the percentage of the total move in USD/JPY captured. One could shorten the time frame of the moving average, say from 52 weeks to 13 weeks. However, this shift provides many more instances in which the closing value crosses the moving average and results in increased false signals, or signals in which the price action moves in the opposite direction of the signal. Whereas the rule with a 52wma produced a total of thirty signals from 1999 to 2008, the price/13wma cross rule provided twenty-six signals from 1999 to 2002. The price/13wma performed similarly, with correct signals only 27 percent of the time, but the average win of 5.8 percent vastly outweighing the average loss of 1.5 percent.

Another way to use moving averages is to define the trend as "up" ("down") when a shorter-term moving average crosses above (below) a longer-term moving average. However, while the smoothing nature of this rule provided fewer whipsaws, it also provided later entry and exit points. Using the cross of the 13- and 52-wma's, ten signals were provided for the entire period from 1999 to 2008. Of these ten, five were profitable, and the 50 percent profitable trade ratio was better than those for the price/wma signals. However, as an offset the average percentage gain provided little advantage over the average percentage loss: 6.9 percent versus 6.1 percent. It appears that the lag introduced by employing two moving averages caused the signal to lose its relationship with the trend we were trying to capture.

EUR/USD and Moving Averages

First, we will consider a buy (sell) signal to be registered when EUR/USD crosses above (below) the 52-week moving average, as we did with USD/JPY. (See **Figure 7.3**.) For EUR/USD between 1999 and 2008, this system generated eighteen signals, nine of which proved profitable. Furthermore, the profitable trades

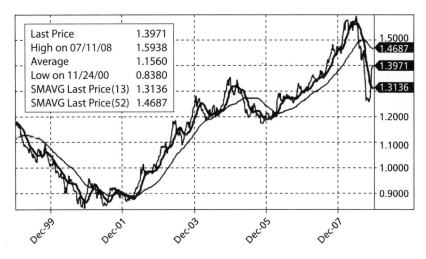

Last Price	1.3971
High on 07/11/08	1.5938
Average	1.1560
Low on 11/24/00	0.8380
SMAVG Last Price(13)	1.3136
SMAVG Last Price(52)	1.4687

Figure 7.3   EUR/USD and 13- and 52-Week Moving Averages

Source: Bloomberg.

averaged 9.4 percent, while the losing trades averaged only 1.6 percent. The profitable signals allowed three trades in excess of 10 percent, including the February 1999 to January 2001 decline from 1.1069 to 0.9570, the April 2002 to April 2004 rally from 0.8926 to 1.1842, and the April 2006 to August 2008 rally from 1.2341 to 1.4687. The lagging nature of the moving-average system was aided considerably by the moderate, yet persistent moves in EUR/USD. During those periods when the price action was non-trending or less persistent, the results suffered. For instance, during the bottoming formation from late 2000 to early 2002, the signals got whipsawed, with seven of the eight signals during the period resulting in losses. And in 2005, when EUR/USD slipped from 1.36 to below 1.20, the signal lagged so much that it registered a short signal in time to take in only a 2.3 percent gain.

Employing the cross of the 13- and 52-week moving averages led to fewer signals with more of a lag. Nine signals were generated, and only three of them were profitable. However, the average of the winning signals was 18.4 percent, while the average of the losing ones was only 3.7 percent. The system generated whipsaws during the 2001 consolidation. During that year, the signals generated four consecutive losing trades totaling 15.1 percent. The sluggish system did capture strong gains during the gradual decline from 1999 to 2000 (15.3 percent) and the rally from 2002 to 2005 (33.5 percent). Despite generating a relatively early signal in May 2006 for the rally towards 1.60, the violence of the sell-off happened too fast for the moving averages to save much of the profits. The exit signal was not provided until October 2008, by which time EUR/USD had already collapsed from 1.60 to 1.38, and so the signal for the 1.20–1.60 rally showed a gain of only 6.5 percent.

USD/CAD and Moving Averages

Employing a rule of being long (short) when the price crosses above (below) the 52-week moving average provided twenty-eight signals during the 1999 to 2008 period. Eight of these signals proved profitable. The low percentage of profitable signals was more than compensated for by the average gain of 7.8

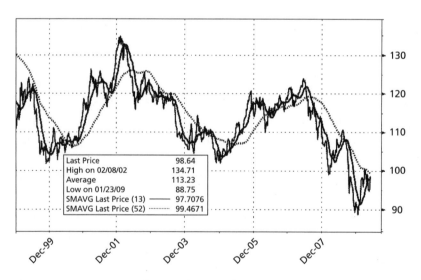

Figure 7.4   USD/CAD and 13- and 52-Week Moving Averages

Source: Bloomberg.

percent versus the average loss of only 1.0 percent. The rule got whipsawed in 2000 when USD/CAD shifted from a gentle downtrend to a gentle uptrend, generating eight consecutive losing signals. Again in 2002, the system got whipsawed as USD/CAD range traded between 1.50 and 1.60, generating four consecutive losses. However, offsetting these periods were strong trends, first from 2002 to 2007 and then in late 2008. Although interrupted by three pullbacks as well as the bottoming formation from late 2007 to mid-2008, the trends allowed the signals to capture gains of 19.5 percent, 14.1 percent, 10.4 percent, 8.6 percent, and 4.4 percent.

By switching the price/week moving-average rule from a 52-week to a 13-week moving average, the number of signals increases from twenty-eight over a ten-year period to thirty-five for the five-year period from 1999 to 2004. The percentage of signals resulting in gains was 34 percent, but the ratio of the average profit to average loss was only 2.7 to 1.1 percent, making the net returns of the system less attractive.

The 13-/52-week moving-average cross signal generated fourteen signals from 1999 to 2008, and the strong, persistent trends in place for much of the period suited the lagging, gradual tracking of the system. Of the fourteen signals, seven were profitable, a strong showing for a trend following rule. Even better was that the average profit of 7.4 percent far exceeded the average loss of 2.8 percent. The rule got severely whipsawed in 2002 as USD/CAD continued to trade flat, providing four consecutive losing signals. Strong countertrend moves also tend to hurt this type of trading signal. During early 2004, USD/CAD rallied from 1.27 to 1.39 over the course of four months. Unfortunately, the rally lasted just long enough to trigger a buy signal just as USD/CAD was resuming the downtrend, and the signal suffered a 5.5 percent loss. Even worse was the experience of the 2006 to 2007 countertrend rally. From June 2006 to February 2007, USD/CAD rallied from 1.10 to 1.18. The rally lasted long enough for the moving-average rule to generate a buy signal in December 2006 at 1.17, near the end and top of the rally. By the time the

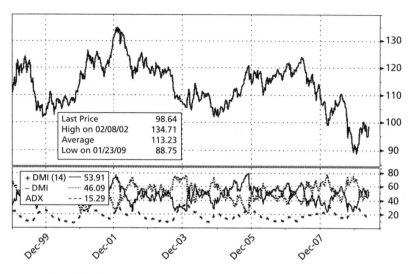

Figure 7.5 USD/JPY and DMI Study

Source: Bloomberg.

moving-average rule reverted to a short signal, USD/CAD had already dropped to 1.06, causing a loss of 8.4 percent.

Average Directional Movement Index (DMI)

The Directional Movement Indicator (DMI) system was developed by J. Welles Wilder Jr. as a means to assess the directional movement of price. The key idea behind the calculation was that in the event of an upward (downward) price trend, a specific day's high (low) would likely be higher (lower) than that of the prior trading day. One can apply the DMI tool to an asset or security in Bloomberg by typing "DMI" after the security code. For instance, to obtain **Figure 7.5**, type "JPY < Curncy > DMI < go >".

Calculation of the DMI

$$+DMI = \text{(average of +DM for previous } n \text{ periods)}/ \\ \text{(average of TR for previous } n \text{ periods)}$$

$$-DMI = \text{(average of } -DM \text{ for previous } n \text{ periods)}/ \\ \text{(average of TR for previous } n \text{ periods)}$$

(7.1)

where

A) n = the DMI period and can be days, weeks, or months.

B) TR (true range) is the greatest of

    a. the difference between the high and low of the current period,

    b. the absolute value of the difference between the current period's high and the prior period's close, and

    c. the absolute value of the difference between the current period's low and the prior period's close.

C) +DM = Positive Directional Movement.

D) −DM = Negative Directional Movement.

For no given period can the Directional Movement be both positive and negative. There are four possibilities:

1) If the current period's high is greater than that of the prior period and the current period's low is higher or equal to that of the prior period,

$$+ DM = \text{current period's high} - \text{prior period's higher,}$$
$$- DM = 0.$$

2) If the current period's low is less than that of the prior period and the current period's high is less than or equal to that of the prior period,

$$+DM = 0,$$
$$-DM = \text{abs(current period's low} - \text{prior period's low).}$$

3) If the current period's high is greater than the prior period's and the current period's low is less than the prior period's, then if the change in the highs is greater apply rule 1) above, but if the change in the lows is greater apply rule 2) above.

4) For any other situation, both DM's = 0.

Calculation of the Average Directional Movement Index (ADX) and ADXR

The ADX measures the strength of a currency pair's trend, be it upward or downward. Generally, an ADX of greater than

25 indicates a trending market while a value of less than 20 indicates a flat, or non-trending, market.

$$\text{ADX} = (\text{average DX over previous } n \text{ periods}) \qquad (7.2)$$

where

$$\text{DX} = 100 \cdot \text{abs}((+\text{DMI}) - (-\text{DMI}))/((+\text{DMI}) + (-\text{DMI})),$$

such that the DX represents the total range of directional movement.

The moving average of the ADX for the current period and that from n periods ago yields the ADXR:

$$\text{ADXR} = [\text{current ADX} + \text{ADX from } n \text{ periods ago}]/2. \quad (7.3)$$

The basic trading rule Welles proposed was to note the high (low) of the day when the +DMI crossed above (below) the −DMI, and both exit a short (long) position and enter a long (short) position on any subsequent day when the price traded above (below) the noted high (low). Note that under this rule the trader is always in a position. We will refer to the crossing higher (lower) of the +DMI as a "bullish (bearish) cross" and the resulting spread as a "bullish (bearish) spread."

USD/JPY and the DMI

The DMI spread for USD/JPY is erratic, with large spreads ceasing almost without warning and many periods of very small spreads. This likely reflects a combination of two factors. First, the Japanese government has historically been very active in attempting to prevent yen strength, with could be responsible for long periods of USD/JPY consolidation. Second, the low yielding yen has historically been used as a funding currency by hedge funds, and this usage has led to periods of USD/JPY strength on the back of speculative "carry trades" and the occasional violent unwinds of risk positions that involved massive covering of short yen-funding positions and led to precipitous declines in USD/JPY.

The very narrow ranges of DMI spread cover five general periods. From February to July of 1999, USD/JPY consolidated around

120. Throughout 2000, USD/JPY managed a modest but very choppy rally in which the February high of 111 was not breached again until November, but the lows of the price action climbed steadily higher. The third period marked by a narrow DMI spread was the September 2002 to August 2003 period, when USD/JPY ground steadily lower at a very modest pace. The fourth period was from March to October of 2004, when USD/JPY was trapped between 105 and 115. The fifth and final period of a narrow spread was 2006, when USD/JPY remained locked in a 110–120 range.

Wide spreads indicative of strong trends were not as long-lasting as for some currencies, but there were ten periods when USD/JPY experienced sharp moves. In each of the periods, USD/JPY moved in excess of fifteen big figures in less than a year and often six months or less.

The ADX and ADXR figures provide a measure of the consolidation or trending in a market and are useful in filtering out DMI signals, with the ADXR providing a smoothing measure. In the case of USD/JPY, the weekly ADXR has ranged from 8 to 30. Readings above 22 have generally been associated with the end of major trends, and declines in the ADXR, especially from the elevated levels, have historically been associated with consolidations. For example, in March 2001, the ADXR crossed above 22 just after USD/JPY had rallied to 126.33. For the next eight months, USD/JPY consolidated and did not reach a new high until December, after the ADXR had not only stabilized but also declined to 16. In January 2004, the ADXR crossed above 22 as USD/JPY closed at 106.79, down from 134 in February 2002 and near the 101 low of November 1999. During the next nine months, the ADXR peaked and sank to 12 as USD/JPY range traded; by the end of October, USD/JPY still traded at 108. More recently, in February 2008, the ADXR crossed above 22. At this time, USD/JPY closed at 103.75, having traded down from 123.44 in June 2007. During the ensuing nine months, USD/JPY enjoyed a bear-market rally as the ADXR fell to 16.31 by September, at which time USD/JPY closed at 106.01. Ignoring DMI cross signals during these periods would have been advisable.

In contrast, an ADXR reading of below 12 has historically been useful as a contrarian signal and consistent with the end of a consolidation range and the beginning of a strong trending market. In July 1999, the ADXR crossed below 12 as USD/JPY closed at 120.99. USD/JPY had range-traded around 120 since February. By July 23, the +DMI had crossed lower, suggesting a bearish trend might develop, and by the end of 1999, the ADXR had risen to 22.34 and the USD/JPY decline had stalled at 101. During October and November 2000, the ADXR remained mired below 10 as USD/JPY traded in a tight 107–108 range. The week of November 10, with USD/JPY at 107.87, the +DMI crossed higher, suggesting the potential beginning of a rally. By March 2001, USD/JPY had rallied to 126 as the ADXR climbed to above 22. As one last example, consider the August 2003 period when the ADXR slipped below 10 as USD/JPY range traded around 120. The week of August 15, with USD/JPY at 119.20, the +DMI crossed lower, indicating a potential breakout to the downside. By January 2004, USD/JPY had fallen to 106 as the ADXR broke above 22.

EUR/USD and the DMI

Figure 7.6 shows that the DMI lines captured the main movements in EUR/USD from 1999 to 2008. In 1999 and 2000, the −DMI was significantly higher than the +DMI line, indicative of a downtrend. The only time the DMI spread and trend-stalled was August to October of 1999. However, by the end of 2000, EUR/USD had reached a bottom, and the DMI spreads became smaller and the ADXR began trending lower, consistent with the bottoming formation that traded until April 2002.

Beginning in April 2002, the DMI spread widened sharply and bullishly and remained that way for most of the time until March 2004. The one exception during this period was when the DMI spread flipped to bearish briefly as EUR/USD corrected to 1.08 before resuming its uptrend. By March 2004, the DMI crossed bearishly and the ADXR began to grind lower, indicative of the consolidation that took place until September 2004. The

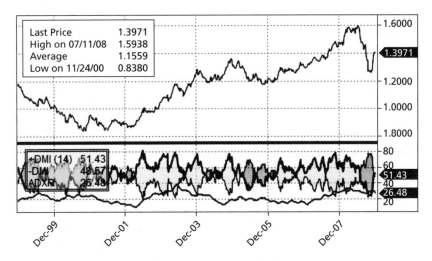

Figure 7.6 EUR/USD and the DMI

Source: Bloomberg.

late 2004 spike to 1.36 was accompanied by a bullish spread of the DMI lines that flipped in April 2005 as EUR/USD corrected below 1.30. The DMI spread widened bearishly through the remainder of 2005 as the currency pair fell towards 1.20, and then the spread narrowed as EUR/USD consolidated around 1.20. In April 2006, the DMI's crossed bullishly with EUR/USD still just above 1.20, and this signal provided an attractive entry point for the rally to 1.60. Despite the suddenness of the sell-off that began in July 2008, the DMI cross was able to react much more quickly than that for the moving-average cross. It switched to a sell signal on August 8, when EUR/USD was trading at 1.50, whereas the 13-/52-week moving-average cross did not register a sell signal until October, when EUR/USD had fallen below 1.40.

Generally, an ADXR above 23 was associated with a mature trending market and a heightened risk of consolidation. For example, in June 1999, the ADXR passed above 23 and EUR/USD consolidated in its bear market and did not close at a new low for another five months. In May 2000, when the ADXR passed above 23, it was presaging the long bottoming formation that

EUR/USD traded between 0.84 and 0.96 before beginning a sustained rally in June 2002. However, the passing of the ADXR above 23 is not a signal to exit positions, but rather to be wary of consolidation. In September 2002, exiting a position based on the ADXR moving above 23 would have caused one to cut a long EUR/USD position at 0.98 and miss the rally to 1.36 over the next 27 months. Similarly, cutting a long position in August 2007 would have taken one out of the rally at 1.37, thereby missing the eventual run-up to 1.60 in the next eleven months.

An ADXR reading at or below 13 has historically represented an extreme low for EUR/USD and signaled an imminent trend reversal. Since 1999, an ADXR below 13 has only occurred on three occasions: early 2002, September to October 2004, and February 2007. In early 2002, the ADXR ground below 13 for the first five months of the year before EUR/USD broke out of its two-year bottoming formation and began a six-year rally. In September 2004, as the ADXR fell below 13, the +DMI crossed higher with EUR/USD at 1.2187, and EUR/USD subsequently jumped to 1.36 by year-end. On the third occasion, February 2007, the ADXR fell below 13, suggesting a consolidation of the rally in EUR/USD around 1.30. However, the ADXR began to rise again, as the rally resumed towards 1.60 by July 2008.

For more moderate ADXR levels between 13 and 23, a declining trend in the ADXR would likely suggest avoiding putting on the trend positions indicated by the DMIs, while a rising ADXR would indicate that one should take advantage of the trend direction indicated by the DMIs.

GBP/USD and the DMI

The DMI spread for GBP/USD suggested only four periods of strongly trending price action. In those periods, the lower of the DMI lines approached 20, while the higher approached 80. In 2000, the spread widened bearishly as GBP/USD fell from nearly 1.65 to 1.40. In 2002 and the beginning of 2003, the currency pair rallied from 1.44 to 1.64. The third period of a strong trend was September 2003 to March 2004, during which time

GBP/USD jumped from 1.64 to 1.89. The fourth strongly trending period suggested by the DMI spread was from July to December 2008, when the currency pair collapsed from 2.00 to below 1.50. (See **Figure 7.7**.)

The DMI spread for GBP is sometimes persistent but moderate. From May 2005 to April 2006, GBP/USD fell modestly from 1.83 to 1.75, with the modest trend eventually stalling into a range trade. From April 2006 to December 2007, GBP/USD climbed steadily from 1.78 to 2.09, but the rally was controlled and persistent; with no explosive moves, the DMI spread remained moderate.

Finally, the DMI spread showed three periods of narrow and unstable spreads. From November 1999 to January 2000, GBP/USD traded at a 1.60–1.64 range before heading lower. From December 2000 to April 2002, the DMI spread remained muted as GBP/USD finished its bottoming formation, while range trading between 1.41 and 1.48. Finally, the DMI spread remained very muted from February to August 2008 as the currency pair consolidated between 1.95 and 2.02.

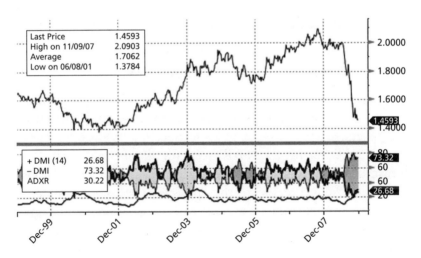

Figure 7.7 GBP/USD and the DMI

Source: Bloomberg.

For GBP/USD during the 1999 to 2008 period, the weekly ADXR associated with mature trends was around 25. In September 2000, the ADXR breached 25 just as GBP/USD closed at 1.4151. The currency pair then consolidated at a 1.40–1.50 range until June 2002. By November 2002, GBP/USD had rallied to 1.58, but the ADXR had reached above 25, and GBP/USD spent the next ten months struggling to breach 1.60. By January 2004, GBP/USD had surged to 1.80, but the ADXR had again breached 25, and GBP/USD spent until April 2006 chopping around from 1.71 to 1.94.

Extreme lows can serve as a warning that consolidations are about to give way to strong trends, and for GBP, 11 or below marked such an extreme. In April 2000, the ADXR slipped to 11.05 just before GBP/USD, at 1.58, began its last leg down towards 1.40 by September. In April 2002, the ADXR had fallen to 8.09 as GBP failed one last test to break below 1.40. The rebound proved to be the beginning of a rally that took GBP/USD to 1.85 less than two years later. The third example of an extreme low was in July 2008, when the ADXR fell to 10.37 as GBP/USD range traded just below 2.00. The 10.37 ADXR reading marked the last period of calm before the violent sell-off that took GBP/USD to below 1.50 by the end of the year.

Parabolic SAR (Stop and Reverse)

The Parabolic SAR ("parabolic" or "SAR") index stems from the work of J. Welles Wilder Jr. The name of the system derives from the general shape the index tends to trace out as a result of price action. Additionally, the "SAR" term highlights the fact that this measure always has a signal. It is never neutral—it merely "stops" one signal "and reverses" to the opposite. The parabolic index is similar to a simple moving-average rule in that it provides a signal when the closing price action crosses the indicator. However, the index contains an "acceleration factor" that allows it to adjust more rapidly to a strong trend. The upside of this characteristic is that the index follows the price action slowly at first—which should alleviate whipsaws, or rapid changes of signals early on—and then progresses more quickly as a trend progresses, thus protecting more profits when the trend ends. Furthermore, because of a quicker exit, the rule also allows for a quicker entry to the next signal. Unfortunately, as with any trend-following indicator, the SAR can get "whipsawed," or provide numerous false signals, should the price action meander aimlessly rather than alternating between strong trends.

The accompanying graph for USD/JPY and the Parabolic SAR study can be created in Bloomberg by typing "JPY < Curncy > PTPS < go >".

Calculating the Parabolic SAR

Conceptually, the parabolic index is based on (1) price action hitting an "extreme" point, at which price action reverses trend, (2) the price posting progressively higher highs or lower lows, and (3) an "acceleration factor." The extreme point represents the highest or lowest point from which price action reverses and begins a trend in the opposite direction.

Specifically, the index is computed as follows:

$$SAR\ (i) = SAR\ (i-1) + AccelerationFactor\ (i-1)$$
$$\cdot (NewHiorLo(i-1) - SAR\ (i-1)) \qquad (7.4)$$

where

A) SAR $(i-1)$ is the value of the index from the prior period;

B) AccelerationFactor is the acceleration factor, which begins at 0.02 and increases by 0.02 (up to a maximum of 0.2) each time the price action establishes a new high (low) of the move up (down); and

C) NewHiorLo$(i-1)$ is the highest or lowest price of the previous period (highest price during rising trends and lowest price during falling trends).

USD/JPY and the Parabolic SAR

Typical of any trend-following indicator, the Parabolic SAR, when applied to USD/JPY, provided more losing than profitable trades, although the winning trades were larger (**Figure 7.8**). From January 1999 to December 2008, this indicator provided thirty-eight signals. Only thirteen, or 34 percent, were profitable signals, but the average gain on a win was 5.8 percent, while the average loss was 3.0 percent. Over the full period, the signals netted an insignificant 0.5 percent gain. The problem, of course, is that the occasional large gain (15.9 percent from September to December 2008, or 11.0 percent from July 2000 to May 2001) got frittered away by strings of smaller losses (eight consecutive losses from December 2005 to July 2007 totaling 17.9 percent).

However, in a strongly trending environment, the few gains overwhelmed the more numerous but smaller losses. For instance, during the rally from 102 to 135 between November 1999 and February 2002, the parabolic system provided eight signals. Of these, only three were correct, but the 23 percent gain on these three outpaced the total 17.5 percent loss on the five losing signals.

Over the course of the nine-year period, the system provided cumulative profits in the first five years. However, most of the

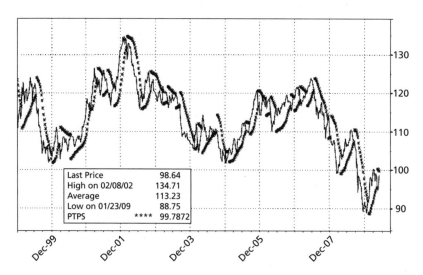

Figure 7.8   USD/JPY with Parabolic SAR

Source: Bloomberg.

last four years of the period, the cumulative returns were negative, as consolidation during 2005 and 2006 caused a plethora of whipsaws, with the signal generating nine losing signals out of a total of eleven. Only the final signal of 2008, the sell signal in September as USD/JPY was collapsing, put the cumulative returns back in positive territory by posting a 15.9 percent gain.

EUR/USD and the Parabolic SAR

The Parabolic SAR signal enjoyed significantly more success with EUR/USD during the 1999 to 2008 period than it did with USD/JPY. The indicator provided thirty-six signals, of which twenty, or 55.6 percent, proved profitable. Not only did the winning trades outnumber the losing ones, the winning ones were on average more profitable (+4.9 percent versus −3.1 percent). (See **Figure 7.9**.)

One particularly successful period was July 2000 through August 2002, which represented the bottoming period for EUR/USD. During the period, the Parabolic SAR provided six consecutive profitable signals. A trend-following system succeeding

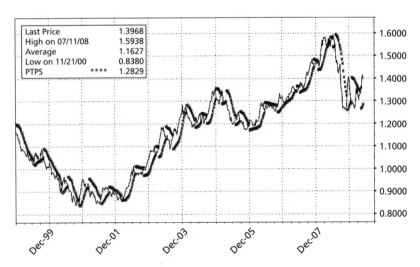

Figure 7.9 EUR/USD and the Parabolic SAR

Source: Bloomberg.

in a non-trending environment is counterintuitive. The reason for the success appears to be that the moves proved to be in sync with the system parameters. The price moves in both directions were of a magnitude and time length such that the Parabolic SAR indicator was able to provide correct up and down signals.

In contrast, during the persistent rally from January 2006 to July 2008, the Parabolic SAR alternated between profitable and losing signals as it was able to ride the upward waves of price action but got whipsawed during the modest pullbacks. However, even during this period when the "win ratio" was only 50 percent, the strong trend allowed the pro-trend profits to outpace the retracement losses.

For the period in general, the signal started off with a serendipitous synchronization of the signal parameters and price action during the bottoming of EUR/USD during 2000 and 2001. This resulted in five consecutive profitable signals. Furthermore, the next signal caught the beginning of the EUR/USD breakout higher in 2002. The signal's effectiveness waned during 2002 and 2003 as the EUR/USD rally was marred by countertrend pullbacks that whipsawed the rule. The cumulative gains lurched up again in late 2003 and early 2004 as EUR/USD rallied to 1.28. From then until late 2008, the cumulative gains treaded water despite the rally in EUR/USD to 1.60 because the rallies were interspersed with consolidations and corrections that created offsetting whipsaw losses. The signal was able to identify the impending sell-off, triggering a sell signal in June with EUR/USD at 1.50, and it also managed to trigger a buy signal in December with EUR/USD at 1.34, catching the rally to 1.39 by year-end.

AUD/USD and the Parabolic SAR

The success of the Parabolic SAR with AUD/USD provided a middle ground between the weak performance on USD/JPY and strong performance on EUR/USD. The indicator provided forty-three signals, of which eighteen, or 42 percent, were profitable.

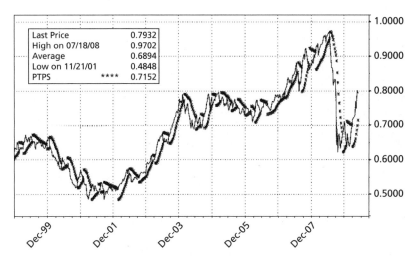

Last Price		0.7932
High on 07/18/08		0.9702
Average		0.6894
Low on 11/21/01		0.4848
PTPS	****	0.7152

Figure 7.10   AUD/USD and the Parabolic SAR

Source: Bloomberg.

On average, the profitable signals led to 6.1 percent gains versus an average 3.2 percent loss for unprofitable signals.

The Parabolic SAR indicator led to two strings of losses. In 2001, the indicator got whipsawed as AUD bottomed near 0.50. During that period the signal provided four consecutive unprofitable signals causing a combined 25.1 percent in losses. The second losing streak occurred from August 2005 to September 2006 as AUD/USD consolidated between 0.71 and 0.78. The consolidation caused the Parabolic SAR indicator to suffer whipsaws that resulted in six consecutive losing signals that resulted in a combined 13.5 percent of losses.

The cumulative gains during the period rose from −13.5 percent as of March 2002 to +15.7 percent at the end of 2008. The signal started the period poorly, accumulating 8 percent of losses as AUD/USD consolidated and peaked in May 1999 at 0.67. Its fortunes reversed with the sharp downtrend that developed into early 2001, and the cumulative returns rose to +11.7 percent. However, the consolidation during 2001, when AUD/USD ranged between 0.48 and 0.54, proved disastrous, with the cumulative profits plunging to −13.5 percent. The steady rally through the beginning of 2004 cause the returns to rise to 17.6 percent, but these were frittered away over the next four years, with the currency consolidating through mid-2006 and then rallying with sharp pullbacks that stripped away gains and left the cumulative profit at −14.9 percent. Except for a huge 26.8 percent gain from registering a sell signal just as AUD/USD began to collapse in August 2008, the cumulative percentage returns from all the signals were significantly negative.

Moving-Average Convergence/ Divergence (MACD) Indicator

Gerald Appel created the Moving-Average Convergence/Divergence (MACD) Indicator in the 1960s as a method for identifying changes in price trend. The indicator creates a signal for a change in trend whenever the difference between two exponential moving averages—the MACD—crosses a smoothed moving average of the MACD, defined as the signal. More specifically, when the MACD crosses below (above) the signal, a top (bottom) is interpreted as having occurred, meaning a downtrend (uptrend) is likely to ensue.

$$MACD = EMA[12] - EMA[26], \qquad (7.5)$$

where

A) EMA = exponential moving average of the closing prices, and
B) [#] = the number of periods in the moving averages (with 12 and 16 being widely recognized defaults).

$$Signal = SMA[9] \ of \ MACD$$

where

A) SMA = smoothed moving average
B) [#] = the number of periods in the moving average (with 9 being the widely recognized default).

USD/JPY and MACD

The graph in **Figure 7.11**, for USD/JPY, can be created in Bloomberg by typing "JPY <curncy> MACD <go>" and adjusting the date and period parameters. We accept the Bloomberg parameters of 12 and 26 for the MACD as well as 9 for the signal periods, as optimal settings will change both over time and depending on the currency pair.

The MACD indicator for USD/JPY during the period from 1999 to 2008 provided thirty-six signals, sixteen (44 percent) of which proved profitable. The 44 percent represents a decent "win" percentage, especially in light of the average win/loss (5.6 percent/1.8 percent, or 3.1). The combination of the winning percentage and the win/loss ratio provided a cumulative return over the entire period of 53.7 percent. However, the maximum drawdown was 16.5 percent.

As with most trend-following systems, the MACD provided some spectacular profits. There were six periods of particular note. In 1999 through the middle of 2000, the parameters of

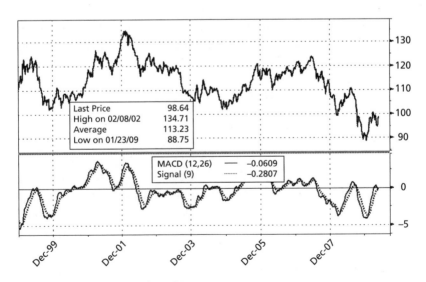

Figure 7.11   USD/JPY and MACD

Source: Bloomberg.

the systems strongly matched the price action, allowing the system to catch part of the upmove in early 1999 (2.5 percent gain), most of the steep drop in the second half of 1999 (12.1 percent gain), and part of the slow grind higher in the first half of 2000 (3.5 percent gain). In September of 2000, the MACD signaled a buy just as USD/JPY was accelerating from 108 to 123. From November 2001 to September 2002, the indicator was able to catch the rally to 135 and the subsequent fall to below 120. In August 2003, the signal registered a sell just as USD/JPY fell from 117 to 107. From October 2004 to September 2005, the signal made another round trip call, profiting first from the sharp 109 to 104 decline from October to February and then from the slow grind higher back towards 110. Finally, the signal generated a total 18.5 percent profit on the move from 108.60 to 90.81.

The signal also had two extended periods during which it suffered significant whipsaw losses. The first lasted from September 2002 to August 2003, when USD/JPY consolidated in the 116 to 126 range, generating seven consecutive losing signals that resulted in a 16.5 percent drawdown on the cumulative returns. In the second instance, from July 2006 to July 2007, USD/JPY ground from 114 to 123, but at a very slow pace and with choppy price action. Consequently, the signal generated five losing recommendations resulting in a drawdown of 9.8 percent.

EUR/USD and MACD

The MACD indicator for EUR/USD during the period from 1999 to 2008 provided thirty-seven signals, nineteen of which proved profitable. (See **Figure 7.12**.) This strong 51 percent winning percentage was offset by a low average win/loss ratio (3.8 percent/3.3 percent) of 1.14. The combination of the winning percentage and the win/loss ratio provided a cumulative return over the entire period of 12.1 percent, but the maximum drawdown was 21.7 percent.

The MACD provided four periods of strong profits. The first period entailed a sell signal in November 1999 that caught the move from 1.03 to 0.95 by June 2000.

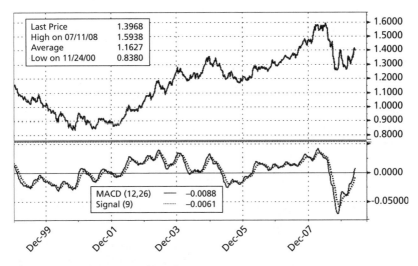

Last Price	1.3968
High on 07/11/08	1.5938
Average	1.1627
Low on 11/24/00	0.8380

| MACD (12,26) | —— | −0.0088 |
| Signal (9) | ········· | −0.0061 |

Figure 7.12   EUR/USD and MACD

Source: Bloomberg.

From August 2000 to August 2002, the signal generated six consecutive profitable signals totaling 20.5 percent. Ironically, this run came mostly during the consolidation bottoming of EUR/USD, which generally whipsaws trend-following indicators. In this case, however, the price action matched the parameters of the signal serendipitously. The 2000 to 2002 profit run was also helped by the indicator signaling a buy just as EUR/USD began to break higher from the bottoming formation. The third period of strong performance came from October 2004 to August 2005, during which time the signal caught both the run up from 1.24 to 1.30 and the retracement from 1.30 to 1.24. In the final period of strong gains, from March to December 2008, the signal caught part of the last bit of the euro rally, the bulk of the move down (from 1.54 to 1.39) and a bit of the end-of-year rally.

The signal experienced two extended periods of significant whipsaw losses. The first lasted from July to October 2004. During that period, the currency ranged in a tight 1.20 to 1.24 range, and the MACD registered four consecutive losing trades totaling 11.7 percent. Then from July 2006 to March 2008, the signals generated nine signals, seven of which lost money. The problem during much of that period was that the currency pair ground steadily higher without much deviation from the trend. As a result the MACD and the signal line moved in very close tandem generating almost random signals. At the very end of the period, the indicator issued a sell signal and then got left behind as EUR/USD began its surge towards 1.60.

Conclusion

This chapter has presented four commonly used trend-following indicators and applied them to five different currency pairs. The time frame used was weekly data, which we believe allowed the indicators to provide signals with relatively long time horizons of at least one month in order to most closely match the horizon of a currency strategist, as compared to those of a tactical trader (minutes to days) or a very high-level policymaker (quarters to years).

Trend-following systems tend to create mostly unprofitable signals but are saved by a few very profitable signals. Think of the traders who employ these signals as surfers. Surfers spend considerable time and energy catching waves that turn out to be small in search of the few really great waves. In a similar fashion, trend-following systems repeatedly signal entry points for what could turn into major trends but more often result in aborted runs. The trade-off is whether the few really good runs make up for the many aborted attempts.

Trend-following systems are most effective in price action that exhibits persistent, lengthy trends with few countertrend moves. Furthermore, trend-following systems will perform well even when a trend reverses—provided that the reversal occurs in a gradual (but not too gradual!) way so as to allow the system to "catch up to," "adapt to," or "learn" the new trend.

Trend-following signals falter in periods of trendless range trading/consolidation and countertrend moves. During consolidation periods, the price action stops moving away from previous values, allowing the lagging indicators to gravitate towards it and each other. As this happens, random price action is more likely to cause the price and/or the indicators to cross over each and trigger a signal. In the case of a countertrend move, the price action actually turns back on and converges with the lagging trend indicators. The result is a countertrend signal because the indicator cannot react, and by the time the indicator does begin to react, the price action has again veered towards and crossed the indicator. Such price action will cause multiple, but generally small, losses referred to as "whipsawing."

None of the technical studies are perfect or static. The search to devise a "perfect," or optimized, system that will stand up over time and across currencies is a sure way to insanity. Different currencies are subject to varying degrees of influences or even totally different influences. For example, we noted that price action in USD/JPY has often been manipulated by Japanese policymakers. The Swiss franc often rallies during sudden periods of geopolitical uncertainty. And the Canadian dollar can enjoy periods of sharp rises on spikes in energy due to price shocks. Furthermore, the price action for any given currency changes over time. Because a signal is optimized over a certain time period is no guarantee that the future price action will have the same characteristics.

Analysts must decide on an individual basis which signals they are most comfortable with. Some may prefer the style of the Parabolic SAR in its attempt to first let a trend develop and then catch the trend to prevent giving away profits in the event of a reversal. Others might prefer a moving average for a general indication of the trend and use other disciplines, including money-management stop-losses, to supplement and compensate for any lags in the signal. Still others may prefer the DMI or MACD signals because of their greater responsiveness to price action. And there are other trend-following systems out there. The key is to avoid blindly reacting to signals randomly because they have caught the attention of some random analyst or trader and to develop instead a familiarity and comfort with, as well as an appreciation for, the benefits and drawbacks of the different indicators so that one can best understand any signals that are given.

Unless one chooses to create black-box trading systems, one should not rely solely on technical trend-following systems. This book aims to present the reader with a variety of tools and disciplines—not just technical analysis. Being conversant in the various disciplines helps to broaden one's perspectives on the multitude of drivers of foreign-exchange markets and to develop stronger relationships with a variety of clients and colleagues who undoubtedly display varying degrees of affinity for different ways to analyze the markets.

8 | Oscillators

Oscillators attempt to mathematically describe a situation in which price action has become overextended and so is likely to reverse. Before discussing oscillators, we must first consider the definition and measurement of being *overextended*. A policymaker might look at a 2 standard-deviation band from a PPP measure and thus not complain about price action being overdone until a currency has already rocketed to one edge or the other of its thirty-year historical band. In the meantime, investors and traders would likely have been groaning about the currency being "overdone" for weeks, if not months. But what are these different market participants looking at? They are likely referring, at least in part, either to a gap between the spot price and reference point that is based on past prices or to a velocity of price direction that has been historically unsustainable. The trader is probably looking at daily data, while an investor or strategist might focus more on weekly data. In this chapter, we will focus on weekly data.

As with trend-following indicators, and indeed, any attempt to generalize a characterization of any market, the actual implementation of an oscillator to provide signals can prove maddening. Oscillators, in particular, tend to suffer along the lines of the old adage that "the markets can prove irrational longer than one can remain solvent." Blindly establishing contrarian positions based on overbought or oversold oscillators has led to colorful analogies describing traders/investors as attempting to catch either "falling knives" or "falling anvils," or, alternatively, as "standing in front of freight trains." Nevertheless, oscillators provide important information that, in conjunction with other measures such as trend, market sentiment/positioning, and valuation, can help traders/investors adopt more profitable positions. The oscillators we will look at in this chapter are the Relative Strength Index (RSI), Bollinger Bands, and slow stochastics.

Relative Strength Index (RSI)

The Relative Strength Index (RSI) attempts to measure the strength of a directional trend in order to identify when the trend has reached a peak or trough and thus is susceptible to either a reversion to trend or trend reversal.

The initial RSI is defined as

$$RSI = 100 - 100/(1 + RS) \qquad (8.1)$$

where RS = average of x days up closes / average of x days down closes.

Subsequent calculations of RSI are defined as

$$RSI = 100 - [100/(1 + [NextAveUp/NextAveDown])] \quad (8.2)$$

where

$$NextAveUp = [([PreviousAveUp \cdot (RSI\ periods - 1)]) + current\ period's\ up\ close]/(RSI\ periods).$$
$$NextAveDown = [([PreviousAveDown \cdot (RSI\ periods - 1)]) + current\ period's\ down\ close]/(RSI\ periods).$$

If the close is unchanged, the current period's up/down close is zero.

The default Bloomberg setting is for fourteen periods, and we will maintain that setting. Furthermore, the RSI reading for a currency is generally interpreted as overbought if it is above 70 percent and oversold if below 30 percent. At such levels, one should begin to question the sustainability of a trend and look for warning signs of at least a consolidation if not an outright reversal of trend. However, one never knows at the time whether an extreme reading is actually the extreme of the move. Rather than trying to guess an extreme, one can define a quantifiable signal as when the RSI crosses back below 70 (a sell signal) or above 30 (a buy signal), and we will use that convention in this section.

The next issue is that the RSI provides no counsel on exiting a position based on such a signal. Note that an extreme RSI reading is generally consistent with a strong trend. A cross of the RSI back into neutral territory is more likely to represent a return to the existing trend for the currency than the establishment of a new trend. Consequently, there will not likely be a point at which an exit signal is registered. Rather, the RSI tends to oscillate for long periods in neutral territory. Thus, some other tool, be it another technical study or simple money-management rules (stop-losses), must be employed with the RSI.

RSI and USD/JPY

Figure 8.1 illustrates the weekly price action for USD/JPY from 1999 to 2008, along with the RSI indicator. The graph can be created in Bloomberg by typing "JPY < curncy > RSI < go >" and adjusting the dates and periodicity accordingly.

The weekly RSI did provide signals around three of the four major turning points circled in the graph. Prior to the December 1999 low at 101.25, the RSI registered a buy in October when the currency closed at 105.10. The RSI registered a sell on February 15, 2002, when USD/JPY closed at 132.61, having just peaked the prior week at 134.71. On December 10, 2004, the RSI crossed above 30 as USD/JPY closed at 105.22 and was in the process of bottoming at 102. The RSI failed to signal one of the major turns—the June 2007 top at 124.13. This likely occurred because the uptrend in USD/JPY had deteriorated after December 2005, which prevented the RSI from rising to an extreme level.

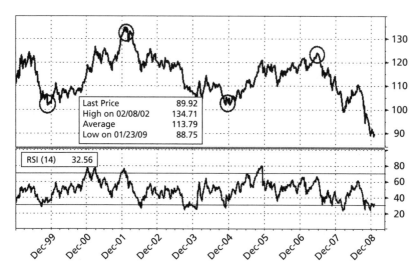

Figure 8.1   USD/JPY, Weekly, January 1999 to January 2009, with RSI Study

Source: Bloomberg.

The RSI provided nine signals at times other than the four major turning points. In five of these cases, the price action consolidated for at least three to four weeks. These periods included January to February 2001, April to June 2001, November 2003 to February 2004, and December 2005 to April 2006. On two occasions, the signal led to a move of five to ten big figures. The first was the July 26, 2002, signal with USD/JPY at 118.80 after which the currency rallied to 125.51 by October 18. The second time was April 4, 2008, when the RSI issued a buy signal with USD/JPY at 101.47, at the beginning of its rally to 110.53. In only one case did the existing trend continue, invalidating the RSI signal, and that occurred in October 2008, likely one of the most volatile periods in financial markets history.

In considering all twelve of the signals, note that only in one extraordinary case did the price trend continue unabated. Of the other eleven instances, six times the price moved at least five big figures, while in the other five cases, the price action stalled for at least three to four weeks.

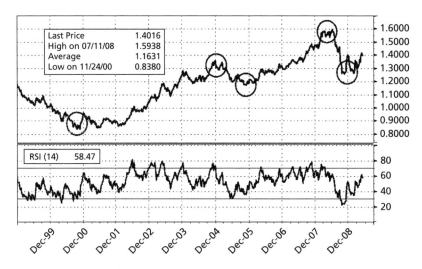

Figure 8.2   EUR/USD, Weekly 1999 to 2008, with RSI Study

Source: Bloomberg.

EUR/USD and the Relative Strength Index

As with USD/JPY, the RSI was largely successful in identifying the major turning points for EUR/USD (circled in accompanying graph), but it also indicated many other periods when the price action had become too steep and needed to pull back towards the trend.

Of the five major turns identified in **Figure 8.2**, the weekly RSI issued appropriate signals four times. The RSI crossed higher on November 3, 2000, with spot at 0.8666, just three weeks before the record weekly closing low of 0.8380. On December 10, 2004, with EUR/USD at 1.3226, the RSI crossed lower; EUR/USD consolidated between 1.29 and 1.35 until May and then moved lower. Around the 1.6038 peak registered in July 2008, the RSI registered not only extreme peaks, but also a negative divergence— that is, the indicator began falling away even as the currency price reached new highs, suggesting even more strongly that the rally was unsustainable. Following the signal of selling when the RSI dropped below 70, one would have shorted EUR/USD in April at 1.5431 on March 21. The final major turn, the bottom from October to December 2008, was accompanied by extreme oversold levels in the RSI, and the RSI crossed back above 30 on December 12 when EUR/USD was 1.3369. The violence of the December rally was such that it surprised even the RSI, which tends to react fairly quickly to price action. The one major turn that the RSI failed to register was the December 2005 bottom at 1.1718. In that case, the price action had been relatively flat around 1.20 since July, which caused the RSI to wane into very neutral territory.

The RSI provided fifteen signals at times other than the major turning points above. In only one case did the price action continue unphased after the signal: in October to November 2007 when EUR/USD continued its march higher, moving from 1.41 to 1.46. In eleven of the fourteen remaining cases, the price action stalled for at least four weeks, and in three cases, the price action reversed for a move of at least 0.05.

Including the four major turns that the RSI correctly signaled for EUR/USD, nineteen weekly signals were provided from 1999 to 2008; in eighteen of those situations, the trend in price at least stopped for three to four weeks, and in seven instances, the price changed direction and moved at least 0.05.

USD/CHF and the Relative Strength Index

A visual inspection of the weekly price action for USD/CHF from 1999 to 2008 suggests five turning points: 1.8077 on November 24, 1999; 1.1310 on December 3, 2004; 1.3186 on November 25, 2005; 0.9954 on March 28, 2008; and 1.2254 on November 21, 2008.

The RSI identified three of the major turns marked by the circles in the accompanying chart in that the indicator crossed from extreme territory near when the high or low in the currency price was made (see **Figure 8.3**). On December 10, 2004, the week after USD/CHF traded the low of 1.1310, the RSI crossed above 30. On April 18, 2008, three weeks after USD/CHF reached a weekly closing low of 0.9954, the RSI crossed above 30 with

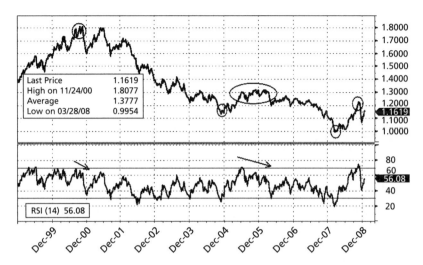

Figure 8.3   USD/CHF, Weekly 1999 to 2008, with RSI Study

Source: Bloomberg.

USD/CHF at 1.0179. In the third instance, the RSI crossed below 70 on December 12, 2008 with USD/CHF at 1.1773, three weeks after the closing high of 1.2254.

The other two instances provide examples of negative divergence, which happens when price continues to make new highs or lows as the momentum indicator begins to fall away from an extreme reading. On September 15, 1999, the RSI reached the highest point during the cycle, 68.05—not quite an overbought level. At that time, USD/CHF closed at 1.7854. During the ensuing two and a half months, USD/CHF would close twice at incrementally higher levels of 1.8057 and then 1.8077, but each time USD/CHF bounced modestly higher, the RSI bounced but to lower levels of 66.22 and then 63.00. This divergence between the currency price action and the RSI is termed a *negative* or *bearish divergence*, and while the RSI never did make it to overbought territory, the divergence should have served as a warning of a coming decline. A similar situation occurred from July 2005 to April 2006. In July, the RSI actually reached 70.24—overbought territory. At the same time, the currency traded to 1.2994. Over the next nine months, the currency made two more attempts to breach 1.30. On November 25, 2005, the currency closed at 1.3186, the high of the move, but the RSI was only able to rise to 63.33. And on March 10, 2006, the currency pair made one last try to breach above 1.30, closing at 1.3174, but this time the RSI rose only to 57.89. This negative, or bearish, divergence provided a strong warning that USD/CHF was headed lower.

The RSI provided ten other signals, only one of which proved incorrect. In that one instance, on May 7, 1999, the rally in USD/CHF continued. However, in six of the remaining cases, the price trend stalled for at least four weeks, and in three cases, the price actually retraced at least 0.05.

USD/CAD and the Relative Strength Index

The RSI identified only two of the four major turns in USD/CAD (identified by circles in **Figure 8.4**) by registering a significant level at the extreme in price. On November 2, 2007, the RSI had dropped to a record low of 12.58 at the same time USD/CAD had dropped to 0.9347, which marked the low (on a weekly closing basis) from

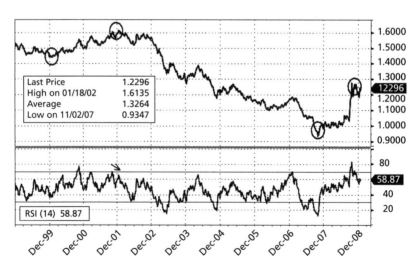

Last Price	1.2296
High on 01/18/02	1.6135
Average	1.3264
Low on 11/02/07	0.9347

RSI (14) 58.87

Figure 8.4 USD/CAD, Weekly 1999 to 2008, with RSI Study

Source: Bloomberg.

which USD/CAD subsequently rallied. The other major turn that the RSI successfully signaled was the October 24, 2008, high of 1.2775. On the third of the major turns, the January 18, 2002, peak of 1.6135, the RSI provided a different type of sell signal: a negative or bearish divergence. This pattern, in which the RSI made successively lower highs even as the currency price rose, started on November 9, 2001, when the RSI reached 69.66 as USD/CAD closed at 1.6028. When USD/CAD closed at the high several weeks later, the RSI could only rise to 64.79, creating the negative divergence signal. Finally, as to the last major turn, the February 4, 2000, low of 1.4408, the RSI did not drop to near an oversold level. However, that likely stemmed from the fact that the currency price was grinding lower at only the slightest of downtrends, and so the indicator was not registering a trend.

The RSI crossed back from extreme levels on eight other occasions, seven of which presaged at least a consolidation of several weeks if not a significant countertrend move. Of the seven instances just mentioned, in five cases, the price action simply stalled. In the other two cases, significant trend reversals ensued. The RSI crossed higher on May 12, 2006, with USD/CAD at 1.1096, and USD/CAD eventually rallied to 1.1842 by February 2002. The very next week, the RSI crossed lower from overbought territory, marking the beginning of a decline from 1.1725 to 1.06 by June 1. The one occasion that the signal did fail was on March 21, 2003, as despite the crossing higher of the RSI, the downward price trend immediately resumed, with USD/CAD dropping from 1.4938 to 1.3342 by June 13. In summary, in nine of the ten RSI signals provided for USD/CAD during the 1999 to 2008 period, the price action at least stalled, and in four of these instances, significant prices reversals ensued.

Findings from RSI Analysis

Applying the RSI study to weekly data for four of the major currencies does provide some meaningful insights. Based on our definition of an RSI signal as the crossing of the level out of the extreme ranges (30 and 70), forty-eight signals were issued. In forty-four cases, the price trend stalled for at least four weeks. In twenty-seven of those forty-four cases, the price action simply stalled in a range. Of the remaining seventeen occurrences, in six cases a modest yet significant countertrend move occurred, and in eleven cases, a major countertrend followed. These results strongly suggest that in the event of such a signal, market participants should consider two options: less agile participants should consider changing existing pro-trend exposure either by buying option protection, by selling out-of-the-money options, or by lightening up on exposure; more agile and/or aggressive players could look to establish countertrend exposure.

Bollinger Bands

Bollinger Bands were developed by John Bollinger and consist of two lines, or bands, plotted a certain number of standard deviations—usually 2—from a middle band (a moving average; Bloomberg's default is 30 periods). Because the bands are based on the standard-deviation concept, the gap between them tends to widen during high volatility periods and narrow when price action is muted. Our primary interest in and use for Bollinger Bands is as a contrarian signal for when price action might either consolidate or even correct.

The price and band section of each graph illustrates when the price action is pushing against the standard-deviation bands. However, the bands can widen, and the middle band, or moving average, also moves. Furthermore, the price action can run back and forth over the upper or lower band, obscuring the relation. This issue is addressed by a second section of the graph for the "%B" index; %B measures the price of the currency relative to the gap between the upper and lower bands and is defined as:

$$(\text{close} - \text{lower band}) / (\text{upper band} - \text{lower band}) \qquad (8.3)$$

The %B section of the graph helps simplify the relationship of the price to the upper and lower bands and actually helps define a quantifiable rule for a signal that we will use in this chapter: when the %B moves back above 0.0 or below 1.0, which would indicate that a currency is correcting back from an extreme variation from its trend, enter a buy or sell signal, respectively.

USD/JPY and Bollinger Bands

Figure 8.5 illustrates the price action for USD/JPY on a weekly basis from 1999 to 2008, the moving average of the weekly closes, the Bollinger Bands, and, in a separate frame below, the price action graph, a line depicting the %B. This graph can be created in Bloomberg by typing "JPY<curncy>BOLL<go>" and adjusting the dates to 1999–2008 and the periodicity to weekly.

Using a trigger definition of the %B either crossing below 1.0 (sell) or above 0.0 (buy), the Bollinger signaled six of the eight major turning points that are circled in the accompanying graph. It missed the first (May 1999) and last (August 2008) because in neither case did the %B cross into overbought territory (above 1.0).

On October 9, 1999, with USD/JPY closing at 105.12, the Bollinger crossed above 0.0, signaling a buy. This presaged a

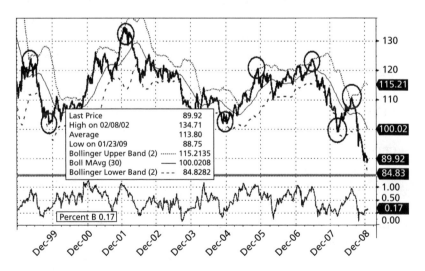

Figure 8.5   USD/JPY and Bollinger Bands

Source: Bloomberg.

consolidation in the currency through November 19. Then there was another slight leg down towards 101 through year-end. However, by March, the lows in the price action were consistently higher. At the next major turn in early 2002, the %B crossed below 1.0 on February 1, when the currency closed at 133.07. Over the next four weeks, the currency range traded as it repeatedly failed to breach 135.00, and by March, a major downtrend had begun. As to the third major turn, on December 10, 2004, the %B crossed above 0.0 with USD/JPY closing at 105.22. The currency had recently tested below 102 and would do so again in coming weeks, but the move lower was over, and by February 2005, the price action had begun to rally. For the fourth turn in December 2005, the %B crossed below 1.0 on a violent move down by the currency from 121 to 115 during the course of the week. Although the violence introduced the risk that the indicator might be severely whipsawed, price action instead simply stabilized, with USD/JPY consolidating into a narrowing range until May, when it broke sharply lower. The fifth major turn forewarned by the %B occurred in mid-2007. On June 29, the %B broke below 1.0 as the currency closed at 123.17. USD/JPY consolidated another two weeks before beginning a downtrend that lasted until March 2008 with the currency falling to 95.76. March 2008 is also the last of the major turns correctly signaled by the %B. On April 4, the %B crossed above zero with USD/JPY closing at 101.47, very early in the rally to 110.66 by August 15.

The %B provided another ten signals outside the periods of the major turns identified for USD/JPY in Figure 8.5. The subsequent price action of these ten occurrences can be categorized four ways: a failed signal (price trend continues), a consolidation (the price retraces less than five big figures), a minor countertrend move (the price retraces five to ten big figures), or a major countertrend move (the price retraces ten or more big figures). Based on these categories, two of the signals resulted in a failed signal. One of these occurred during the highly anomalous period of October 2008, while for the other (October 2003), price action continued for another four big figures before consolidating in the subsequent nine months. Five of the signals resulted in consolidation, one resulted in a minor countertrend move, and two resulted in major countertrend moves.

Given that we artificially broke out the eight major turns identified at the beginning of the discussion, let's add those back in to the categorization of the results for the signals. Our universe is now eighteen incidents. Of these, the %B missed two opportunities and provided two failed signals. Of the remaining fourteen cases, the %B led to five consolidations, one minor retracement, two major retracements, and six trend reversals. Based on these results, one should consider %B signals as an opportunity at least to sell out-of-the-money options, if not to adopt outright countertrend positions.

EUR/USD and Bollinger Bands

The %B cross-trigger signaled all five of the major turns identified by circles in **Figure 8.6**. On September 22, 2000, the %B issued a buy signal as EUR/USD closed at 0.8766. Subsequently, the currency dropped to 0.8230, at which point the %B issued a second

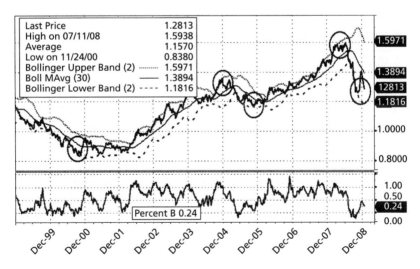

Figure 8.6 EUR/USD and Bollinger Bands

Source: Bloomberg.

signal on the very week that the currency established its lifetime low. At the December 2004 peak, the %B issued another "double" signal, first on December 17 with EUR/USD at 1.3307, and again on January 7, 2005, after the currency had dropped to 1.3054. For the third turn, the 1.1640 low in November 2005, the signal is less proximate. The sharp decline from near 1.30 in May 2005 to 1.18 by July had caused the %B to drop below 0.0, and as the move lost momentum, the %B began to issue buy signals, with the last one being on July 15 when EUR/USD closed at 1.2035. This was four months before and four big figures above the eventual bottom, but it did signal the stall in price around 1.20 that lasted until April 2006. From April to July 2008, EUR/USD consolidated, vainly trying to breach 1.60. The %B issued another "double" signal, first on March 21 with EUR/USD at 1.5431 and again on April 18 when the currency closed at 1.5851. Finally, on November 21, 2008, the %B issued a buy signal. The currency pair closed at 1.2587, just off its 1.2330 low on October 31.

In addition to the above five signals, the %B issued another fifteen signals during the period. One of these proved to be a false signal in that the price action continued to trend, but this occurred during the anomalous September 2008 period. Twelve of the signals resulted in a consolidation of EUR/USD for at least three or four weeks. The remaining two resulted in moderate countertrend moves (less than 0.05).

Consequently, for a universe of twenty signals issued by the %B over the 1999 to 2008 period, twelve resulted in consolidations that one could have profited from by selling out-of-the-money options; seven resulted in significant countertrend moves that would have benefited from outright positions; and only one signal failed, and that occurred in the midst of the most extraordinary period of recent financial history.

USD/CAD and Bollinger Bands

The %B cross trigger signaled all four of the major turns identified by circles in **Figure 8.7**. Around the January 2000 low of 1.4320, the %B issued two signals, the first on January 7 with USD/CAD

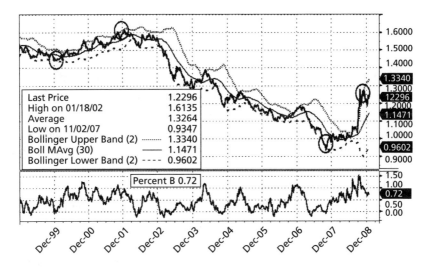

Figure 8.7 USD/CAD and Bollinger Bands

Source: Bloomberg.

at 1.4558 and the second on January 28 with the currency at 1.4463. On November 16, 2001, the %B registered a sell signal with USD/CAD closing at 1.5901. Over the next four months, the currency traded a 1.58 to 1.62 range before eventually beginning a multi-year decline. The end of that decline, representing the third major turn for USD/CAD, came during the week of November 9, 2007, when the currency traded a low of 0.9058. That same week, the %B issued a buy signal when the currency closed at 0.9448. In the final major turn, as USD/CAD struggled to breach 1.30 from October to December of 2008, the %B registered a double sell signal, first on November 7 when the currency had dropped to 1.1893, and again on November 28 when the price closed at 1.2398.

In addition to the four signals above, the %B registered another nineteen signals. The results are still quite positive, but not as good as for the EUR/USD or USD/JPY. In five of the cases, the existing trend persisted, leading to a failed call. Only one of those failed calls can be discounted as part of the September to October 2008 crisis. The others occurred during the persistent downward march during 2003 and 2004. We vividly remember being victim to one of these signals, losing on a countertrend rally call in October 2004. At that time, USD/CAD closed at 1.2529, but rather than consolidating or rebounding, it plunged to 1.1718 in November before starting a bear-market rally to 1.2734. Of the remaining fourteen signals, seven resulted in a consolidation of price action for at least three to four weeks, six resulted in moves of 0.05 to 0.10, and one resulted in a move in excess of 0.10.

Overall, out of twenty-three signals, subsequent price action reversed significantly in eleven cases, consolidated in seven instances, and continued in the existing trend five times. This analysis suggests that the %B signal indicates opportunities either to sell out-of-the-money option credit spreads, or covered options, or to adopt outright countertrend exposure.

GBP/USD and Bollinger Bands

The %B cross-trigger signaled four of the five major turns identified by circles in **Figure 8.8**. On October 8, 1999, the %B crossed lower, with GBP/USD at 1.6514. For two weeks it crossed back into extreme territory but crossed back lower again on October 22 with the currency at 1.6525. That week, the currency had posted a medium-term high of 1.6746 and would head lower throughout the following year. By September 2000, GBP/USD had fallen to 1.40, a level the currency would continue to test until April 2002. On June 15, 2001, the %B issued a buy signal on the same week that the currency traded its low (1.3682) of the entire 1999 to 2008 period. The third major turn correctly signaled by the %B was that in December 2004. On December 24, 2004, the %B crossed lower, the week after the currency had traded its high of 1.9550. The %B missed the signal around the December 2005 1.7049 low, likely a function of the fact that the currency had dropped precipitously to 1.7273 around mid-year with the result that the marginal new low in December did not constitute an extreme trend. The %B did catch the next major turn—that from the high of 2.1161 established the week of November 9, 2007.

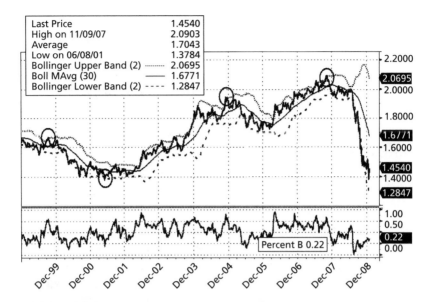

Last Price	1.4540
High on 11/09/07	2.0903
Average	1.7043
Low on 06/08/01	1.3784
Bollinger Upper Band (2) ⋯⋯	2.0695
Boll MAvg (30) ———	1.6771
Bollinger Lower Band (2) - - - -	1.2847

Figure 8.8   GBP/USD and Bollinger Bands

Source: Bloomberg.

The following week, the %B crossed lower with GBP/USD still elevated at 2.0547.

The %B indicator rule provided an additional eighteen signals during the nine-year period. In three cases, the signal failed as the existing trend continued on. In two of those cases, January 2004 and June 2005, the trend continued for another few weeks, causing the %B to revert back to an extreme, and then exhausted itself, at which point the %B provided signals that presaged significant countertrend moves. The third case was in September 2008, when the violence of the global crisis overwhelmed the indicator. In nine of the fifteen remaining incidents, the price action stalled for a period of at least four weeks. In four cases, the price action reversed by 0.05 to 0.10, and in two cases, countertrend moves in excess of 0.10 followed.

Including the four major moves that the %B captured, then, the indicator provided twenty-two signals, after eighteen of which the price trend stalled for at least four weeks. In eight of those eighteen cases, significant price action developed that was counter to the existing trend.

Findings from the Bollinger Band Analysis

Bollinger Bands applied to weekly data provide an excellent warning system of an interruption to an existing trend. For the four currencies we examined, the indicator issued eighty-one signals during the 1999 to 2008 time period. Of those eighty-one, only 13.6 percent (eleven) of the signals were incorrect (the trend continued unabated); 40.7 percent of the time (thirty-three occurrences), the price action consolidated in a narrow range for at least four weeks; and 45.7 percent of the time, a significant counter-trend or even a new opposing trend developed. Bollinger Band signals provide an excellent opportunity to pare back on existing risk by taking steps that could include (1) selling out-of-the-money options; (2) buying option protection; or (3) switching one's net exposure to take advantage of a move in the opposite direction.

Slow Stochastics

The slow stochastics (SStoch) study represents another commonly used oscillator that builds on the concept of the RSI discussed in the previous section. The SStoch is based on the notion that as the price of a currency rises (falls), the closing values tend to lie closer to the upper (lower) end of the price range. The study is comprised of two lines, one of which derives from the difference between the closing and low prices relative to the difference between the high and low prices, while the other represents a moving average of the first line. The *slow* in slow stochastics emanates from a further transformation of the measures to smooth them. More specifically, the line that plots the difference between the closing and low prices relative to the high price is referred to as the %K line, while the line plotting the difference between the closing and high prices is referred to as the %D line.

%K: an unsmoothed Relative Strength Indicator,   (8.4)

where

%K = [(current close − lowest low price for period)/(highest high price for period − lowest price for period) · 100.
%D: a simple moving average of the %K,
%D = (%K1 + %K2 + %K3 + ⋯ + %Kn) / n, where n represents the number of time periods examined.

To calculate the "slow stochastics," a further transformation is required in which the %D measure is smoothed even further with moving averages:

$$\%DS = (\%D1 + \%D2 + \%D3 + \cdots + \%Dn)/n \qquad (8.5)$$

$$\%DSS \; (slow) = (\%DS1 + \%DS2 + \%DS3 + \cdots + \%DSn)/n \quad (8.6)$$

Price action is said to be overbought when the lines are above 70–75 and oversold when below 25–30. Furthermore, the study can be used to call a turn when the lines turn and cross over each other: a buy when they cross higher and a sell when they cross lower. The crossing signals are considered particularly important when the lines are in overbought or oversold territory. However, they can also be used to identify the ends of countertrend corrections that the RSI and Bollinger Band signals alone proved unable to capture. On relatively rare occasions, the price of the currency continues to make new highs (lows) even as the indicator lines turn lower (higher). Such patterns are referred to as *price divergences* and often interpreted as sell (buy) signals.

USD/JPY and Slow Stochastics

Figure 8.9 reveals that the slow stochastics indicator did correctly identify the price action as overbought and oversold at the five extremes identified by visual inspection. In October 1999, with USD/JPY at 105.50, the stochastics crossed higher while in oversold territory. The subsequent drop in USD/JPY to 101.87 caused the stochastics to flip back to a sell signal, but by January 7, the stochastics turned higher with the currency pair at 105.34.

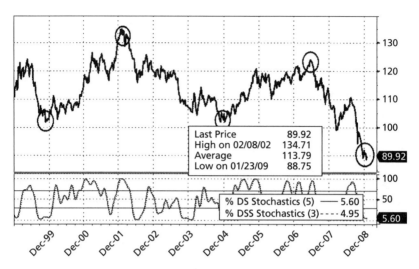

Figure 8.9   USD/JPY, Weekly, January 1999 to January 2009

Source: Bloomberg.

In February 2002, the stochastics crossed lower while in over-bought territory. The USD/JPY closed the week at 134.71, the high close of the entire move. During the December 2004 to January 2005 period, USD/JPY bottomed around 102. The stochastic initially crossed higher in oversold territory December 24 and got whipsawed as the price action consolidated, but then turned higher again with USD/JPY at 105.65. On June 22, 2007, USD/JPY closed at a multi-year high of 123.89. A few weeks later, on July 20, the stochastics crossed lower in overbought territory with the currency at 121.27. Finally, on January 23, 2009, USD/JPY closed at a multi-year low of 88.75, but that same day, the stochastics crossed high in oversold territory, catching the exact bottom (at least on a weekly basis) of the collapse in USD/JPY.

Whereas with the RSI, once a signal was triggered it couldn't be "un-triggered" until the RSI had moved to the opposite extreme, with the slow stochastics we can set the signal for whenever the stochastics cross—even if they are in neutral territory. Using this signal definition created many more signals—sixty-three, of which twenty-seven, or 43 percent, were correct; the average profit on successful signals was 4.2 percent against the average loss of 2.5 percent. As a result, at the end of the period, the cumulative return was 23.3 percent. When the cumulative returns and draw-downs (cumulative return less the maximum cumulative return reached) are taken into account, the signal appears less attractive. On three occasions, the drawdown reached below 15 percent, including a −25.2 percent reading in March 2008. The problem for the slow stochastic cross signal was that it got whipsawed during the consolidations of January to September of 2003, November 2003 to October 2004, and April 2006 to April 2008. Even when small gains were made during these periods, the profits would be lost on sharp corrections with which the stochastics could not keep pace.

The disappointing results of the above experiment are a reminder that slow stochastics are an oscillator and designed to highlight extreme values and potential turning points. Perhaps by using sto-chastic crosses within the neutral zone only to exit positions and not enter new ones, the signal would work better. When this was attempted, the number of signals fell to forty-two, eighteen of which proved correct, so that the ratio of correct signals, 43 per-cent, did not change. However, average of the profitable trades rose to 5.0 percent while the average loss moderated to 2.3 percent. Consequently, the cumulative profit at the end of 2008 reached 35.4 percent, and the drawdowns were reduced: the 18 percent drawdown during 2001 slipped to 8.6 percent, and that of 19.3 percent in January 2005 slipped to 13.2 percent. Unfortunately, the 25.2 percent drawdown of March 2008 slipped only to 23.1 percent as the initial decline in the currency starting in mid-2007 pushed the stochastics into oversold territory quickly, and few of the bear-market rallies proved enough to push the stochastics back up into neutral territory. As a result, the signal was triggered for many of the small corrective rallies.

EUR/USD and the Slow Stochastics

The weekly slow stochastic study captured each of the five major turning points for EUR/USD during the 1999 to 2008 period (see **Figure 8.10**). On November 24, 2000, EUR/USD closed at

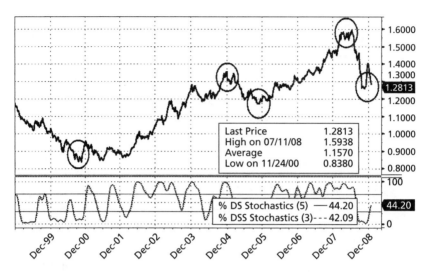

Figure 8.10   EUR/USD, Weekly from 1999 to 2008, with Slow Stochastics Study

Source: Bloomberg.

the record low of 0.8390. One week later, the slow stochastics crossed higher in oversold territory. By the time EUR/USD peaked at 1.3554 on December 31, 2004, the slow stochastics had already turned lower in overbought territory two weeks earlier while EUR/USD was at 1.3307. By December 2, 2005, the currency had completed its pullback and closed at 1.1718. Three weeks later, with the currency still at 1.1869, the stochastics crossed higher in oversold territory. Finally, on July 11, 2008, the euro closed at a record high of 1.5938 versus the U.S. dollar, and three weeks later, with EUR/USD still at 1.5564, the stochastics crossed lower in overbought territory.

As in the analysis of USD/JPY, the stochastics crossed many times in addition to the major turns identified visually. As we will never know in real time whether a major turn is being made, we need to evaluate all the signals. To start, we will evaluate the signal made whenever the stochastics cross, regardless of whether they are in neutral, overbought, or oversold territory. This results in sixty-one signals, twenty-seven of which (44 percent) ended up being correct; the average gain (+4.4 percent) outpaced the average loss (−2.6 percent) by a wide margin. The trading rule provides cumulative profits of 28.9 percent, but there are two drawdown periods in excess of 20 percent. The first drawdown period, which began in April 1999 as the decline in EUR/USD dragged on from 1.10 towards 1.00, caused the RSI to reach an extreme oversold level and then whipsaw on modest pullbacks. This drawdown worsened to June 2000 because the bear market continued relentlessly with the slightest of pullbacks causing whipsaws to the oversold indicator. The second period of worsening drawdown occurred from June 2006 until June 2008 as the persistent, slow grind from 1.26 to above 1.55 left the indicator pinned in overbought territory and whipsawing on the very slight pullbacks. These drawdown periods highlight the key drawback of oscillators—that price trends can continue in spite of their already having persisted a long time by historical standards.

Stripping out the entry signals that occur when the stochastics were in neutral territory added value when applied to USD/JPY. Unfortunately, this adjustment actually made things worse when applied to EUR/USD. Stripping out the neutral cross signals reduced the number of signals from sixty-one to forty-two. The number of profitable signals fell even more, from twenty-seven to fifteen, or from 44 to 35 percent. And the advantage of the average gain to the average loss fell to 4.1 percent for gains and 2.5 percent for losses. Lastly, while the drawdown in 2000 was not so bad (19.7 percent versus 24.0 percent), the one in 2008 was considerably worse (29.8 percent versus 21.3 percent). These results illustrate one of our core themes: no indicator or study works across different currencies or even within a currency over time.

GBP/USD and the Slow Stochastics

The weekly slow stochastic study captured each of the six major turning points for GBP/USD ("cable") during the 1999 to 2008 period (see **Figure 8.11**). In October 1999, GBP/USD closed at 1.6697, which turned out to be a high before the currency's next leg down to the 2001 low. The signal from the stochastics came a few weeks later, in November, after the currency had slipped

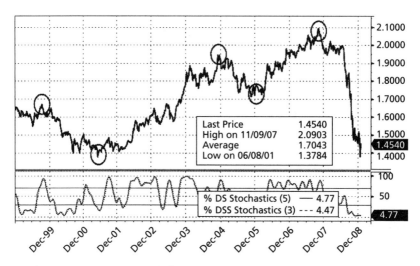

Figure 8.11 GBP/USD, Weekly from 1999 to 2008, with Slow Stochastics Study

Source: Bloomberg.

towards 1.61. Although GBP/USD traded roughly a 1.40–1.50 range for two years from June 2000 to June 2002, the lowest weekly close, 1.3784, came on June 8, 2001. Two weeks later, on June 29, 2001, the stochastics turned up with the currency pair trading at 1.4153, very close to the bottom. The next key turning point for GBP came with the 1.9439 close on December 3, 2004. The stochastics took a month to begin turning lower, but that could have been because the price action held near 1.95 for a couple of weeks. In any event, the signal to sell was provided on January 7, 2005, at 1.8712, as GBP/USD was headed for the next key turning point, 1.7142, on November 25, 2005. Once again, the stochastics took a month to turn, but on December 23, 2005, with the currency at 1.7334, they provided a buy signal for the rally that saw GBP eventually test 2.10. That test of 2.10 came on November 9, 2007, when GBP/USD closed at 2.0903. Three weeks late, with the currency closing at 2.0563, the stochastics signaled a sell very close to what turned out to be the peak in Cable.

Just as for USD/JPY and EUR/USD, the weekly stochastics provided numerous other signals during the nine-year period. We first look at signals as defined by any cross regardless of whether the stochastics are in extreme territory. Unfortunately, on the whole the results were disastrous. By the end of 2008, the signal had generated a cumulative 16.2 percent loss. The maximum cumulative profit for the entire period came in March 1999—a 1.3 percent gain. The rest of the nine years was all downhill. Sixty-seven signals were triggered, but only twenty-six, or 39 percent, were profitable. Worse, the average win/loss ratio stood at 1.01, meaning that the profitable signals were not strong enough to offset their lack of frequency. There was only one period when the indicator provided any measure of success. That occurred from April 2005 to March 2006, when the indicator synced up with the downturn and bottom in the currency from 1.90 to 1.71 and provided four consecutive profitable signals totaling 10.6 percent.

Stripping out the entry signals that occurred when the stochastics were in neutral territory only managed to cut the losses by providing fewer signals. The number fell to 44, and the percentage profitable trades rose only marginally to 41 percent (eighteen), but the average win/loss ratio fell to 0.94 (+2.0 percent versus −2.1 percent). At no point did the indicator provide a positive cumulative return; it ended 2008 with a cumulative loss of 25.5 percent, and it suffered a 30.2 percent drawdown.

AUD/USD and the Slow Stochastics

The weekly slow stochastics study captured each of the five major turning points for AUD/USD between 1999 and 2008 (circled in **Figure 8.12**). In January 2000, AUD/USD traded back towards the top of the 0.63–0.67 range it had plied since April 1999 and then began a descent to below 0.50 by 2001. The stochastics issued a sell signal on February 11, 2000, when AUD/USD was still at 0.6305. In March 2001, AUD/USD's descent had stopped, and the currency would range trade for roughly a year before beginning a multi-year rally. AUD/USD closed at 0.4855 on March 30, 2001, and on April 27, 2001, the stochastics had crossed higher from deeply oversold territory. By 2004, AUD/USD's rally had reached a plateau, and for three years the currency would range trade between 0.70 and 0.80. On February 13, 2004,

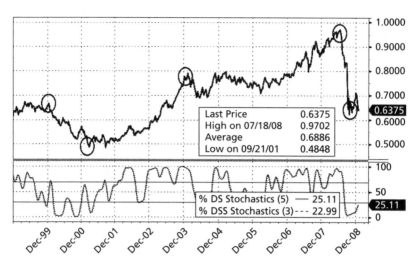

Figure 8.12   AUD/USD, Weekly from 1999 to 2008, with Slow Stochastics Study

Source: Bloomberg.

AUD/USD closed at 0.7898, marking the end of the uptrend from 2002. The stochastics had actually turned lower in over-bought territory several weeks earlier, on December 19, 2003, with the currency price at 0.7359. The next major turning point for the currency did not come until July 2008, when AUD/USD closed at a peak of 0.9702. The trend had been decelerating since May, and so the stochastics had turned lower on June 20 with the currency at 0.9533. The final turn came on October 24, 2008, when AUD/USD made a bottom at 0.6225 (weekly closing basis). The week before, the stochastics had begun to turn higher presaging the ensuing rally.

The weekly stochastics provided sixty-seven signals during the 1999 to 2008 period, including any cross of the stochastics regardless of whether they were in neutral or extreme territory. Of these, thirty-one, or 46 percent, were correct. The profitable trades averaged 3.8 percent, while the losing ones averaged 2.6 percent, allowing the rule to generate a 26.6 percent cumulative profit at the end of 2008. However, the cumulative drawdown could be severe, as it registered as much as 11.7 percent in December 1999, 18.9 percent in September 2001, and 23.0 percent in November 2007.

The rule had three particularly bad periods. It got whipsawed by trendless trading twice, first as the AUD/USD traded flat around 0.65 in the second half of 1999 and a second time during 2005 and 2006 as the currency remained range bound between 0.70 and 0.80. The third period of distress was August and September of 2001, when the currency took three significant losses on volatile price action not in sync with the parameters of the stochastics.

Stripping out the stochastic crosses at less extreme levels—other than to exit existing positions—helped somewhat; the number of signals fell to forty-five, but the percentage of correct signals remained steady at 46 percent. What did change for the positive was that the average profit rose to 4.0 percent and the average loss moderated to 2.2 percent. Consequently, the drawdowns were less severe, often below 10 percent. Unfortunately, the grinding nature of the flat trading from 2005 to 2006 and the moderate but persistent rally from 2006 to 2007 still caused a drawdown of 20.5 percent by early 2008.

Key Findings for Slow Stochastics

Attempting to use slow stochastics for both entry and exit points, especially when using all stochastic crosses, even those in neutral territory, pushed the indicator too far and led to unsatisfactory results. Of the four currencies on which the indicator rule was tested, the percentage of profitable signals ranged from 36 to 47 percent, while the ratio of the profits from correct signals to losses from incorrect signals generally exceeded 1.0 (range of 0.9 to 2.2). And for all currencies tested, the cumulative returns from applying the rules experienced severe drawdowns, ranging from 21.6 percent to 38.7 percent.

Conclusion

Oscillator indicators are very useful in identifying periods when the distribution of ensuing returns will likely be skewed in one direction. The RSI and Bollinger Band indicators proved able to pinpoint times when a roughly 90 percent probability existed that a trend would cease for at least four weeks. The 10 percent of the time that the signals failed, they were overwhelmed by extraordinarily powerful trends, the most extraordinary one being the historic U.S. dollar rally during the August to December 2008 financial crisis.

Because the slow stochastics indicator provided two lines that cross, we attempted to push this indicator further by using it to determine entry and exit points. That test did not work out very well. The performance of the slow stochastics indicator morphed into something like a trend-following system that provided successful signals less than 50 percent of the time and experienced extended periods of incorrect signals with dramatic drawdowns as the indicator got whipsawed because the price action did not match the parameters of the indicator.

This chapter has described the value added by oscillators, as well as their limitations. Applied to weekly data, these indicators provide excellent and reliable warnings of when an existing trend is likely to stall, suffer a countertrend move, and even reverse completely. They identify exceptional circumstances. They should *not* be used to try to identify anything but exceptional circumstances. As we saw when pushing the slow stochastics study towards selecting entry and exit points for trades, the results were unsatisfactory.

The warnings of the oscillator signals can be used to take meaningful action. At these points, one should consider taking at least partial profits on existing positions, insuring the position by buying protective options, generating some extra revenue by selling out-of-the-money options, eliminating exposure altogether, and at the most extreme, adopting exposure in the opposite direction.

9 Technical Pattern Recognition

Another class of technical analysis involves the characterization of price patterns, also called pattern recognition. In some cases, the analysis's main purpose is to identify critical points, either price levels or time frames, for price action. As to price levels, the patterns provide areas of potential support or resistance for price action; as to time frame, the developing patterns often suggest a time at which a pattern (price support or resistance suggested by the pattern) will be confirmed (not broken) or denied (broken). In other cases, the analysis aims at interpreting whether the patterns within the price action indicate strength in a trend or indecision on the part of the market participants.

Critics of pattern recognition often reserve their severest diatribes for the fickle nature of the analysis. Strategists will often find that a technician's determined support for a position not only evaporates but actually turns to an opposing view with the passing of one day of adverse price action. However, the key to appreciating pattern recognition is to perceive the suggested price levels and time frames not as predictions of when a particular price action is going to occur (that is, when prices will reach a ceiling and fail), but rather of the time and/or price level at which the market participants are going to make a key decision about future price action.

Fibonacci Ratios/Levels

Fibonacci ratios are derived from a combination of numbers used to form the Fibonacci sequence, named after the Italian mathematician, Leonardo Fibonacci, who originally calculated it sometime in the twelfth or thirteenth century. Each term of this sequence is simply the sum of the prior two terms (1, 1, 2, 3, 5, 8, 13, …). Furthermore, the quotient of each of the adjacent terms is roughly 1.618, or 0.618, and these ratios have been found to exist throughout nature. For example, the ratio of female to male bees in any honeybee hive is 1.618. In technical analysis, not just the 61.8 percent ratio, but also the 50 percent and the 76.4 percent ratios (along with these numbers subtracted from 100 percent) have been deemed significant. Fibonacci ratios can be used in arcs, fans, and support/resistance levels, although we discuss only the support/resistance levels in this text.

Fibonacci levels can show up in long-term charts. For instance, as **Figure 9.1** illustrates, from April 2001 to July 2008, AUD/USD rallied from 0.4775 to 0.9850, or 5,075 pips. From July 2008 to October 2008, AUD/USD collapsed to 0.6009, or 3,841 pips.

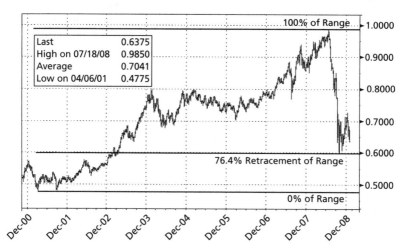

Figure 9.1   AUD/USD, Weekly, 1999 to 2009, with 76.4 Percent Fibonacci Retracement

Source: Bloomberg.

A 76.4 percent retracement would have led to a bottom at 0.5972, a miss of only 38 pips, or 0.7 percent of the entire range. During October 2008, as the freefall in AUD/USD that had started in July began to show some signs of stabilizing, many traders and investors, in the utter chaos that reigned during the crisis, would have been looking for a level at which the currency might finally bottom. The 76.4 percent retracement figure was one such level. The most aggressive traders would have adopted a bullish position the week of October 24, the week before the low actually traded, with a stop-loss below the 0.5972 level. The more faint of heart would have waited till the next week to see the 76.4 percent level tested and held before putting on the same position with the same stop-loss. Even lesser souls might have waited for further confirmation from other signals, and as we noted in the last chapter, on the week of November 14, the %B from the Bollinger Band indicator crossed bullishly from oversold territory.

A second example is provided by USD/CHF during 2008. In the early weeks of 2008, concerns mounted regarding the viability of the U.S. banking system, and rumors circulated of

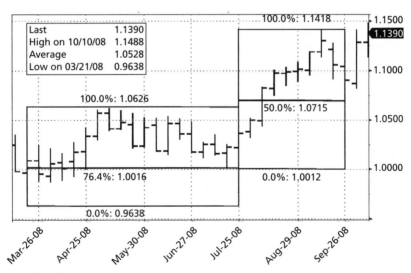

Figure 9.2   USD/CHF and Fibonacci Retracements During 2008

Source: Bloomberg.

imminent bank failures. In the face of this existential threat to the global financial system, USD/CHF collapsed on safe-haven buying of the Swiss franc against the dollar. Finally, Bear Stearns swooned, caught only at the last moment by a government "supported" acquisition by JPMorgan. The next week, that of March 28, 2008, USD/CHF traded a post–Bretton Woods low of 0.9638. As the situation stabilized, USD/CHF began to rally, but then some large U.S. banks began to waver and rumors began to circulate that even Fannie Mae and Freddie Mac—quasi–government guaranteed entities—might fail. USD/CHF began trending lower again in May, and by the week of July 18 had dropped to 1.0012. The decline to this level represented almost a perfect 76.4 percent retracement of the March to May rally from 0.9638 to 1.0626, which lay at 1.0016. The near-precise hold of this level set the stage for another run up in USD/CHF's rally to 1.1418. Weekly oscillators did not provide confirmation of the hold at 1.0012, but the daily Bollinger Band %B did touch 0.0 the day USD/CHF bottomed and rebounded the next day along with the currency.

From the week of July 18 to that of September 12, USD/CHF rallied 1,406 pips from 1.0012 to 1.1418. That rally ended with the actual collapse of Lehman Brothers, and yet another specter of global financial Armageddon drove yet another wave of Swiss franc safe-haven buying. Over the next two weeks, USD/CHF plunged 722 pips before stopping at 1.0696. The hold at this level represented yet another near-precise Fibonacci retracement, as the 50 percent retracement level was at 1.0715. As with the bottom on July 18, the bottom here was corroborated by the daily %B statistic of the Bollinger Band indicator, which dropped to 0.0 the day USD/CHF fell to 1.0696 and rebounded the next day along with the currency.

Head-and-Shoulders Patterns

A head-and-shoulders pattern is comprised of an initial "shoulder," in which price action establishes a high; a retreat; a renewed rally to a new high—the "head"; another retreat; and yet another rally

Figure 9.3   USD/JPY, Weekly, with Head-and-Shoulders Pattern

Source: Bloomberg.

that does not achieve a new high—the second shoulder. The lows established after the initial shoulder and head comprise the base of the "neckline." This neckline extends forward in time and provides support, a breach of which suggests a target decline equal in magnitude to the height from the neck to the top of the head.

Figure 9.3 illustrates the head-and-shoulders pattern USD/JPY traced out from 2001 to 2003. During early 2001, USD/JPY rallied from 114 to a top of 127 the week of April 6. The price action eventually rolled over and established a low of 116 the week of September 21. This completed the first shoulder of the formation. USD/JPY went on to rally towards 135 by February of 2002, where the price stalled and rolled over to establish a low near 116 the week of July 19, 2002. This completed the head of the formation. The price action went on to rally just short of 126 before fading away, suggesting the second shoulder of the head-and-shoulders formation. The key to the formation would be a break below neckline support, the line between the bottoms traded at the beginning and end of the head. The resulting, slightly downtrending neckline provided support just above 115 that held in May 2003. When the support gave way in September of 2003, the breach of the neckline support opened the way for a significant decline of roughly twenty big figures (the height of the head). Subsequently, USD/JPY did trade down towards 105. While that was short of the twenty big-figure decline to 95 that the pattern would have suggested, the range trading between 105 and 110 in late 2003 and early 2004 was consistent with the range in place prior to the head-and-shoulders formation.

Of course, having conjured up the concept of a head-and-shoulders formation, one could further imagine the possibility of an "inverted" head-and-shoulders pattern. GBP/USD traded an inverted—or upside-down—head-and-shoulders formation from June 2006 to April 2007 (see **Figure 9.4**). From June to September 2006, GBP/USD plunged from 1.82 to nearly 1.73, stabilized, and then rallied to 1.85. This price action traced out an initial shoulder. From September 2006 to February 2007, the currency fell to almost 1.70—a new low—stabilized, and then rallied towards 1.79. This price action created a head and a downward sloping neckline. Then from February to April, GBP/USD

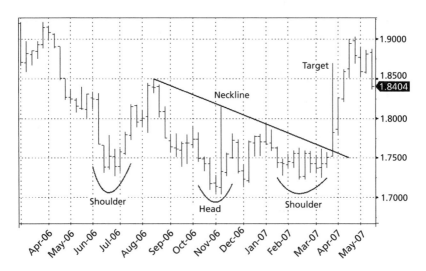

Figure 9.4   GBP/USD, Weekly, with Inverted Head-and-Shoulders Pattern

Source: Bloomberg.

retreated to around 1.7250 before stabilizing and beginning to rally. The breach of neckline resistance at 1.7588 precipitated an explosive move higher and consolidation for six months around the indicated target level of 1.8716. Note that the price action reached the target in this instance, unlike the USD/JPY scenario above; however, in both cases, upon the completion of the head-and-shoulders pattern, the price action accelerated to the pre-formation range and stabilized. In the case of GBP/USD, that range was the 1.85–1.90 region.

Channels

Some people tend to see price action as a series of rough "channels" in which the price moves higher at a relatively constant pace and volatility, such that lines drawn along the highs and the lows of the move are parallel. A breakout from the bottom (top) of an ascending (descending) channel would provide a sell (buy) signal.

USD/CAD is one currency that particularly exemplifies this quality, and **Figure 9.5** illustrates the price action. In this example,

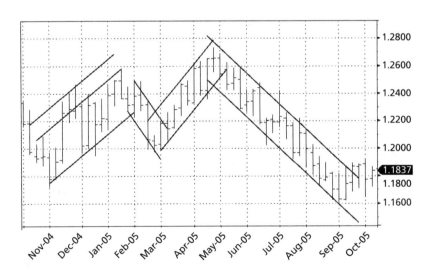

Figure 9.5   USD/CAD, Weekly, with Channel Patterns

Source: Bloomberg.

someone would have been attempting to catch the first uptrending channel from below 1.18 in November 2004 to above 1.25 in February 2005, the downtrending channel from 1.25 to below 1.20 in March, the uptrending channel to 1.27 in May and then the long downtrending channel to 1.16 in September. Ideally, these four trades would have captured 3,000 pips of profit. However, this would have required being willing to sell at the extremes of each channel with the existing trends still fully intact.

The actual implementation of the channel pattern recognition is, as stated above, to sell when the price drops out of the bottom of an uptrending channel and to buy when the price breaks above the top of a downtrending channel. In the case of USD/CAD from November 2004 to October 2005, this would have entailed buying at roughly 1.21 in December, selling around 1.22 in March, buying around 1.22 in April, selling around 1.25 in June, and then buying around 1.18 in October. These signals would have netted 1,100 pips of profit, considerably smaller than the 3,000 alluded to above, but still impressive.

A breach of a particularly well-defined channel is generally viewed as more indicative of a decisive break. The "well-defined" channel usually derives from a horizontal range, which makes sense, intuitively. The bounds of a horizontal range can be concisely described by two unchanging numbers. Consequently, more traders and investors can position over a longer period of time based on one particular level, and this allows for a more explosive move should either boundary be breached. As an example, consider the EUR/USD trading pattern during 2008, illustrated in **Figure 9.6**.

As EUR/USD peaked around a record high 1.60 during mid-2008, it traced out not only a double-top, but also a horizontal channel formation. The high of 1.6019 established in April was retested and slightly breached (1.6038) in July, and this created a double-top pattern. During the March to August period, EUR/USD also tested but failed to breach the 1.5275 support level in May and June, and this became the channel support. After EUR/USD failed to break above 1.60 in July, it turned lower

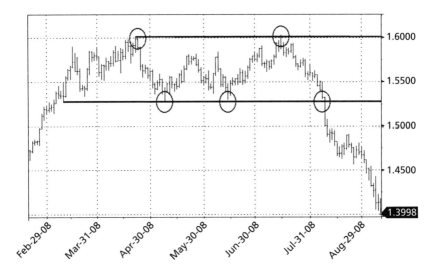

Figure 9.6 EUR/USD, Daily with Channel Pattern

Source: Bloomberg.

and then tested the channel support for one day. The following day, August 8, EUR/USD broke through the support, and the breach led to a violent plunge of roughly thirteen big figures by mid-September.

Multiple Tops/Bottoms and Triangles/Wedges

Market participants often push the price of a currency to test and retest a high or low, causing the price action to trace out double- or triple-tops or bottoms. Each time these levels are tested and hold, they gain significance to a technical analyst. They also likely attract the attention of traders and investors, who increasingly place orders (i.e., stop-loss, options) around the levels. The increased attention tends to serve as a magnet for price action, which often leads to the debate of whether technical analysis is "real" or whether it is merely "self-fulfilling prophecy." While the debate presents an interesting intellectual issue, it does not illuminate the discussion about the obvious relevance of the levels. Our point is merely

Figure 9.7 AUD/USD, Weekly, with Triple-Top and Rising Wedge

Source: Bloomberg.

that if a level is important enough for a critical mass of market participants, it is important for the analyst to be aware of it.

A "triangle" or "wedge" is formed when price action consolidates into a narrowing range. A narrowing as the price level increases (decreases) is often viewed as bearish (bullish). Regardless of the bias as the wedges or triangles are forming, a breakout in either direction is interpreted as indicative of the future price trend.

In early 2007, AUD/USD presented an interesting dilemma. **Figure 9.7** illustrates that the price failed three times from February 2004 to January 2007 right near the psychologically important 0.8000 level. The third failure in January 2007 could have been expected to yield a fairly sizable retreat for the currency. However, after a retreat in the wake of the second failure at 0.80 in March 2005, the price action began to form a wedge pattern, and this time, the rising lows compressed the price action to such a point that bulls were able to push the price decisively through the resistance. This scenario highlights that pattern recognition sometimes fails to "forecast" future price action. However, the episode also highlights that pattern recognition is important for

Figure 9.8 USD/CAD, Daily, with Triple-Top and Rising Wedge

Source: Bloomberg.

money and risk management in that it at least enables traders and investors to determine when the market psychology has reached a tipping point and that one's directional view is best abandoned.

As another example, consider USD/CAD during late 2008. USD/CAD formed a triple-top at 1.3017 during the fourth quarter of 2008 (see **Figure 9.8**). The top was initiated on October 28, 2008. The currency dropped back to 1.1472 by November 4, establishing the beginning of what would become upward trendline support from late September. USD/CAD surged a second time towards 1.30, but failed again, and it corrected back to 1.2127 on November 25, confirming the uptrend support. USD/CAD then ground higher along the uptrend support, eventually failing a third time to breach 1.30. USD/CAD turned lower and tested the uptrend support line three consecutive days. However, on December 11, it finally broke lower, leading to a decline to 1.1819 by December 18.

From late 1999 to late 2000, USD/JPY traded in an ever-narrowing range (see **Figure 9.9**). The bottom had been put in around 101 during the last weeks of 1999. Subsequent bottoms

Figure 9.9 USD/JPY Symmetrical Triangle, or Wedge, Formation

Source: Bloomberg.

were established at 102.07 in March 2000, 103.93 in June, and 104.77 in September. As to the downtrending resistance, the initial high was established at 111.73 in February, followed by 110.08 in May, 109.80 in August, 109.58 in October, and 109.29 in November. Both trend lines appeared to be approaching a collision with about the same angle, providing little inkling as the direction of the breakout. On the week of November 24, 2000, the price action broke above the downtrending resistance, jumping from an open of 108.79 to a close of 111.28. This explosive breach opened the way for a sustained rally to 126.84 by April 2001.

Japanese Candlestick Patterns

The Japanese initiated the use of technical analysis in the seventeenth century in the trade of rice, but candlestick technical analysis did not appear until after 1850, with much of the credit for the development of this type of analysis going to a rice trader named Munehisa Homma.

A candle consists of a "body," or the "wax" of the candle, which represents the range between the open and the close for the day

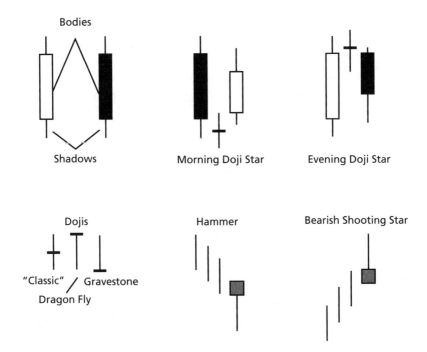

Figure 9.10 Examples of Japanese Candlesticks

Source: Investopedia.

(see **Figure 9.10**). To distinguish "up" days from "down" days, candle bodies that are either white or green are those for which the price closed higher for the period, while black or red candles denote those days when the price fell. The figures also contain a thin line—the "wick," referred to as the "shadow"—that represents the range between the low and the high of a period. The shadow above the body is called the "upper shadow," while that below the body is called the "lower shadow."

The length of the body relative to the overall shadow is considered to reflect the decisiveness of price action for a given period. A long body that leaves only a bit of shadow showing is considered very decisive. Strong rallies and sharp bear markets tend to be marked by long bodies. In contrast, a body that is tiny relative to the shadow occurs when the market closes at nearly the same price it opened and is considered the mark of an indecisive market.

A *doji* is a candlestick in which the body has little height (ideally just a thin line with the open and closing levels equal), leaving a relatively long shadow. It is a mark of an indecisive market and is often considered a warning of imminent changes in trend direction. In the classic doji, the shadow is moderate, and the upper and lower shadows are of approximately equal length. In contrast, a *long-legged doji* has a very long shadow. In a *gravestone doji*, the tiny body lies at the bottom of the shadow. The price action started at the low, tested higher, but then retraced. This is considered very bearish if it occurs in an uptrend. Finally, a *dragonfly doji* is one in which the body lies at the top of the shadow; the prices opened at the high, tested lower, but then rebounded. The dragonfly is considered bullish if it occurs in a downtrend. Interpretation of the candlesticks should never be performed in isolation. Instead, one must consider the groupings of the candlesticks.

For instance, the *morning doji star* is refers to a three-day bullish reversal pattern that marks the end of a downtrend. The first day is a down day with a long body, consistent with the extant trend. The following day opens lower and but forms a doji—a mark of indecision on the part of the market. The last day is an up day with a relatively long body and a close above the midpoint of the first session's body. Conversely, the *evening doji star* refers to a three-day bearish reversal pattern that marks the end of an uptrend. The market remains broadly bullish on the first day, consistent with the trend, creating a large body. On the second day, the price moves immediately higher, but eventually retreats to create an indecisive doji. On the third day, the market retreats in force, creating a long body with a close below the midpoint of the first day's body.

A "hammer" is another candlestick that—in the right context—can be considered a signal for a trend reversal. Hammer candlesticks occur when a security moves significantly lower after the open, but rebounds to close far above the intraday low. Hammers forming in downtrends are considered bullish. If this candlestick forms during an advance, it is called a *hanging man*. Conversely, the *shooting star* is a bearish reversal Japanese candlestick pattern. In an uptrend, the security opens higher and rallies even more, but then closes near where it opened. The candlestick has a long upper shadow/wick and a small body.

Conclusion

This chapter has introduced some of the key concepts in the pattern recognition subset of technical analysis. Most important is the need to approach this subject without any prejudgment. Some analysts hold these concepts in high regard, others in utter disdain. Be pragmatic, not dogmatic, in applying the analysis. There is value in having the ability to connect and converse with a client or colleague who finds these useful. There is no value in engaging in heated discussions about whether pattern analysis has any intellectual or statistical merit.

Patterns can develop over any time horizon, which, for the purposes of this book, would generally encompass days, months, and in some cases, years. We have observed 76.4 percent Fibonacci retracements that took over seven years to develop, as in the case for AUD/USD between April 2001 and July 2008, and others that took as few as ten weeks in the case of USD/CHF from July to September of 2008. We looked at scenarios for head-and-shoulders formations, one of which took the better part of three years to create (USD/JPY, 2001–2003), and another which was completed in nine months (GBP/USD, July 2006–April 2007). We encountered wedges, channels, and multiple tops, some of which lasted a couple months (USD/CAD, October–December 2008), and others that dragged on upwards of a year (USD/JPY, December 1999–November 2000).

Patterns can represent either well-defined mathematical relationships or more amorphous relationships that attempt to assess the "animal spirits" of the market. Fibonacci retracements are mathematical constructs, and so while one might quibble over whether a retracement overshooting a retracement level by 0.6 percent or 1.1 percent is significant enough to negate the signal, there is no refuting the calculation of the level. Beyond Fibonacci retracements, however, the pattern analysis becomes a bit less objective and a bit more subjective. Okay, so a failure of USD/CAD to breach 1.30 on three occasions in late 2008 is pretty straightforward, right? Well, in one instance, the price topped at 1.3017, while on another it stopped at 1.2984—not exactly horizontal resistance, but likely good enough for traders and investors to set stops and triggers zeroed in on 1.3000. Wedges and non-horizontal channels become even more nebulous. The various highs and lows make drawing one line that captures the pattern exactly quite difficult. If one uses a particular close but ignores another because it looks too aberrational to include, one changes the slope of the line, which can greatly affect when support or resistance is eventually tested and/or broken. Even assuming one can draw an indisputable line, the coordinates of the support and/or resistance change daily, providing traders and investors with moving targets, very few of which the market can ever really home in on as being critical. Furthermore, analysts of Japanese candlesticks are careful to warn that one must never consider a single candlestick in isolation, but rather that one must consider the "context" of the surrounding candlesticks. The variability of the nuance in candlesticks makes hard, quantifiable analysis rather difficult.

Nevertheless, pattern analysis represents one more "arrow" in one's analytical "quiver." And from a purely pragmatic perspective, if enough people in any situation believe something, that thing stands a very good chance of becoming reality. Furthermore, the patterns make no hard and fast predictions about price action. If one interprets the support and resistance levels the charts indicate as simply support and resistance levels that can either be held or broken, their utility rises. As we have previously stated, the real value in pattern analysis lies in identifying potential inflection points for price action or psychological tipping points for market participants, and adjusting one's positions and outlook based on the resolution of the price around these points.

Case
Studies

E ach chapter so far has focused on one particular aspect of currency analysis starting from very high–level macroeconomic theory, then zooming in to inter-market fair value analysis, and then focusing even more specifically on tactical considerations like positioning and technical patterns. In reality, the tools presented separately so far are all brought to bear in a fully informed investment or trading decision. This chapter will present several historical examples and explain the complete analysis that is best undertaken.

EUR/USD Peaks at 1.60
During Mid-2008

To the extent that the crisis during 2008 confronted policymakers, investors, and traders with the most intense situation any had dealt with in their careers or seen in their lifetimes, the fact that the price action in EUR/USD pushed long-term valuations to extremes is not surprising. Oftentimes, currencies get pushed to over- or undervalued territory without the danger signals being registered on the longer-term measures. Generally, by the time a long-term valuation, such as PPP, registers "over-done" for a currency and prompts a high-level policymaker to lament the "volatility" in the currency, the traders and investors have been experiencing a series of "overdone" situations—or "living the dream"—for months. On many occasions in our careers, the complaints of policymakers regarding "excessive" currency moves have prompted cynical responses on trading floors to the effect, "... and where exactly have you (the policymaker) been the last several months (or years)!?"

During 2008, EUR/USD spiked on concerns regarding the health and viability of the U.S. banking and financial system. EUR/USD rose to a record high during March 2008 as the U.S. government was forced to broker a last-minute deal in which JPMorgan purchased a faltering Bear Stearns. The currency stabilized at an extremely high price above 1.50 for the next four months as the market stuck with the perception that the crisis was U.S.-centric and that the financial system and economy of the euro area would skate past the problems with relatively minor damage. Eventually, however, EUR/USD proved susceptible to the spreading crisis, with forced hedge fund liquidations causing unwinds of long EUR/USD positions and the realization that Europe would eventually be sucked into the vortex of skyrocketing financial losses and the grinding economic slowdown.

Long-Term Regression Model Analysis: Extremely Overvalued

As discussed in Chapter 4, EUR/USD had been persistently overvalued relative to the estimation of a long-term regression model that used the CPI ratio, 10-year bond spread, S&P 500, and the average of the U.S. and German 10-year yields. The persistent overvaluation likely stemmed partly from negativity about the U.S. dollar due to unpopular U.S. foreign policy that began building in December 2002 and seemed to peak with the reelection of George W. Bush in 2004. Additionally, concerns regarding the U.S. subprime mortgages had begun to grow beginning in 2005. As the subprime crisis broadened out and fears regarding the viability of the U.S. banking system began to surface, EUR/USD spiked further into overvalued territory. By March 2008, the currency pair had risen 5.7 standard deviations above the estimated fair value of 1.30. At 1.60, EUR/USD was as clearly and extraordinarily overvalued as it had been undervalued at 0.84 in 2000 during the height of the Internet equity bubble. (See **Figure 10.1**.)

Weekly, Inter-Market Regression: Identified Top, Hinted at Impending Sell-Off

As we mentioned at the beginning of the chapter, often by the time a currency has reached an extreme based on long-term relationships, the shorter-term investors and traders have adjusted and wonder why the policymakers have taken so long to "catch on" to the volatility. Indeed, by May, after EUR/USD had tested above

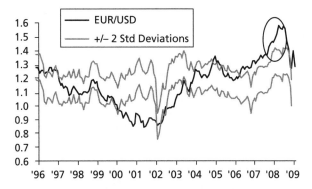

Figure 10.1   EUR/USD and Long-Term Regression Standard-Deviation Band

1.60, the weekly, inter-market regression analysis showed that the price action of EUR/USD was moving in tandem with other assets in the marketplace.

Specifically, the model as of May 2 attained an adjusted R-squared of 0.9672 using fifty-two weeks of weekly closing prices for the following variables: oil, the U.S. 2-year note yield, the German-U.S. 2-year note spread, and the German 10-year yield. The coefficients for oil, the U.S. 2-year yield, and the German-U.S. 2-year yield spread were all positive. The positive oil coefficient is consistent with U.S. dollar weakness being associated with higher commodity prices. The positive 2-year yield spread coefficient is consistent with a yield advantage accruing to a currency's advantage. The positive U.S. 2-year yield coefficient can be tied to the move away from U.S. assets, while the negative coefficient for the German 10-year yield is consistent with a move by investors towards safe, non-U.S. government bonds. The model indicated that while a price of 1.60 put the currency pair at the top of its 2 standard-deviation envelope, that price was not significantly overvalued. Thus, the model supported the notion that EUR/USD was topping but not the notion that it should correct substantially in the short term (which it didn't).

As EUR/USD remained in an elevated 1.50–1.60 trading range through August, the dynamics of the weekly model changed.

By August 8, when EUR/USD began collapsing, the model had shifted such that only oil from the May 2 model remained significant. The other variables in the equation now included the U.S. 3-month Libor yield; the EU less U.S. 3-month Libor yield spread; gold; and the S&P 500. The model signaled clearly that EUR/USD was overbought in April when the currency pair first tested 1.60, suggesting the rally would stall. The model estimate drifted higher through early August, indicating support for the currency pair continuing to range at very elevated levels. By August 8, the model estimate was beginning to decline, and although EUR/USD was collapsing faster, pushing the currency near the bottom of the 2 standard-deviation band, the currency was not significantly undervalued at the end of the model's time period.

Daily, Inter-Market Regression: Identified Top, Hinted at Impending Sell-Off

In Chapter 4, we detailed the change in the daily regression model between May 1 and November 1, 2008. Recall that as of May 1, the regression showed that gold, the 3-month Euribor yield, the U.S. 2-year yield, the average of the U.S. and German 10-year yields, and the S&P 500 exhibited a significant relation with EUR/USD. This model signaled that EUR/USD was overbought in late April when it tested 1.60 and pointed to the turn lower going into May. However, as of May 1, the correction in EUR/USD had brought it to the low end of the 2 standard-deviation band of the model, and the implied upside potential for the currency was realized in coming months. The model at the end of the consolidation period (August 8) reflects a moderate change in the significant variables. Gold, the S&P, and the U.S. 2-year yield remained significant. However, the 3-month Euribor was replaced by the U.S. 3-month Libor, and the average of the German and U.S. 10-year yields was replaced by the 2-year yield spread and oil. The model estimate peaked on July 15 at 1.5975 and began to trend lower towards the bottom of the sixty-day range by the beginning of August. However, the violence of the collapse in EUR/USD on August 8 (from a close of 1.5325 on August 7 to 1.5005) caused the currency to fall to more than 3 standard deviations below the estimated value.

Positioning/Sentiment: Mixed Signals

Positioning and sentiment analysis from the CFTC and risk reversals provided a "split decision." The non-commercial position deviation actually provided a buy signal, while the risk reversal deviation provided a sell signal.

The non-commercial community did not trust the rally beyond the 2004 high of 1.3666, let alone the spike to 1.60. That market segment had already begun paring back its long positions when EUR/USD traded above 1.3666 in 2007, and it actually shifted to a net short position as EUR/USD stabilized above 1.50. If any signal were indicated, the percent long measure of 43 percent in May 2008, which represented the lowest reading since November 2005, after EUR/USD had corrected to below 1.20 and resumed at its multi-year rally, would have suggested EUR/USD should go higher.

In contrast to the CFTC non-commercial positioning, the risk reversal did indicate an imminent move lower—or at least consolidation—in EUR/USD. Looking at the level of the risk reversal relative to the level of EUR/USD, one can see that options market participants, just like the non-commercial futures traders, began to pare back EUR-bullish positions as EUR/USD rallied in 2007 above the 2004 high of 1.3666. However, as EUR/USD spiked in early 2008, the risk reversal bottomed and traded positive (premium for calls) in May 2008. By July, the risk reversal had risen to +0.14, a high since September 2007, when the rally in EUR/USD stalled below 1.50, and such a risk reversal level could have been interpreted as a warning of a correction during mid-2008. Transforming the risk reversal and EUR/USD data to deviations from their 130-day moving averages would have provided an even stronger signal for an imminent correction in EUR/USD. By July 2008, the risk-reversal deviation had climbed to 0.65, the highest reading in data back to 2004.

Given the contradictory signals provided by the CFTC and risk reversal, one would have been conflicted, but the macroeconomic and regression analysis all suggested EUR/USD should at least not rally further or that it was extremely overvalued, and thus so far the analysis would have been leading towards a bearish stance for EUR/USD.

Technical Analysis: Bearish Signals

A variety of oscillator technical signals corroborated the other studies that warned of an impending move down in EUR/USD. The weekly RSI exhibited a negative divergence. That is, the indicator moved lower from overbought territory at the same time that the price action of EUR/USD was stable. This apparent loss of momentum—or lift—for EUR/USD signaled that the price action would imminently roll over. (See **Figure 10.2**.)

The weekly slow stochastics indicator provided a similar negative divergence, with the %DS and %DSS lines both moving below overbought territory (which is defined as stochastic readings above 70) as EUR/USD remained stable. Additionally, the slow

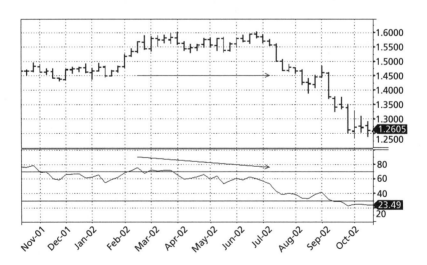

Figure 10.2   EUR/USD, Weekly, with RSI

Source: Bloomberg.

stochastics "crossed lower from overbought territory." More specifically, the %DS line crossed below the %DSS on August 1, the week before EUR/USD broke sharply lower out of its four-month trading range, and then both lines crossed below 70.

Finally, EUR/USD traced out very obvious bearish patterns. First, the 1.60 level proved to be a double-top. In other words, EUR/USD established a high just above 1.60, retreated, rallied to just above 1.60 a second time, and failed again. Especially when coupled with the falling RSI and the negative divergences on both the RSI and slow stochastics, aggressive market participants could have argued for entering short EUR/USD positions as early as July 15 at the close (1.5911). More conservative traders and investors would have waited for the price action to break out of the channel formation formed between roughly 1.53 and 1.60 during the April to August period, and established a short on the August 8 close of 1.5005.

Bottom Line for the EUR/USD Spike to 1.60

The analysis above shows that while not unanimous, the preponderance of the evidence from the high-level macroeconomics on down through the tactical positioning and technical analysis indicated that EUR/USD should have been sold between 1.50 and 1.60 on a medium- to long-term basis.

USD/CAD Bear Market Rally in 2004–2005

Our second case study involves the bear market rally experienced by USD/CAD from November 2004 to May 2005, in which USD/CAD rose ten big figures from 1.17 to 1.27 in the course of a seventy–big figure bear market (1.60 to 0.90) that spanned almost six years (2002–2007). In September 2004, USD/CAD was moving sharply lower, breaching below the 1.2682 low established in January of that year to establish a new low since 1993. The breach to a multi-year low caused the move to accelerate, and USD/CAD had broken below 1.20 by mid-November. At this point, USD/ CAD stalled for roughly three weeks before beginning a six-month rally. Below we will discuss the analysis that would have been undertaken in November 2004 and would have allowed investors and traders to have scaled back on their short positions, moved to the sidelines altogether, or even established long positions.

Long-Term Regression Model Analysis: Signaled Start but Not End of Rally

The long-term, fair-value regression model for USD/CAD (see **Figure 10.3**) is based on the consumer price index ratio between the United States and Canada, the spread between the countries' 10-year government bond yields, the Bank of Canada's energy

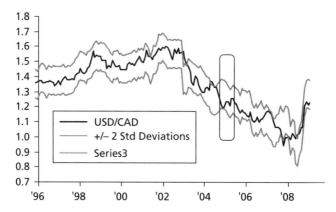

Figure 10.3   USD/CAD and Confidence Bands from Long-Term Regression Model

Source: Data from Bloomberg; calculations by T. J. Marta.

and non-energy price indexes, and a variable that accounts for a structural break (U.S. dollar–negative) due to the impact of unpopular U.S. foreign policy after late 2002. This model achieved an adjusted R-squared of 0.92 and a standard error of 4.6 big figures. USD/CAD was undervalued by more than 2 standard deviations only once during the USD/CAD bear market, at least until the very end of the bear market in late 2008. The one month when the currency pair registered significantly undervalued was November 2004, when USD/CAD closed the month at 1.1874, 2.1 standard deviations below the model's fair value of 1.29. Subsequently, USD/CAD rallied to close May 2005 at 1.2548, less than 0.03 standard deviations away from the estimated fair value.

Weekly, Inter-Market Regression: Signaled Start but Not End of Rally

When the USD/CAD bear market rally began in November, the weekly model based on the preceding fifty-two weeks of weekly closing data provided little warning that it was about to begin, as the currency closed at 1.1775, well within the 2 standard-deviation band of the model. The model provided a relatively good fit (adjusted R-squared of 0.9154) and was based on three variables: the *JoC* base metals index, Canadian 3-month Libor yield, and U.S. less Canadian 2-year yield spread. As would be expected, the coefficients for both base metals and the Canadian Libor yield were negative as increases in both were bullish for the Canadian dollar (and so bearish for USD/CAD). The coefficient for the 2-year yield spread was positive, consistent with the notion that yield advantage helps a currency. The model was able to signal the top and bottom of the choppy price action at the beginning of the period from December 2003 and January 2004 and caught the peak in price action during May along with the turn lower through to November. However, at the very end of the period, the model had begun to turn higher as base metals and the Canadian Libor yield peaked while the U.S.-Canadian 2-year yield spread consolidated. Consequently, when USD/CAD closed at 1.1775 on November 26, it was 2.16 standard deviations below the model estimate, signaling at least a temporary end to the move down.

As the rally drew to a close on May 20, 2005, USD/CAD closed at the upper part of the 2 standard-deviation range estimated by the regression model at that time but was not significantly over-valued (z-score of 1.36). The model for the period was simpler, with only two significant variables, base metals and Canadian 3-month Libor yield, but its adjusted R-squared remained high at 0.9176. This model provided no evidence regarding the potential for the downtrend in USD/CAD to resume.

Daily, Inter-Market Regression: No Signal for Start or End of Rally

Despite the strong bullish signal provided by the long-term fair-value model, the shorter-term model showed no valuation problems. The short-term model was based on sixty days of daily closing data for six variables: the Canadian 3-month yield, the U.S.-Canadian 2-year government note yield spread, the U.S. 10-year government note yield, the U.S.-Canadian 10-year government note yield spread, the price of crude oil, and the level of the *JoC* industrial metals price index. The adjusted R-squared of the model was 0.97. During the sixty-day period of the model, USD/CAD had moved to or below the bottom of the 2 standard deviation envelope three times, and in each case USD/CAD consolidated before resuming its downtrend. However, in late November, the model showed that USD/CAD lay practically in the middle of its range, providing no inkling that the price would soon rally sharply.

By the time the rally peaked on May 16, 2005, the optimized daily model had shifted significantly, and the descriptive power had fallen from an adjusted R-squared of 0.97 to 0.84. The base metals index was no longer significant, although oil remained. The U.S. 10-year yield was significant and negatively signed, perhaps reflecting the effect of cross-border capital flows. In any event, USD/CAD ended the period only moderately overvalued; the z-score at the close on May 16 was only 1.34, with the actual close of 1.2694 versus a model estimate of 1.2601. The daily regression provided little warning that the rally in USD/CAD was over.

Positioning/Sentiment: Signaled the Rally and Its End

Both the CFTC position and risk-reversal data provided strong bullish signals in November 2004 and bearish signals in May 2005.

The net long, non-commercial CFTC position for CAD reached 49,000 contracts in October 2004, a record in data back to 2000, and thus a very bullish signal for USD/CAD. Note that by the time the rally ended at 1.27 in May 2005, the net position had swung to the opposite extreme—negative 33,500, thus suggesting the rally was over.

The detrending of the CFTC data by measuring the percentage of long non-commercial contracts to overall non-commercial positions and the deviation of USD/CAD from its 26-week moving average provided a similar, strongly bullish signal for USD/CAD. In September 2004, the percent long position had reached 90 percent and remained in the high 80s through mid-October as the deviation for USD/CAD from its trend reached 8.6 big figures, among the ten widest deviations back to 2000. As to the end of the rally, the percent long measure again signaled a change was imminent, as percentage fell to 19 percent, a low since 2003.

The 3-month, 25-delta risk-reversal data showed very similar, very strong bullish signals for USD/CAD in November 2004. The risk reversal had dropped to −0.375, the most extreme skew in favor of USD/CAD puts since January of 2004, when the foreign-exchange rate had begun a fourteen–big figure bear market rally from 1.26 to 1.40 that spanned four months. By the time that previous rally had ended, the risk reversal had risen to 0.075, and the result of the November 2004 to May 2005 rally was similar: the risk reversal rose to 0.075. Consequently, the risk-reversal data provided strong signals that the price trend was about to reverse.

The detrending of the risk-reversal and foreign-exchange data by measuring their deviations from their 130-day moving averages provides a similar signal (see **Figure 10.4**). In November 2004, the risk-reversal deviation had fallen to a record 0.29 below trend. At the same time, USD/CAD had dropped to almost eleven big figures below trend, a low since June 2003, just before USD/CAD rallied almost nine big figures in less than two months. By May 2005, the risk-reversal deviation had risen to +0.18, an eleven-month high. While the deviation had gone higher early in 2004 (+0.496), the +0.18 reading should have been enough to raise at least some degree of caution.

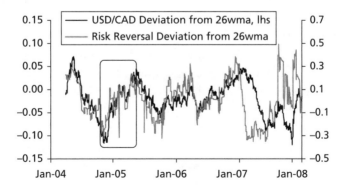

Figure 10.4   USD/CAD and Risk Reversal: Deviations from Trend

Technical Analysis: Oscillators Caught Move; Trend Following of More Limited Help

The first oscillator we look at is the weekly slow stochastics. Remember that it is composed of %DS and %DSS lines and that we are looking for their levels (above 70–75 is overbought and below 25–30 is oversold) and also the relationship of the two lines (%DS above [below] %DSS is bullish [bearish]). On November 19, 2004, the %DS line fell to 1.41, a low for the series back to 2000 (and also subsequently). Of the prior four occasions that the DS% fell below 10, the subsequent cross higher of the DS% over the DSS% line corresponded with a bear-market rally of nine to fourteen big figures over two to four months. Consequently, the low reading on November 19 and the subsequent cross higher on December 3 provided a very strong, clear buy signal. As to the end of the rally in May, the %DS line crossed above 70 the week of May 13, 2005, an overbought signal, although the outright sell signal—%DS cross below %DSS—did not occur until the week of June 17.

A second oscillator study, the RSI, provided similar signals. The weekly RSI dropped below 20 during only three periods over the course of the nearly six-year decline in USD/CAD. On the first two occasions, the low reading presaged significant bear-market rallies of nine and ten big figures over two and six months. The third occasion was the last spike lower of USD/CAD to the record low of 0.9058 registered in November 2007. During the week of November 26, 2004, the RSI dropped below 20, a clearly oversold signal. As to signaling the end of the rally, the RSI reached 57.18, a high since May 2004, when the previous bear-market rally had ended. Now, generally a reading above 70 is required to acknowledge a bearish reversal signal. However, in a persistent downtrend, the RSI rarely gets to 70, and so within the context of a multi-year downtrend, the 57.18 reading should have at least indicated investors and traders should be cautious about the continued rally.

We looked at two trend-following measures for this period: a moving-average cross and the ADX. A 13- and 52-week moving average cross rule lags so completely that it missed the entire move.

Shortening the moving average rule to a 15- and 45-day cross still got into the position late (December 20 at 1.2289) and then got whipsawed as the price action traded with the uptrending channel pattern. The ADX provided a better warning of both the start and end of the rally. The ADX reached a one-year high of 36.00 the week ending December 3, suggesting that the trend had run its course and might stall. By July 1, 2005, six weeks after the bear-market rally had actually ended, the ADX had dropped to a nearly one-year low of 15.18, suggesting a heightened risk that the bear-market rally was finished and the downtrend would resume.

Bottom-Line for the USD/CAD November 2004 to May 2005 Bear-Market Rally

The long-term fair-value regression, positioning, and technical oscillators all provided strong bullish signals that presented a near-unanimous buy recommendation in November 2004. Only the short-term fair-value regression failed to provide a corroborating signal, although it merely provided a neutral—not conflicting—reading. None of the analysis we would have performed at the time would have indicated that we should not have at least protected our short USD/CAD positions if we did not also establish long exposure. The end of the rally was less obvious from our analysis. None of the fair-value regressions indicated that USD/CAD was overbought. However, the positioning and technical analyses both indicated the situation had gone too far. There was enough warning that anyone who had taken advantage of the rally should have been looking to at least protect profits.

AUD/USD Bottoming around 0.5000 from March 2001 to January 2003

Our third case study involves the bottoming AUD/USD established in March 2001, the resulting consolidation phase, and the eventual break higher in January 2003. After falling sharply during the Asian crisis of 1998, AUD/USD managed a modest rally during 1999, along with risk assets generally (and the dot-com bubble particularly), but then faltered and established new lows as the Internet bubble burst. With the United States slipping into recession in March 2001, AUD/USD fell even further to a record low 0.4775 in the first week of April and retested that level on safe-haven flows to the U.S. dollar in the wake of 9/11. Subsequently, AUD/USD managed to grind higher, but it could not break above 0.5700–0.5750 resistance for good until January 2003.

Long-Term, Regression-Model Analysis: Captures Bottoming for AUD/USD, but Does Not Show Undervaluation

The long-term, fair-value regression model for AUD/USD is based on the CPI ratio between Australia and the United States (relatively high CPI wearing down a currency), the spread between the countries' 10-year government bond yields (yield advantage benefiting a currency), the *JoC*'s base metals index (A$ as a commodity

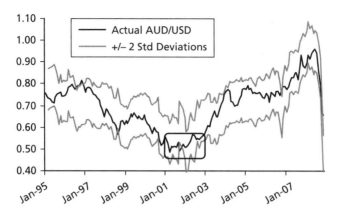

Figure 10.5   AUD/USD and Confidence Bands from Long-Term Regression Model

currency), and the U.S. 3-month Libor yield (higher yields consistent with stronger global growth, which is A$-positive). This model achieved an adjusted R-squared of 0.82 and a standard error of 0.0471. (See **Figure 10.5**.)

The long-term model's estimation of the bottoming phase for AUD/USD can be explained as either "good news" or "bad news." The good news is that the model proved robust enough to describe most of the bottoming process. The model estimate did spike in the immediate aftermath of 9/11 due to a spike in U.S. inflation during September and October, but that effect was temporary and the model normalized. Further "good news" is that because the model estimate was robust, an accurate assessment of the outlook for the explanatory variables would have yielded a profitable outlook for AUD/USD. The "bad news" is that because of the model's robustness in capturing the bottom, AUD/USD never appeared significantly undervalued.

Weekly, Inter-Market Regression: Moved Lower with Foreign Exchange at Bottom, Moved Higher with Spot at Breakout

The fifty-two-week model regressed on the April 6, 2001, record low close provided a decent description of the price action during the period, attaining an adjusted R-squared of 0.83. The significant variables were the S&P 500, the price of gold, the price of oil, and the Australian less U.S. 3-month yield spread. The coefficients for the S&P 500 and gold were positive, which is also not surprising given that (1) both the Australian dollar and the S&P 500 are both considered "risk assets" and (2) the Australian dollar's reputation as a gold currency. The yield spread coefficient was positive, consistent with a yield advantage helping a currency. Only the coefficient for the price of oil was counterintuitively signed (negative). The model estimate managed to capture the move lower through 2000, including the rallies in May to June 2000 and November 2000 to January 2001.

AUD/USD failed to gain any appreciable ground until January 2003, when it was finally able to close above 0.5750 for the first time since August 2000. The week ending January 10, 2003, AUD/USD closed at 0.5835. The model regressed for the fifty-two weeks up to January 10 was highly significant (adjusted R-squared of 0.934) and contained five variables: the S&P 500, *JoC* base metals index, gold, and the Australian less U.S. 3-month Libor yield spread. The model was able to describe the January to June 2002 rally, the June 21 peak and subsequent decline, and the final rally of the period that began in August of 2002. As of January 10, 2003, AUD/USD was trading above the model estimate, but not above the 2 standard-deviation band. While no oversold condition was signaled, the model was trending higher and supported the price action.

Daily, Inter-Market Regression: Corroborated Move Lower, Signaled Against 2003 Break Higher

The daily, inter-market regression for AUD using 60 days of daily data as of April 2, 2001, when AUD/USD bottomed at 0.4789 (closing basis), achieved an adjusted R-squared of 0.96 using four independent variables: gold, the Australian 3-month yield, the U.S. 10-year yield, and the S&P 500. The positive coefficients for gold, the Australian 3-month yield, and the S&P 500 are intuitive in light of the Australian dollar's reputation as a gold currency and the notions that higher Australian yields should support the currency and that higher equity prices are consistent with stronger growth currencies like the Australian dollar. The negative coefficient for the U.S. 10-year yield is consistent with investor appetite for U.S. Treasuries being a drain on risk currencies. The model estimate managed to catch not only general downtrend for AUD/USD during the period, but also when that downtrend might stall (January 22, February 13, and March 15) or resume (February 2, March 2, and March 19). However, the model estimate did not signal that AUD/USD was significantly undervalued when it bottomed on April 2.

By January 10, 2003, AUD/USD had convincingly broken above 0.5750 resistance and was moving higher. The daily model at that stage had an adjusted R-squared of 0.71 and relied on four variables: gold, *JoC* base metals index, S&P 500, and the Australian 3-month Libor yield. The coefficients for gold, base metals, and the S&P 500 were all positive, as would be expected. That for the Australian 3-month yield was negative, perhaps as lower rates were perceived as supportive of growth. In early January, AUD/USD had rallied significantly. While the rally was supported by a spike in base metal prices, the foreign exchange move outpaced the model estimate, and so AUD/USD closed January 10 more than 2 standard deviations above the estimated value. This misvaluation could have been interpreted as a sell signal, although the fact that the model estimates had clearly begun to rise in early January might have suggested that the rally would merely consolidate and not actually retrace.

Positioning/Sentiment: Warned of Bottom, Hinted at Correction Instead of the Breakout

The risk-reversal data are not available prior to October 2003, at least from Bloomberg. The CFTC position data provided no warning of the bottom or the eventual breakout that took place.

- The net short, non-commercial CFTC position had fallen to a significant, if not extreme, net short of 3,132 contracts in April 2001, just after AUD/USD bottomed. In January 2003, the non-commercial position was overweight, actually signaling the potential for a correction rather than a breakout higher. In December 2002, the non-commercial net long had risen to over 17,000 contracts, a high since mid-2002 when AUD/USD had corrected from over 0.57 to 0.53. That extreme net long level, in combination with the paring back of the position towards 11,373 contracts by January 10, 2003, would have suggested that AUD/USD should retrace.

- The detrending of the CFTC data by using the net long percentage for the CFTC position provided similar signals. In late March and again in early April, the net long percentage fell to 0.26, while AUD/USD fell to below 0.49 (weekly closing basis)—well below the 26-week moving average of around 0.53. Regarding the January 2003 period, the data provided a very clear signal, with the net long percentage rising to 99.9 percent.

Technical Analysis: Oscillators Signaled Bottom, but Not Breakout; Trend Followers Warned of Bottom and Breakout

The slow stochastics oscillator indicator provided a strong warning that AUD/USD had bottomed in April 2001, but provided a mixed message as to the eventual breakout in January 2003. By the week of March 30, 2001, the %DS line had dropped below 30 (an oversold reading), and the slower moving %DSS line dropped below 30 the following week. By April 27, the %DS line had crossed above the %DSS line, confirming a move higher. As to January 2003, the %DS and %DSS lines were both over 70, suggesting that AUD/USD was overbought. Conflicting with this reading was the crossover rule for the %DS–%DSS lines, in which %DS greater (less) than %DSS is considered bullish (bearish). At the time of the breakout higher in January 2003, the crossover rule remained bullish, thus offsetting the overbought reading deriving from the 70+ readings.

The RSI oscillator provided a strong oversold signal in March 2001, but registered overbought during the January 2003 breakout. The week of March 30, 2001, the RSI fell below 30, a clear signal that AUD/USD was extremely oversold. As AUD/USD stabilized, the RSI moved back into the 30–70 "neutral" range, albeit with a slight upward drift. By January 10, 2003, the RSI moved above 70, suggesting the currency pair was overbought, exactly the wrong signal for the rally that ensued.

As to trend following, 13- and 52-week moving average crossover rule, with its long lag, benefited from the long consolidation period AUD/USD traded in 2001. The 13-week moving average remained below the 52-week moving average until January 2002, nine months after AUD/USD reached the April 2001 low. Consequently, the moving average cross switched from short to long when AUD/USD closed 0.5167, not giving up much ground (from a long-term perspective) on the short signal from the 0.4775, and getting into a long position much earlier than the eventual break higher at 0.5835 in January 2003. The DMI/ADX indicator was similarly most helpful in calling an early end to the consolidation that occurred after the April 2001 bottom. In 2000 and 2001, as AUD/USD trended lower, the ADX increased to reflect the growing downtrend. The ADX actually peaked at 40.43 in November 2000 when AUD/USD closed at 0.5235. Even as AUD/USD tested below 0.5000 during the next year, the ADX began to drop off, reflecting the stall in the downtrend. By March 1, 2002, the ADX had dropped to 8.61, a low in data back to 1998, and this would have suggested that the consolidation was nearing an end. At the same time, the +DMI had crossed above the −DMI, indicating the breakout would be to the upside.

Bottom Line for the AUD/USD March 2001 to January 2003 Bottom

For the most part, the move lower in AUD/USD to April 2001, consolidation through January 2003, and subsequent rally were all gentle enough and persistent enough that the long-term regression and trend-following technical analyses outperformed

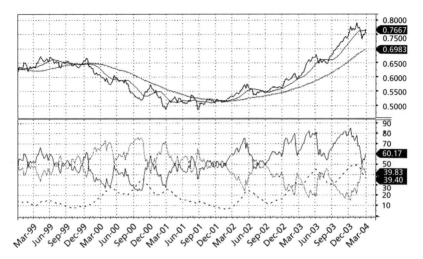

Figure 10.6   AUD/USD with Moving-Average Crossover and DMI/ADX Indicators

Source: Bloomberg.

position/sentiment indicators and technical oscillators, which are contrarian in nature (See **Figure 10.6**.).

As to the bottom in March, the long-term regression model was able to adapt to the slowly evolving price developments and so captured the loss of momentum for the downtrend. The weekly and daily inter-market regressions both corroborated the move lower in AUD/USD, but failed to register oversold signals. The CFTC non-commercial positioning did provide warning that AUD/USD was bottoming in March and April 2001. The technical analysis oscillators—both the slow stochastics and the relative strength indexes—also managed to signal strong oversold conditions. The one trend-following signal that warned of a potential end to the downtrend was ADX, which suggested the momentum had been waning since November 2000. In total, the evidence from our analysis did not provide an urgent signal that AUD/USD had bottomed in early 2001, but movements of regression variables and the oversold technical indicators at least pointed to the loss of power to the downtrend, consistent with the nearly two-year consolidation that followed.

Identifying the breakout of the bottoming range in January 2003 was more problematic if only because breaking out of a range usually pushes technical and positioning oscillators into overbought (or oversold) territory. The RSI and the slow stochastics were both in overbought territory in January 2003, as was the CFTC non-commercial net long position. However, the trend-following indexes and the moving-average crossover had presented a bullish signal, and the ADX had reached an extremely low level suggesting a trend was about to begin. The daily inter-market regression model also suggested that AUD/USD at least needed to consolidate, as the currency rally had outpaced moves in the explanatory variables. The slower moving weekly and monthly regression models were able to keep pace and corroborate the notion that AUD/USD's rally was rationally based. Overall, the analysis for January 2003 suggested that AUD/USD's move higher would continue, but that it would likely suffer a short-term consolidation or pullback in order to allow some of the overextension in some indicators to moderate. AUD/USD's rally did grind at a slower pace in coming weeks, taking until mid-March 2003 to finally breach 0.6000.

GBP/USD Spike and Overvaluation from November 2004 through May 2005

In November 2004, President George W. Bush won reelection in a very tight race. Historically, the election of an incumbent president is generally bullish for the U.S. dollar. However, the controversy of U.S. foreign policy in the wake of the 9/11 attacks, along with rising concerns regarding the U.S. twin deficits, had caused the international community to sell the U.S. dollar. Consequently, when Bush won reelection, the international community held its own "vote," selling the U.S. dollar in torrents such that the U.S. dollar index closed down 0.9 percent the day after the election, among the 5 percent most extreme daily price moves between January 2000 and December 2004. The U.S. dollar selling continued, and within weeks, GBP/USD climbed to test 1.95 and held a 1.85–1.95 range until May 2005.

Long-Term, Regression-Model Analysis: Captured Spike That Put GBP/USD into Overvalued Territory

The long-term model for GBP/USD we created is based on six significant variables: the ratio of UK to U.S. CPI inflation rates, the UK 10-year yield, the U.S. 3-month Libor yield, the differentials for the 3-month Libor and 2-year note yields, and the

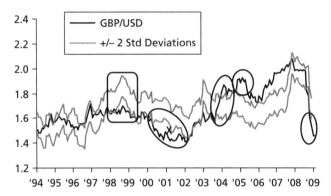

Figure 10.7   GBP/USD and 2 Standard-Deviation Bands of Long-Term Regression-Model Estimate

price of oil. The model has an adjusted R-squared of 0.89 and a standard error of 0.04. **Figure 10.7** illustrates the fit of the estimate.

Particularly noteworthy are the periods during which the model failed to describe the actual price action very well. GBP was clearly weighted in 1998 during the run-up to the advent of the euro and again in 2000 and 2001, due first to the Internet bubble and then to a sharp rise in U.S. dollar–denominated corporate debt issuance. In 2003 and 2004, the weights of foreign policy as well as the current account and budget deficits on the U.S. dollar were readily apparent, with GBP/USD trading from the bottom to the top of the estimated range. Beginning in 2006, the U.S. dollar began to suffer further on concerns that subprime mortgages would harm the U.S. economy. However, by late 2008, the investment community realized that the world was not decoupled from the U.S. crisis, and GBP/USD became significantly undervalued as investors worried about the solvency of UK banks and the United Kingdom itself.

The rest of this chapter focuses on the November 2004 to May 2005 period when GBP/USD spiked well above the range estimated by the long-term regression model. From November 1, 2004, through the end of the year, GBP/USD spiked from 1.83

to 1.95. However, during that same time, oil fell from $50 to $43 a barrel, the UK 3-month yield advantage narrowed more than 40bp, and the 2-year yield advantage narrowed 60bp. Consequently, despite a GBP-supportive rise in the U.S. 3-month yield and decline in the UK 10-year yield, the estimated value for GBP/USD fell from 1.74 at the end of October 2004 to 1.70 by December 31. Even when the spot rate began to correct in February 2005 and fell to 1.59 by October, it did not fall fast enough to bring it back within 2 standard deviations of the estimated value. The long-term regression estimate for GBP/USD clearly signaled that the currency pair was overvalued.

Weekly, Inter-Market Regression:
No Warning of Break Higher;
Warned of Consolidation After Decline in May

The 52-week regression for GBP/USD as of October 29, 2004, provided a poor description of price action. The regression was based on three variables, the 3-month Libor yield spread, the S&P 500, and oil, but achieved an adjusted R-squared of only 0.54. The model did support the move higher in late 2003/early 2004 and also captured the range trading that occurred from January through October of 2004. However, as of October 29, the model showed no signs of the spike in GBP/USD that developed in November and December 2004.

By May 27, 2005, the weekly inter-market regression had shifted considerably. There were four significant variables, only one of which was present in the model for October 29, 2004: the S&P 500. The other variables included the 2-year and 10-year note yield spreads and the U.S. 3-month Libor yield. The model's adjusted R-squared was 0.61. It managed to capture the late 2004 spike and some of the subsequent drift lower in GBP/USD. However, by the end of May, the actual spot price was moving lower at a faster pace and the model was suggesting that GBP/USD was bordering on being 2 standard deviations undervalued. The suggestion of GBP/USD being undervalued by the model did presage the consolidation that occurred over the next four weeks.

Daily, Inter-Market Regression: Supported Late November Rise, the Topping and Sell-Off Through May, and Eventual Consolidation

The sixty-day, daily inter-market regression as of November 23, 2004, corroborated the move higher during the period. The model was based on four variables, the UK 3-month Libor, the UK less U.S. 3-month Libor yield spread, oil, and the S&P 500, and it achieved an adjusted R-squared of 0.87. The model's ability to trend upward during the rally supported continued strength in GBP/USD, although it failed to provide a warning of the steepness of the spike during the remainder of 2004.

On December 20, 2004, GBP/USD closed at what eventually proved to be an intermediate top of 1.9467. The daily, inter-market model at this point was based on three variables (oil, S&P 500, and U.S. 3-month Libor yield) and achieved an adjusted R-squared of 0.93. The model captured the overall uptrend from early October. However, the spike from 1.87 in late November to 1.94 by December 6 took the actual spot price from the bottom to the top of the 2 standard-deviation envelope. By December 10, the model estimate had begun to level off, suggesting that "fair value" lay between 1.90 and 1.96, supportive of the view that GBP/USD had reached a top.

By May 16, GBP/USD had broken below the 1.85–1.95 range it had traded since November. The daily, inter-market model at this point was based on five variables (S&P 500, the U.S. 3-month Libor yield, the UK 2- and 10-year yields, and the UK less U.S. 2-year yield spread) and achieved an adjusted R-squared of 0.70. The model estimate had started to trend lower during March, presaging the late March sell-off in GBP/USD, and also trended lower beginning in late April, supporting the move lower in GBP/USD during that period. However, by May 16, the spot price had moved down too sharply and registered as 2.2 standard deviations undervalued, suggesting the subsequent consolidation in price action that occurred through late June.

Positioning/Sentiment: Supported Rise from November to December 2004; Warned of Top in December 2004; Warned of Consolidation in July 2005

- The net long, non-commercial CFTC position as GBP/USD broke above 1.80 in October switched from a net short to a net long position. By the week of November 26, the net long position had grown to a record 33,000 contracts and continued to grind higher to a high of 38,000 contracts for the week of December 17. The percentage of long non-commercial contracts to the total non-commercial contracts shifted similarly, from 43 percent in October (a low since August 2003) to 95 percent by December 17. These shifts fully supported the powerful move higher by spot, but they also provided a strong warning that GBP/USD was overbought and needed to consolidate and eventually correct, as it did over the next five months. By July, when GBP/USD had collapsed back below 1.75, the non-commercial position had shifted to a record net short position of −22,000 contracts and the net long percentage had collapsed to 23 percent, again supportive of the move lower, but also a warning of the need for the price action to at least consolidate, which it did for almost a year.

Risk Reversals: Supported Spike; Warned of Top, Supported Move Lower in May and Consolidation after July

- The risk-reversal skew as GBP/USD broke above 1.80 in October shifted from −0.1 (in favor of puts) on October 15 to +0.25 by November 5. By December 10, when GBP/USD closed at 1.9147, the skew had risen to +0.45, a high since February 2004 when GBP/USD peaked before falling back to 1.75 by May 2004. The +0.45 risk reversal skew proved to represent the peak for the risk reversal during the November 2004 to May 2005 period. By mid-May, as GBP/USD fell below the 1.85–1.95 range it had held since November, the risk-reversal skew slipped to -0.2, an extreme in data back to October 2003. By July, when GBP/USD had fallen all the way below 1.75, the risk reversal had established a new record low of -0.5.

Using the deviations of GBP/USD and the risk reversal from their 130-day moving averages provides a similar description of the market sentiment and price action. As GBP/USD broke above 1.80 in October 2004, the deviation in the risk reversal shifted from negative to positive, and by the time GBP/USD spiked to 1.95 in December, the risk-reversal deviation had spiked to a record high 0.399, which provided a very strong warning of an end to the spike in the currency pair. As GBP/USD leveled off in the following months, the risk-reversal deviation moderated and turned negative. By July, the risk-reversal deviation had followed the collapse in the currency price by dropping to a record -0.47, which highlighted the potential for GBP/USD to at least consolidate, if not rally.

Technical Analysis: Oscillators Supported Spike, Warned of Top; Trend Followers Late / Inconsistent

The weekly slow stochastics study failed to cross into oversold territory, meaning neither the %DS nor the %DSS fell below 30. Consequently, it did not provide a clear rally signal for GBP. However, the %DS did drop to 34.83 and then cross above the %DSS line on the week ended October 29 with GBP/USD at 1.8372. The upward signal continued even as the %DS and %DSS crossed above 70 (into overbought territory) by December 2004, providing a clear warning of a consolidation or correction in GBP/USD. The %DS and %DSS lines dropped below 70 by February 2005 and continued trending lower. When GBP/USD fell below 1.85 in May, the stochastics continued to decline. By June, both lines had crossed below 30 (thus into oversold territory), and by July, when GBP/USD had fallen below 1.75, the stochastics were clearly oversold and beginning to stabilize, suggesting the consolidation that actually developed during the ensuing months.

The weekly RSI was trending upward during October, consistent with the rise of GBP/USD. It continued higher until December 3, when it peaked in overbought territory at 73, suggesting the currency pair rally would stall and/or reverse. The RSI began to trend lower as the price action drifted lower in coming months. It did not register oversold (below 30) until July as GBP/USD was testing below 1.75.

The trend-following rule of the 13-/52-week moving-average crossover lagged the move. It crossed higher the week ending November 26, when GBP/USD first tested above 1.90. However, it did not cross lower until June 2005, when GBP/USD had already closed below 1.85.

The weekly directional movement indicator, DMI/ADX, provided reasonable warnings of the start of the move higher in November 2004 as well as the potential for a move lower in May 2005, although it did little to help warn of the top near 1.95. In November, the ADX had dropped to below 20, the lowest level since May 2002, just before GBP/USD broke from 1.45 to above 1.55 in three months. The positive DMI was above the negative DMI, suggesting the break would be to the topside, which is what ensued. By November, the ADX had topped out at a fairly neutral reading of 27, providing little support for short positioning. The ADX continued to grind lower as GBP/USD range traded in coming months. By May, it had fallen to 15.84, strongly suggesting a breakout for price action, and the −DMI was above the +DMI, suggesting the move would be to the downside, which is what happened over the course of the next two months.

Bottom Line for the GBP/USD During November 2004 to May 2005 Spike

The long-term regression, fair-value estimate provided a clear indication that the late 2004 price action was highly aberrational and that, even after the correction in May 2005, further weakness was warranted into 2006. The weekly, inter-market regression models missed the spike in late November, but managed to signal in May 2005 that the sharp fall in GBP/USD needed to abate. The daily, inter-market regression models had managed to capture the initial uptrend, the topping of price action in December, declines through May, and the need for consolidation in May. The positioning and sentiment indicators, both the CFTC non-commercial positions and the 3-month, 25-delta risk reversals, moved in concert with the spike in November and December 2004 as well as the collapses in both May and July 2005. Additionally, they provided a clear overbought signal in December 2004 that warned of a top and a clear oversold signal in July 2005 that warned of a bottom. The technical analysis signals did not provide uniform indicators of imminent price action, but by employing various tools, signals could be extracted. For instance, in late October, the slow stochastic crossed higher and the RSI dropped to an oversold level with a bullish bias. In December, as GBP/USD peaked around 1.95, both the slow stochastics and RSIs had moved into extremely overbought territory. In May, the break lower in GBP/USD below the 1.85–1.95 range was signaled by the ADX, which had fallen to an extreme low that indicated a trend would begin, and the +DMI, which was below the −DMI, signaled a move to the downside. By July, when GBP/USD had taken another tumble lower to below 1.75, the relative strength index and slow stochastics both registered severely oversold conditions.

Conclusion

The examples in this section provide an overview of how an analyst, investor, and/or trader might apply the various analytical techniques—macroeconomic, inter-market, positioning, and technical analysis—in order to provide a better, stronger rationale for either initiating, lightening up on, or exiting currency exposure. There is no single, exact formulation for how the different analytical techniques fit together, any more than there is any single, exact formulation for how to apply any one of the techniques over time. However, by deploying the wide range of tools, one can better determine the extent to which a variety of views of the data support an investment and/or trading position.

CONCLUSION

We wrote this book with two goals in mind. The first was to provide an overview of the various disciplines a strategist can deploy in analyzing major foreign currencies, from high-level PPP and productivity considerations, to the issue of relative business cycles along with monetary and fiscal policy impacts, to global financial flows and inter-market correlations, and finally to the tactical level of technical and positioning analysis. Our second goal was to show that the different disciplines are best employed not in isolation but rather in concert with one another. Usually a variety of influences have an impact on price actions, and one must be able to discern which elements are relevant at any given time and then how the significant ones interact with each other and the currency price. Recognition of the various analytical disciplines will allow one at least to ask the right questions, while a proficiency will lead to optimal investment decisions. Additionally, foreign-exchange strategists collaborate with many different types of individuals of the course of a career, and having the broadest possible appreciation of how different people look at the currency markets will enable one to connect with and provide the most value to the broadest universe of clients— whether internal to your organization or external.

As to the various disciplines or paradigms we considered, think of the analogy of trying to zoom in on a particular house somewhere on the Earth from outer space. First we would start with a high-level view of the globe, which would provide overall context. Then we might home in on a particular continent, trading some scope for granularity. We would then zoom closer on a country, then a region, closer to a city, on downward to a section, then a neighborhood, then a street, and finally the particular house. By starting with a consideration of PPP and concluding with a focus on technical analysis, the analyst is able to establish a view or position that takes best advantage of all the considerations for an investment. By looking at the big picture, one is unlikely to establish a position counter to the desires of a currency's policymakers, while by looking at the tactical picture one can avoid entering a position at a time when the short-term momentum is moving in the opposite direction—which could make holding the position prohibitively costly and painful.

There might be certain periods when a currency trades based on very high–level macroeconomic and/or political considerations, such as when a currency pair reaches an extreme PPP valuation, prompting strong remarks or actions from policymakers that focus market participants' attention on those factors. The 1985 Plaza Accord—an agreement between France, West Germany, Japan, the United Kingdom, and the United States to cause the U.S. dollar to depreciate versus the yen and mark—and the Louvre Accord of 1987—the agreement to stop the U.S. dollar devaluation—both stemmed from such considerations. Subsequently, the Japanese policymakers have been the most active among developed countries in intervening in the foreign-exchange markets, although euro strength has precipitated intermittent expressions of concern from European leaders. China's government has been the most active in foreign-exchange interventions in recent years, tightly controlling the daily-trading ranges of currencies in order to control the trading band of their currency, the yuan. In late 2008 and early 2009, the U.S. dollar came under pressure due to concerns that the massive fiscal and monetary stimulus policymakers in the United States were undertaking would be endurable only if it was "inflated away" or monetized by the creation of more U.S. dollars.

Alternatively, the relative growth outlook might dominate price action, especially when the economic cycles are out of sync. Part of the U.S. dollar's decline from 2005 to 2008 stemmed from the notion that prospects for growth in the United States were declining due to the overleveraging of U.S. consumers, along with the belief that the problems were U.S.-centric and that the rest of the world would decouple from the U.S. economy. However, subsequently, part of the dollar's rise in late 2008 derived from the realization that while the U.S. economy was among the first to slow under the weight of the deleveraging crisis, the world economy had at best de-synchronized—but not completely decoupled—from the U.S. economy.

At times, the drivers are less "big picture" in nature. For example, inter-market relationships, such as those with equities, bonds, gold, oil, or base metals, often exhibit a much stronger correlation with the price of a currency. The Canadian dollar is often characterized as an "oil" currency, although for varying periods, it has proved to be more of a "tech stock" currency (2000), a natural gas currency (2005 in the wake of Hurricane Katrina), and a base metal currency. During the early 2000s, the euro was characterized as a "bond" currency due to its decline during the Internet boom when bonds lagged, but as the euro eventually rebounded along with stocks, the value of the euro was correlated more strongly with the price of oil and interest-rate spreads. The Australian dollar and Swiss franc are both sometimes referred to as "gold" currencies, and while the correlations between gold and the two have generally been strongly positive, there have also been extended periods when the correlations have moved to strongly negative. The key in this regard is to be aware of the possible drivers of price action and know which of those drivers are exhibiting strong correlations at any given time.

At other times, value is determined by the often subjective whim of human sentiment and emotion. Excessive buying by one or more market segments—we looked at the options and futures non-commercial segments—can suggest heightened risk that a trend in the price action for a currency will reverse or at least consolidate. But the human element touches all of the above analytic techniques in more subtle ways. The waxing and waning of regression coefficients and t-statistics attest to the variability of humans' perceptions of the factors that determine a currency's value.

Finally, technical analysis often helps shape price action. Currencies tend to exhibit significant and persistent trends over time, and "riding" these trends can prove quite profitable. In contrast, oscillators can allow investors and traders to take advantage of consolidations, or even reversals of trends. Pattern recognition, often derided as so much "tea-leaf reading," can provide insights to price action, if only because the patterns can create self-fulfilling prophecies. However, even when patterns are "broken," they still point out critical levels at which market participants will either confirm their outlook for a currency or shift to a new paradigm. Technical analysis—while tactical in nature because it provides specific levels as support, resistance, and/or targets—does not have to be applied to only short-term data; recall the 7-year, 76.5 percent retracement for AUD/USD or the 3-year head-and-shoulder that USD/JPY traced out.

This book has offered insight into the richness of analysis that needs to be brought to bear in working with currencies. Anyone reading this book with an eye towards some "holy grail" of valuation methods or a "black box" style approach has no doubt been disappointed. The book provides only the elements of analysis and attempts to illustrate some permutations of how currency price action has evolved during various episodes in history. One can go through a checklist to ensure one has at least accounted for a broad variety of valuation measures; however, these valuations must be continuously tweaked, optimized, and questioned as the market evolves with each new input of information.

We hope that this book has provided a solid foundation from which to expand your study and knowledge of the foreign-exchange markets, and we wish you a rewarding and profitable experience with foreign-exchange trading and investing.

INDEX

ADX. *See* Average Directional Movement
Index
ADXR, 148–152, 154
AIG, 89, 90
Asian currency crises, 52, 228
Australia
ASX 200 Index, 77, 81, 82, 88
inflation in, 66, 67, 229–230
interest rates in, 66, 67, 77, 79, 81,
88–90, 229–232
Australian dollar (AUD), 32, 97, 118–119
base metals and, 81, 82, 88, 90–91,
229–232
gold and, 32, 66, 77, 79, 81, 88–90,
231–232, 247
hedge funds and, 121
oil and, 77–79, 81, 82, 88, 90–91
Australian dollar and U.S. dollar
(AUD/USD), 248
Bollinger Bands, 197
case study (March 2001–January
2003), 228–236
daily regression analysis, 88–91,
231–232, 235
DMI (ADX) and, 235, 236
Fibonacci ratios/levels, 196–197,
209
monthly regression analysis, 65–67,
229–230, 234–235
moving averages, 234, 236

non-commercial positions, 111–113,
232–233, 235, 236
Parabolic SAR, 158–160
risk reversals, 120, 129–130
RSI, 234–236
S&P 500 Index and, 77, 78, 88,
231–232
slow stochastics, 191–193, 233, 235,
236
triangles/wedges and multiple tops/
bottoms, 204–205
weekly regression analysis, 77–82,
230–231, 235
autoregressive integrated moving average
(ARIMA), 59
Average Directional Movement Index
(ADX)
AUD/USD and, 235, 236
calculation of, 148
GBP/USD and, 243, 244
overview of, 147–149
USD/CAD and, 226–227

balance of payments. *See* current account
entries
Bank of Canada
Commodity Price Index, 64, 222–223
Ex-Energy Commodity Price Index,
64, 223
interest rates and, 24

Bank of England, 24
Bank of International Settlements, 50
Bank of Japan, 24, 126
base metals
    Australian dollar and, 81, 82, 90–91,
        229–232
    Canadian dollar and, 64, 66, 72–75,
        86–88, 223–224, 247
    JoC base metals index, 66, 81, 86–88,
        90–91, 223–224, 229–232
    U.S. dollar and, 64, 66, 72–75, 81,
        82, 86–88, 90–91, 223–224,
        229–232
bearish (negative) divergence, defined, 173
Bear Stearns, 71, 81, 87, 88, 114, 125,
    197, 213–214
Bernanke, Ben, 22, 34
Bloomberg Professional Service
    Bollinger Bands, 176, 177
    CIX custom indexes, 115
    DMI tool, 146
    moving averages, 139
    risk reversals, 118, 119, 124, 232
    RSI, 168
    ticker codes, 118
body (wax) candlestick pattern, 206–207
Bollinger, John, 176
Bollinger Bands, 168, 185
    AUD/USD, 197
    calculation of, 176
    EUR/USD, 179–181
    findings from analysis, 184, 193–194
    GBP/USD, 182–184
    overview of, 176–177, 184
    USD/CAD, 180–182
    USD/CHF, 198
    USD/JPY, 177–179, 181
Bretton Woods Conference, 33, 38
British pound sterling (GBP), 97, 118–119
    oil and, 238–240
    as reserve currency, 38–40
    special drawing rights and, 39
British pound sterling and U.S. dollar
    (GBP/USD), 16
    Bollinger Bands, 182–184
    case study (November 2004–May
        2005), 236–244
    daily regression analysis, 240, 243–244

DMI, 152–154
DMI (ADX), 243, 244
    head-and-shoulders patterns,
        200–201, 209
    interest-rate parities, 45–47
    monthly regression analysis, 237–239,
        243
    moving averages, 243
    non-commercial positions, 102–106,
        241, 244
    risk reversals, 122–124, 241–242, 244
    RSI, 243, 244
    S&P 500 Index and, 239, 240
    slow stochastics, 189–191, 242, 244
    weekly regression analysis, 239, 243
Bush, George W., 62, 214, 237

Canada, 31
    Bank of, 24, 64, 222–223
    inflation in, 64, 221–222
    interest rates in, 64, 72–74, 76,
        85–86, 221–224
    Toronto Stock Exchange (TSX),
        72–74, 76, 86
Canadian dollar (CAD), 97, 118–119,
    165
    base metals and, 64, 66, 72–75,
        86–88, 223–224, 247
    natural gas and, 64, 72–75, 86, 87
    oil and, 32, 64, 73, 75, 86, 87,
        223–224, 247
Canadian dollar and U.S. dollar
    (CAD/USD), 32
    Bollinger Bands, 180–182
    case study (2004–2005), 221–227
    channels, 201–202, 209
    daily regression analysis, 85–88,
        223–224, 227
    DMI (ADX) and, 226–227
    monthly regression analysis, 64–65,
        221–222, 227
    moving averages, 140, 144–146,
        226–227
    non-commercial positions, 102–103,
        109–111, 224–225
    risk reversals, 120, 127–128, 225
    RSI, 174–175, 226
    slow stochastics, 226

triangles/wedges and multiple tops/
bottoms, 205, 209, 210
weekly regression analysis, 72–77,
222–223
candlestick patterns
overview of, 206, 210
types of, 207–209
capital flows, 49–51
CFTC. *See* Commodity Futures Trading
Commission
channels
EUR/USD, 202–203, 219
overview of, 201
USD/CAD, 201–202, 209
CHF. *See* Swiss franc; Swiss franc and
U.S. dollar
China, 1, 8, 22, 30, 60
Chinese central bank, 38
current-account deficit, 41
current-account surplus, 35–37,
40–41, 52
new reserve currency proposed by,
24, 38–41
U.S. Treasury securities held by, 25,
39, 52, 53
Chinese yuan (CNY)
control/promotion of, 41, 246
fixed exchange rate for, 36–37, 40
swaps, 41
Colosio, Luis Donald, 57
commodities, 31–32, 41, 59, 63, 68
See also Commodity Futures Trading
Commission
base metals, 64, 66, 72–75, 81, 82,
86, 87, 88, 90–91, 223–224,
229–232, 247
gold, 19, 33, 38, 66, 77, 79, 81,
82, 85, 88–90, 216, 231–232,
247
natural gas, 64, 72–75, 86
oil, 32, 41, 64, 69–71, 73, 75, 77–79,
81, 82, 86, 88, 90–91, 215,
223–224, 238–240, 247
Commodity Futures Trading
Commission (CFTC), 94, 118,
120, 132, 217–218
AUD/USD non-commercial positions,
111–113, 232–233, 235, 236

Commitments of Traders (COT)
reports, 97–98
creation of, 97
EUR/USD non-commercial
positions, 100–104, 217–218
GBP/USD non-commercial
positions, 102–106, 241,
244
non-commercial positions, overview
of, 4, 94, 247–248
NZD/USD non-commercial
positions, 113–115
USD/CAD non-commercial
positions, 102–103, 109–111,
224–225
USD/CHF non-commercial
positions, 102–103, 106–107
USD/JPY non-commercial positions,
102–103, 107–109
consumer price index (CPI)
Australian, 66, 67, 229–230
Canadian, 221–222
European, 18–19, 62–64, 214
U.K., 237–238
U.S., 18–19, 62–64, 66, 67, 214,
221–222, 229–230, 237–238
crude oil. *See* oil
current account, 43–44
exchange rates and balance of
payments model, 55–58
interest rates, effect of, 55–56
parity conditions and, 51–55
zero balance, 27–28
current-account deficits, 35
Chinese, 41
Mexican, 28, 55–58
U.S., 35–36, 38–39, 41, 51–55
current-account surpluses, 54
Chinese, 35–37, 40–41, 52
German, 35
Indonesian, 41
Japanese, 35
Korean, 41
U.S., 41

deflation, 75
Federal Reserve and, 26
DEM. *See* German mark and U.S. dollar

Directional Movement Index (DMI),
165, 234–236, 243, 244
    ADX, 147–149, 226–227, 235, 236,
        243, 244
    ADXR, 148–152, 154
    AUD/USD and ADX, 235, 236
    calculation of, 146–147
    EUR/USD, 150–152
    GBP/USD, 152–154
    GBP/USD and ADX, 243, 244
    overview of, 137, 146, 165
    USD/CAD and ADX, 226–227
    USD/JPY, 148–150
doji candlestick pattern, 208
dollar. *See under nation of origin,*
        e.g., Australian dollar; Australian
        dollar and U.S. dollar;
Dow Jones Industrial Average, 51
dragonfly doji candlestick pattern, 208
Duisenberg, Wim, 69

ECB. *See* European Central Bank
England. *See* British pound; British
        pound and U.S. dollar;
        United Kingdom
Euribor, 82–83, 216
euro (EUR), 97, 98, 118–119, 246
    as bond currency, 61, 63, 69–71, 247
    creation of, 30, 60, 61, 63
    gold and, 82, 85, 216
    hedge funds and, 104, 121, 214
    oil and, 69–71, 215, 247
    as reserve currency, 30, 38–40
    special drawing rights and, 39
euro and U.S. dollar (EUR/USD), 1, 8,
        18–19, 22–26, 29, 30, 45
    Bollinger Bands, 179–181
    case study (mid-2008), 212–219
    channels, 202–203, 219
    daily regression analysis, 82–85,
        216–217
    DMI, 150–152
    equity market, 50
    interest-rate parities, 48–49
    MACD, 162–164
    monthly regression analysis, 61–64,
        214
    moving averages, 142–144

non-commercial positions, 100–104,
        217–218
    Parabolic SAR, 157–158
    risk reversals, 118–122, 217–218
    RSI, 171–172, 189, 218, 219
    S&P 500 Index and, 61, 63, 69, 70,
        82, 83, 214, 216
    slow stochastics, 187–190, 218–219
    weekly regression analysis, 68–72,
        214–216
Europe/European Union, 1, 26
    See also euro; euro and U.S. dollar
    inflation in, 18–19, 61–62, 214
European Central Bank (ECB), 69
    interest rates and, 8, 24
evening doji star candlestick pattern,
        208
"Exchange Rates and Capital Flows"
        (IMF), 50

fair-value regression, long term.
        See regression analysis, monthly
fair-value regression, medium term.
        See regression analysis, weekly
fair-value regression, short term.
        See regression analysis, daily
Fannie Mae, 80, 83–84, 89, 90, 198
Federal Reserve, 31
    Bernanke, 22, 34
    deflation and, 26
    Greenspan, 22, 29–30, 94
    inflation and, 8, 26, 85, 86
    interest rates and, 8, 22–24, 26, 34,
        39, 69, 78, 81, 85–87, 89, 90
Fibonacci, Leonardo, 196
Fibonacci ratios/levels
    AUD/USD, 196–197, 209
    overview of, 196, 209
    USD/CHF, 197–198, 209
Fisher effect, 44, 47–48
foreign exchange (forex), overview of,
        1–3
forward exchange rates, 44–49
franc. *See* Swiss franc; Swiss franc and
        U.S. dollar
France, 246
Freddie Mac, 80, 83–84, 89, 90, 198
Froot, Kenneth, 33

fundamental analysis
    overview of, 3, 8–9
    parity conditions, 44–58
    purchasing power parity (PPP), 3,
        11–27, 43, 44, 95, 167, 213, 245,
        246
    real exchange rate analysis, 3, 27–41
    regression analysis, 3, 59–91, 95,
        214–217, 221–224, 227, 229–232,
        234–235, 237–240, 243–244

GBP. *See* British pound sterling; British
    pound sterling and U.S. dollar
German mark and U.S. dollar
    (DEM/USD), 29
    Louvre Accord (1987), 246
    Plaza Accord (1985), 246
Germany, 246
    current-account surplus, 35
    interest rates in, 48–49, 61, 63, 64,
        69–71, 82–83, 214–216
gold
    Australian dollar and, 66, 77, 79, 81,
        88–90, 231–232, 247
    euro and, 82, 85, 216
    Swiss franc and, 247
    U.S. dollar and, 19, 33, 38, 77, 79,
        81, 82, 85, 88–90, 216, 231–232
gravestone doji candlestick pattern,
    208
Great Depression of the 1930s, 8
Great Society programs, 33
Greenspan, Alan, 22, 29–30, 94
G-10 nations, 30, 94
G-20 nations, 24, 34, 39

hammer candlestick pattern, 208
hanging man candlestick pattern, 208
head-and-shoulders patterns
    GBP/USD, 200–201, 209
    overview of, 198–199
    USD/JPY, 199–201, 209, 248
hedge funds
    Australian dollar and, 121
    euro and, 104, 121, 214
    Japanese yen and, 121, 148
    Swiss franc and, 121
    U.S. dollar and, 104, 214

Homma, Munchisa, 206
Hurricane Katrina, 67, 75, 76, 247

ICP (International Comparison
    Program), 20–21
IMF. *See* International Monetary Fund
India, 60
Indonesia, 41
inflation
    Australian, 66, 67, 229–230
    Canadian, 64, 221–222
    consumer price index (CPI), 18–19,
        62–64, 66, 67, 214, 229–230,
        237–238
    European, 18–19, 61–62, 214
    Federal Reserve and, 8, 26, 85, 86
    Japanese, 16
    parities, 44–45
    personal consumption expenditure
        deflator, 18
    producer price index, 18, 19
    U.K., 16, 48, 237–238
    U.S., 8, 16, 18–19, 48, 61–62, 64,
        66, 67, 70, 85, 86, 214, 221–222,
        229–230, 237–238
    wholesale price index, 19
interest-rate parities, 43
    covered, 45–49
    Fisher effect, 44, 47–48
    overview of, 45
    uncovered, 47–49
interest rates, 68, 247
    Australian, 66, 67, 77, 79, 81, 88–90,
        229–232
    Canadian, 64, 72–74, 76, 85–86,
        221–224
    current account, effect on, 55–56
    Euribor, 82–83, 216
    European Central Bank and, 8, 24
    Federal Reserve and, 8, 22–24, 26,
        34, 39, 69, 78, 81, 85–87,
        89, 90
    German, 48–49, 61, 63, 64, 69–71,
        82–83, 214–216
    Japanese, 45, 148
    Libor, 66, 69–74, 76–79, 86, 87, 89,
        90, 216, 223, 230, 231, 237–240
    Mexican, 57–58

interest rates (*continued*)
quantitative easing, 8, 23–24, 26, 31, 39
U.K., 45–48, 237–240
U.S., 8, 22–24, 26, 34, 39, 45–48, 56, 57, 61, 63, 64, 66, 67, 69–74, 76–79, 81–83, 85–90, 214–216, 221–224, 229–232, 237–240
International Comparison Program (ICP), 20–21
International Monetary Fund (IMF), 20, 38, 41
"Exchange Rates and Capital Flows," 50
special drawing rights (SDR), 24–25, 34, 39–41
Internet (dot-com) bubble, 62, 73–74, 229, 238
Iraq, U.S. 2003 invasion of, 30, 62, 64, 66–67, 70, 94

Japan, 31, 45, 246
Bank of, 24, 126
current-account surplus, 35
inflation in, 16
interest rates in, 45, 148
Japanese candlestick patterns.
See candlestick patterns
Japanese yen (JPY), 8, 37, 97, 118–119
hedge funds and, 121, 148
as reserve currency, 38–40
special drawing rights and, 39
Japanese yen and U.S. dollar (JPY/USD), 12–14, 16, 24, 29, 45, 94, 165
Bollinger Bands, 177–179, 181
DMI, 148–150
equity market, 49–50
head-and-shoulders patterns, 199–201, 209, 248
interest-rate parities, 45
Louvre Accord (1987), 246
MACD, 161–162
moving averages, 138–142
non-commercial positions, 102–103, 107–109
Parabolic SAR, 155–158
Plaza Accord (1985), 246
risk reversals, 125–127

RSI, 169–170
slow stochastics, 185–190
triangles/wedges and multiple tops/bottoms, 205–206, 209
Johnson, Lyndon, 33
Journal of Commerce (*JoC*) base metals index, 66, 81, 86–88, 90–91, 223–224, 229–232
JPMorgan Chase, 71, 198, 213–214
JPY. *See* Japanese yen; Japanese yen and U.S. dollar

Keynes, John Maynard, 14, 38, 94
Korea, 41
krona, Swedish (SEK), 32
krone, Norwegian (NOK), 32

law of one prince, 11–12
Lehman Brothers, 85, 89, 90, 123, 198
Libor, 66, 69–74, 76–79, 86, 87, 89, 90, 216, 223, 230, 231, 237–240
long-legged doji candlestick pattern, 208
Long-Term Capital Management (LTCM), 66
Louvre Accord (1987), 246

MACD. *See* Moving Average Convergence Divergence Index
mark. *See* German mark and U.S. dollar
Mexico
current-account deficit, 28, 55–58
interest rates, 57–58
Mexican peso (MXN)
currency crises, 28, 52, 55–58
U.S. dollar and, 8, 22–23
morning doji star candlestick pattern, 208
Moving-Average Convergence Divergence Index (MACD)
calculation of, 160
EUR/USD, 162–164
overview of, 137, 160, 165
USD/JPY, 161–162
moving averages
AUD/USD, 234, 236
EUR/USD, 142–144
GBP/USD, 243
overview of, 137, 139–140, 165

USD/CAD, 140, 144–146, 226–227
USD/JPY, 138–142
multiple tops/bottoms and triangles/
    wedges. *See* triangles/wedges and
    multiple tops/bottoms
Mundell, Robert, 38, 40
MXN. *See* Mexican peso

NAFTA (North American Free Trade
    Agreement), 57
Nasdaq, 61, 94
natural gas
    Canadian dollar and, 64, 72–75, 86, 87
    U.S. dollar and, 64, 72–75, 86, 87
negative (bearish) divergence, defined,
    173
New Zealand dollar (NZD), 32, 97,
    118–119
New Zealand dollar and U.S. dollar
    (NZD/USD)
    non-commercial positions, 113–115
    risk reversals, 130–131
9/11 terrorist attacks, 30, 32, 62, 74, 78,
    79, 110, 230, 237
Nixon, Richard, 33, 38
Nobel Prize, 38
non-commercial positions. *See* Commodity
    Futures Trading Commission
North American Free Trade Agreement
    (NAFTA), 57
Norwegian krone (NOK), 32
NZD. *See* New Zealand dollar;
    New Zealand dollar and
    U.S. dollar

oil
    Australian dollar and, 77–79, 81, 82,
        88, 90–91
    British pound sterling and, 238–240
    Canadian dollar and, 32, 64, 73, 75,
        86, 87, 223–224, 247
    euro and, 69–71, 215, 247
    U.S. dollar and, 41, 64, 69–71, 73,
        75, 77–79, 81, 82, 86–88, 90–91,
        215, 223–224, 238–240
Organization for Economic Cooperation
    and Development (OECD), 11,
    20

oscillators
    Bollinger Bands, 168, 176–185,
        193–194, 197, 198
    overview of, 135, 167–168, 193–194,
        248
    Relative Strength Index (RSI),
        168–176, 184–186, 189, 193–194,
        218, 219, 226, 234–236, 243, 244
    slow stochastics (SStoch), 168,
        184–194, 218–219, 226, 233,
        235, 236, 242, 244
overextended, defined, 167

Parabolic SAR, 165
    AUD/USD, 158–160
    calculation of, 155
    EUR/USD, 157–158
    overview of, 137, 154, 165
    USD/JPY, 155–158
parity conditions
    capital flows, 49–51
    current account and, 51–55
    Fisher effect, 44, 47–48
    forward exchange rate, 44–49
    inflation rates, 44–45
    interest rates, 43–49
    overview of, 43–45
pattern recognition
    candlestick patterns, 206–210
    channels, 201–203, 209, 219
    Fibonacci ratios/levels, 196–198,
        209
    head-and-shoulders patterns,
        198–201, 209, 248
    overview of, 135, 195, 209, 248
    triangles/wedges and multiple tops/
        bottoms, 203–206, 209, 210
personal consumption expenditure
    deflator, 18
peso. *See* Mexican peso
Plaza Accord (1985), 246
positioning analysis
    See also Commodity Futures Trading
        Commission
    CIX custom indexes om Bloomberg,
        115
    overview of, 3–4, 94–95, 97–103,
        116, 132, 247–248

positioning analysis (*continued*)
  risk reversals, 4, 94, 117–132,
    217–218, 225, 241–242, 244
pound. *See* British pound sterling;
  British pound sterling and
  U.S. dollar
Powell, Colin, 70
price divergences, defined, 185
producer price index, 18, 19
purchasing power parity (PPP), 27, 43,
    44, 167, 213, 245, 246
  absolute, 14–15, 19
  calculation of, 18–21
  law of one prince, 11–12
  overview of, 3, 11–14, 95
  relative, 15–16, 19
  usefulness of, in exchange-rate
    analysis, 16–21

real exchange rate analysis
  external and internal balance, 27–41
  fiscal changes and long-run real
    equilibrium exchange rate, 33–34
  international investment and
    exchange rates, 34–41
  overview of, 3
  productivity shocks and long-run
    equilibrium exchange rate, 29–31
  real effective exchange rate (REER)
    analysis, 3
  terms of trade and exchange rates,
    31–32
regression analysis, daily
  AUD/USD, 88–91, 231–232, 235
  EUR/USD, 82–85, 216–217
  GBP/USD, 240, 243–244
  overview of, 3, 60, 82, 91
  USD/CAD, 85–88, 223–224, 227
regression analysis, monthly
  AUD/USD,   65–67,   229–230,
    234–235
  EUR/USD, 61–64, 214
  GBP/USD, 237–239, 243
  overview of, 3, 59–60, 91
  USD/CAD, 64–65, 221–222, 227
regression analysis, weekly
  AUD/USD, 77–82, 230–231, 235
  EUR/USD, 68–72, 214–216

GBP/USD, 239, 243
  overview of, 3, 60, 67–68, 91
  USD/CAD, 72–77, 222–223
Relative Strength Index (RSI), 184–186
  AUD/USD, 234–236
  calculation of, 168
  EUR/USD, 171–172, 189, 218, 219
  findings from analysis, 175–176,
    193–194
  GBP/USD, 243, 244
  overview of, 168–169, 176
  USD/CAD, 174–175, 226
  USD/CHF, 172–174
  USD/JPY, 169–170
risk reversals
  AUD/USD and, 120, 129–130
  correlation with price action, analysis
    of, 118–120
  EUR/USD and, 118–122, 217–218
  GBP/USD and, 122–124, 241–242,
    244
  NZD/USD and, 130–131
  overview of, 4, 94, 117–118, 131–132
  USD/CAD and, 120, 127–128, 225
  USD/CHF and, 120, 124–125
  USD/JPY and, 125–127
Rogoff, Kenneth, 33
RSI. *See* Relative Strength Index
Russia, debt default in, 52, 66

S&P/ASX 200 Index, 77, 81, 82, 88
S&P 500 Index, 214, 216, 231, 232,
    239, 240
  AUD/USD and, 77, 78, 88,
    231–232
  EUR/USD and, 61, 63, 69, 70, 82,
    83, 214, 216
  GBP/USD and, 239, 240
S&P Toronto Stock Exchange (TSX)
  Index, 72–74
SAR. *See* Parabolic SAR
SEK (Swedish krona), 32
sentiment and positioning.
    See Commodity Futures Trading
    Commission; positioning analysis
shadow (wick) candlestick pattern, 207
shooting star candlestick pattern,
    208–209

slow stochastics (SStoch), 168
   AUD/USD, 191–193, 233, 235, 236
   calculation of, 184
   EUR/USD, 187–190, 218–219
   findings from analysis, 193, 194
   GBP/USD, 189–191, 242, 244
   overview of, 184–185
   USD/CAD, 226
   USD/JPY, 185–190
special drawing rights (SDR), 24–25, 34,
      39–41
sterling. *See* British pound sterling;
      British pound sterling and
      U.S. dollar
stochastics. *See* slow stochastics
Swedish krona (SEK), 32
Swiss franc (CHF), 97, 118–119, 165
   gold and, 247
   hedge funds and, 121
   as reserve currency, 38, 39
Swiss franc and U.S. dollar
      (CHF/USD), 22–23
   Bollinger Bands, 198
   Fibonacci ratios/levels, 197–198,
      209
   non-commercial positions, 102–103,
      106–107
   risk reversals, 120, 124–125
   RSI, 172–174
Switzerland, 31
   Swiss National Bank, 24

technical analysis
   oscillators, 135, 167–194, 198,
      218–219, 226, 233–236,
      242–244, 248
   overview of, 4–5, 95, 134–135, 248
   pattern recognition, 135, 195–210,
      248
   trend-following indicators, 135,
      137–166, 226–227, 234, 236,
      243, 248
Toronto Stock Exchange (TSX), 72–74,
      76, 86
trend-following indicators
   Directional Movement Index (DMI),
      137, 146–154, 165, 226–227,
      235, 236, 243

Moving Average Convergence
      Divergence Index (MACD), 137,
      160–165
moving averages, 137–146, 165,
      226–227, 234, 236, 243
   overview of, 135, 137–139,
      164–166, 248
Parabolic SAR, 137, 154–160,
      165
triangles/wedges and multiple tops/
      bottoms
   AUD/USD, 204–205
   overview of, 203–204
   USD/CAD, 205, 209, 210*
   USD/JPY, 205–206, 209

United Kingdom, 31, 45–48, 246
   See also British pound sterling;
      British pound sterling and
      U.S. dollar
   Bank of England, 24
   inflation in, 16, 48, 237–238
   interest rates in, 45–48, 237–240
United Nations (UN), 70
U.S. Department of State, 70
U.S. dollar (USD), 2, 9, 246–247
   base metals and, 64, 66, 72–75, 81,
      82, 86–88, 90–91, 223–224,
      229–232
   current-account deficit and, 51–55
   German mark and, 29
   gold and, 19, 33, 38, 77, 79, 81, 82,
      85, 88–90, 216,
      231–232
   hedge funds and, 104, 214
   Iraq, 2003 U.S. invasion of, 30, 62,
      64, 66–67, 70, 94
   Mexican peso and, 8, 22–23
   natural gas and, 64, 72–75, 86, 87
   9/11 terrorist attacks, 30, 32, 62, 74,
      78, 79, 110, 230, 237
   oil and, 41, 64, 69–71, 73, 75,
      77–79, 81, 82, 86–88, 90–91,
      215, 223–224, 238–240
   overvalued or not?, 21–26
   as reserve currency, 23–25, 34–36,
      38–41
   special drawing rights and, 39

U.S. dollar and Australian dollar
(USD/AUD), 248
Bollinger Bands, 197
case study (March 2001–January 2003),
228–236
daily regression analysis, 88–91,
231–232, 235
DMI (ADX) and, 235, 236
Fibonacci ratios/levels, 196–197, 209
monthly regression analysis, 65–67,
229–230, 234–235
moving averages, 234, 236
non-commercial positions,
111–113, 232–233, 235, 236
Parabolic SAR, 158–160
risk reversals, 120, 129–130
RSI, 234–236
S&P 500 Index and, 77, 78, 88,
231–232
slow stochastics, 191–193, 233, 235,
236
triangles/wedges and multiple tops/
bottoms, 204–205
weekly regression analysis, 77–82,
230–231, 235
U.S. dollar and British pound sterling
(USD/GBP), 16
Bollinger Bands, 182–184
case study (November 2004–May
2005), 236–244
daily regression analysis, 240,
243–244
DMI, 152–154
DMI (ADX), 243, 244
head-and-shoulders patterns,
200–201, 209
interest-rate parities, 45–47
monthly regression analysis, 237–239,
243
moving averages, 243
non-commercial positions, 102–106,
241, 244
risk reversals, 122–124, 241–242,
244
RSI, 243, 244
S&P 500 Index and, 239, 240
slow stochastics, 189–191, 242, 244
weekly regression analysis, 239, 243

U.S. dollar and Canadian dollar
(USD/CAD), 32
Bollinger Bands, 180–182
case study (2004–2005), 221–227
channels, 201–202, 209
daily regression analysis, 85–88,
223–224, 227
DMI (ADX) and, 226–227
monthly regression analysis, 64–65,
221–222, 227
moving averages, 140, 144–146,
226–227
non-commercial positions, 102–103,
109–111, 224–225
risk reversals, 120, 127–128, 225
RSI, 174–175, 226
slow stochastics, 226
triangles/wedges and multiple tops/
bottoms, 205, 209, 210
weekly regression analysis, 72–77,
222–223
U.S. dollar and euro (USD/EUR), 1, 8,
18–19, 22–26, 29, 30, 45
Bollinger Bands, 179–181
case study (mid-2008), 212–219
channels, 202–203, 219
daily regression analysis, 82–85,
216–217
DMI, 150–152
equity market, 50
interest-rate parities, 48–49
monthly regression analysis, 61–64, 214
MACD, 162–164
moving averages, 142–144
non-commercial positions, 100–104,
217–218
Parabolic SAR, 157–158
risk reversals, 118–122, 217–218
RSI, 171–172, 189, 218, 219
S&P 500 Index and, 61, 63, 69, 70,
82, 83, 214, 216
slow stochastics, 187–190, 218–219
weekly regression analysis, 68–72,
214–216
U.S. dollar and German mark
(USD/DEM), 29
Louvre Accord (1987), 246
Plaza Accord (1985), 246

U.S. dollar and Japanese yen
(USD/JPY), 12–14, 16, 24, 29,
45, 94, 165
  Bollinger Bands, 177–179, 181
  DMI, 148–150
  equity market, 49–50
  head-and-shoulders patterns,
  199–201, 209, 248
  interest-rate parities, 45
  Louvre Accord (1987), 246
  MACD, 161–162
  moving averages, 138–142
  non-commercial positions, 102–103,
  107–109
  Parabolic SAR, 155–158
  Plaza Accord (1985), 246
  risk reversals, 125–127
  RSI, 169–170
  slow stochastics, 185–190
  triangles/wedges and multiple tops/
  bottoms, 205–206, 209
U.S. dollar and New Zealand dollar
(USD/NZD)
  non-commercial positions, 113–115
  risk reversals, 130–131
U.S. dollar and Swiss franc (USD/CHF),
22–23
  Bollinger Bands, 198
  Fibonacci ratios/levels, 197–198, 209

  non-commercial positions, 102–103,
  106–107
  risk reversals, 120, 124–125
  RSI, 172–174
U.S. Treasury securities, 22
  2-year, 69–71, 73, 76–77, 82–83,
  85–87, 215, 216, 223–224,
  237–239
  10-year, 61, 63, 64, 69, 70, 76,
  82–83, 86–88, 90, 214, 216,
  221–224, 229–232, 239
  foreign investment in, 25–26, 30–31,
  36, 39, 52, 53

Vietnam War, 33

wax (body) candlestick pattern,
206–207
wedges. *See* triangles/wedges and
  multiple tops/bottoms
wholesale price index, 19
wick (shadow) candlestick pattern, 207
Wilder, J. Welles, Jr., 146, 154

yen. *See* Japanese yen; Japanese yen and
  U.S. dollar
yuan. *See* Chinese yuan

Zhou Xiochuan, 38, 39

ABOUT THE AUTHORS

T. J. Marta is founder and chief market strategist of Marta on the Markets. He is the editor and publisher of the daily Morning Minute and contributor to several financial publications. With more than twenty years of business and Wall Street experience, Marta, a respected market strategist, is widely sought after as a commentator, speaker, and guest lecturer. Marta holds degrees from Wharton (BS, economics) and NYU (MBA). He lives in central New Jersey with his wife and two children.

Joseph Brusuelas is an economist who currently works for Moody's Economy.com and was named the forecaster of the month for August 2009 by Marketwatch.com. Brusuelas has more than a decade of experience as an economist and has worked in academia and banking since 1989. He lives in Stamford, Connecticut, with his wife Amanda and their beloved St. Bernard, Jake.

ABOUT BLOOMBERG

Bloomberg L.P., founded in 1981, is a global information services, news, and media company. Headquartered in New York, Bloomberg has sales and news operations worldwide.

Serving customers on six continents, Bloomberg, through its wholly-owned subsidiary Bloomberg Finance L.P., holds a unique position within the financial services industry by providing an unparalleled range of features in a single package known as the Bloomberg Professional® service. By addressing the demand for investment performance and efficiency through an exceptional combination of information, analytic, electronic trading, and straight-through-processing tools, Bloomberg has built a worldwide customer base of corporations, issuers, financial intermediaries, and institutional investors.

Bloomberg News, founded in 1990, provides stories and columns on business, general news, politics, and sports to leading newspapers and magazines throughout the world. Bloomberg Television, a 24-hour business and financial news network, is produced and distributed globally in seven languages. Bloomberg Radio is an international radio network anchored by flagship station Bloomberg 1130 (WBBR-AM) in New York.

In addition to the Bloomberg Press line of books, Bloomberg publishes *Bloomberg Markets* magazine.

To learn more about Bloomberg, call a sales representative at:

London: +44-20-7330-7500
New York: +1-212-318-2000
Tokyo: +81-3-3201-8900